# The Arthurian Tarot Course

# The Arthurian Tarot Course

*A Quest For All Seasons*

## Caitlín Matthews

Thorsons

*An Imprint of* HarperCollins*Publishers*

Thorsons
An Imprint of HarperCollins*Publishers*
77–85 Fulham Palace Road,
Hammersmith, London W6 8JB

First published by Thorsons 1993
1  3  5  7  9  10  8  6  4  2

A catalogue record for this book
is available from the British Library

ISBN 1 85538 258 X

Phototypeset by Harper Phototypesetters Limited,
Northampton, England
Printed in Great Britain by
Mackays of Chatham, Kent

*For Miranda Gray*
*with deepest appreciation*

# Contents

# Acknowledgements

I warmly appreciate the enthusiasm which *The Arthurian Tarot* and *Hallowquest* have received from readers worldwide. This book extends the work that I started with my husband, John Matthews, and to him I give grateful thanks. Much of the material within this course originated from our joint Grail workshops given over many years. Thanks to all readers who kept chasing me for this course: I hadn't forgotten you, it just took longer to beam down than I anticipated. I also acknowledge the brave band who joined us on the *Hallowquest* course at Hawkwood in December 1990 who sang, divined and danced without complaint in one of the most complex rituals we've ever attempted. Especial thanks to all members of the Lyceum Domus Sophiae Terrae et Sanctae Gradalis who enacted the four quests in a semi-spontaneous ritual format throughout 1992.

# Introduction

This book is intended to serve as a practical workbook for those who have enjoyed working with *The Arthurian Tarot*. It does not duplicate material from either that book or its companion volume, *Hallowquest*, which contains much of the Celto-Arthurian background for the cards themselves. Here you will find a year's coursework for deepening your understanding of yourself and your relationship with the Arthurian and Grail mysteries. All you will need is your Arthurian Tarot, *Hallowquest*, a large loose-leaf notebook and lots of dedication.

In keeping with the earlier books, I have concentrated on helping the reader study the inner correlatives of the cards: to create inner landscapes, to explore the cards' relevance to the reader, to manifest the cards' symbolism through the agency of the unfolding year and through ritual enactment. This may seem very odd to those who are used to tarot as divination, but these images arise from the depths of a tradition which conveyed its teachings through story and symbol. (There are enough new readings within to satisfy most appetites!) I believe that it is by these means that we restore the Hallows or sacred treasures to our earth and activate them once more.

The recreation of the inner landscape within us is a potent method of exploring our lives and reattuning ourselves to our true desire and purpose. By this means, we simultaneously create pathways by which the living reality of the archetypes of these cards can manifest within our world: this two-way exchange is at the heart of the Arthurian and Grail mysteries. When you have actually travelled this inner landscape for yourself, you will know the cards and what they stand for in a much more intimate way. You will also have helped create pathways which those who come after you can walk with more ease.

Readers who use tarot solely for divination will find their skills considerably enhanced by the newly devised, self-exploratory spreads in this book, and that the 'voice of the oracle' will take on accents of profound wisdom.

The material is split into 60 manageable lessons which you can either work through at your own speed, or else set yourself a schedule of study which will last just over a year. You will find tasks, meditations, seasonal rituals and practical guidance to help you on your way. Your own input, however, is more important than the text, for this is your own workbook from which you will make inner journeys, answer questions and recreate the Otherworldly realities in your own life.

To maintain a course of study requires a great deal of self-discipline. You have only yourself to urge you on. Some days will seem hopeless and you will feel disinclined to continue. The repetition of meditation or ritual formats will often seem boring and pointless. On these days you will need to make special efforts to rededicate your work.

In any self-study course certain questions of procedure will always arise. I have tried to anticipate general questions and give examples of how you should arrange your work. It is impossible to adjust the course to all requirements and you may have to find creative solutions for yourself. This should be regarded as a challenge not a disaster. It is evident from certain letters I receive that some students succumb to easy despair and seem incapable of independent thought; they want it all done for them. I'm sorry to say that the path of the Hallows is about finding what works for you, about discovering answers by means of self-questioning. It matters not whether you wear purple or pink robes, or whether you speak your rituals in authentic ancient languages; in the last analysis, only your whole-hearted service to the universe will bring the endorsement you seek, through the validation of compassionate action.

Whatever your age, race, abode or experience you are a skilful inhabitant of the sacred planet earth. You have the priceless heritage of life from your ancestors, you inherit the riches and responsibilities of your planet. You are a precious human being with the gifts of love and laughter within you. Step upon your path with joy and purposeful desire as the Seeker in the Wasteland and never stop asking the questions, 'Why are things like this? What can *I* do?'

Caitlín Matthews
23 October 1991–25 September 1992

*Note:* The reference numerals in the text refer to the Bibliography on p.261. Male and female pronouns appear in alternation: all instructions in this course refer equally to women as to men.

# Before You Begin

Read through this section swiftly before you begin the course; it contains guidance for those times when you encounter basic difficulties or procedural practice as you study. I have tried to anticipate the common problems which most often trouble students because they have no level-headed friend or experienced teacher to hand. In a course of this nature, I cannot be at your elbow to prompt and guide. You will have to use your common sense and find creative solutions for yourself.

## 1. How Much Meditation Should I Do?

Meditation time cannot be measured quantitively. Sometimes a three-minute session will yield a few years' work, while a half-hour session will be arid and unsatisfying. Regularity of work is important. Find your own level and try and stick to it, without being hopelessly rigid. Your own written records cannot be too detailed. In these, you should *always* record new realizations and skills that occur to you: these will be the basis of all your future experience. Bald recitals of what you saw or experienced are less valuable than records of the *quality* of your experience. Check how you felt.

## 2. Why Do I Feel So Ill/Disinclined to Meditate?

Any new procedure will make you feel tired and out of sorts. If you are unused to meditating, you are using parts of yourself that may not have been used before. If your psyche aches, then it probably means you've exercised it well. Often physical problems like headaches, backaches and twitching may afflict you. Check all normal causes, such as the position and height of your chair and the lighting, first. If the same problem recurs only when you sit to meditate, it's just the body's way of telling you it's unused to this routine. There is nothing here that practice will not alleviate.

## 3. Why Has My Life/Relationship/Job Got So Difficult Since I Started This Course?

If you are really meditating hard and discovering about yourself, this will have the effect of changing you. When *you* change, everything about you changes. Cosy but stale relationships where neither person has questioned anything have a tendency to go supernova suddenly, leaving a large black hole in your life. Similarly, other circumstances may reconstellate themselves. This is often upheaving and distressing: it does not mean that the malign forces of the universe are out to zap you personally. When you've cleared the ground, you will come through and survive to form more fulfilling relationships, and so on.

## 4. Why Does Nothing Happen When I Try to Visualize the Cards?

You may be someone with a poorly developed visualitive skill. This can be improved by simple visualization exercises. Start by visualizing your home: its rooms, shelves, contents of drawers and so forth. Visualize colours, sounds, textures, smells and tastes, so that your five senses are engaged. Visualization is based upon simple observation.

Visualitive problems may mean that you gain better impressions from other senses. You may naturally *feel* or *sense* impressions rather than *see* them. Some people gain their experience from a welter of different senses. Always trust and capitalize on your existing skills. If your meditational experience remains patchy, it may be that you are someone who doesn't like to lose control and that you've not yet reached a space of inner freedom where things may be allowed to happen. Gently encourage yourself and have fun experimenting with new methods of receiving impressions. Give yourself permission.

You may find it useful to keep a blank tape running to record your meditations aloud. You need to keep a running commentary on what you are experiencing, describing even what seem to you to be 'surface impressions', for example, 'I'm going into the Grail Castle and there's a door ahead of me. Inside it's dark, but I think I can see a little dog. It barks at me to come forward . . . . My mind's wandering a bit now. I listen again to the dog and ask it to help me . . . .' This is also very helpful for those who have intensive, multi-layered meditative impressions.

## 5. How Can I Find Time and Space in My Family Home to Meditate?

Anyone who needs quiet meditation time has either to live alone or come to an agreement with the rest of the household. Set a realistic time aside and ask everyone to respect your privacy. Give very young children their own special time and they will learn to respect yours. Put a sign on your door to indicate when you are meditating. You do not need to set up visible altars and shrines, waft incense about or dress up in robes if this is going to cause trouble at home.

# 6. What If I'm Deluding Myself?

Our society is unsupportive of people living in more than one reality. Indeed, some people have to be insulated from other kinds of reality for their own sanity ~ these places are called mental institutions or the real world, depending on your standpoint. Certain things happen in meditation. If you are seriously unhappy about anything that you experience, you are probably discovering things about yourself which life has shielded you from until now, and which your brain has hidden away in a back cupboard. What you do about this is your responsibility. If this much reality frightens you or makes you feel guilty or disoriented to the point of delusion, then you should probably not be doing any esoteric work at all, never mind this course. Alternatively, if you are able to trust the experience you are having, it will probably change very soon and you will understand things in ways which might not seem possible now.

# 7. I'm Worried that the Advice/Messages of Meditational or Inner Guides May be Wrong

The rules for esoteric work, like those for ordinary life, are much the same. The moral standards that are right for you obtain also in the innerworlds. If an inner entity, however respected or admired, suggests you do something that your integrity revolts at ~ DON'T DO IT. The same goes for any walk of life: devious salesman, proselytizing evangelists, threatening youths or lustful employers may try to have power over us, but we must do what our integrity dictates. It frequently happens that, because we are ignorant of innerworlds, we feel that we must sublimate our instincts and good sense. When in doubt, always follow your common sense. If a person or situation makes you feel doubtful of their intentions, ask questions or flee. Good spiritual discernment is not hard to develop. Do not confuse challenge or difficulty with evil intention: check the grain of truth every time. Discernment is hard if you yourself are upset, ill or out of sorts. The best thing is not to meditate if you are under the weather. Always ask pertinent questions to clarify meditational answers.

# 8. How Do I Know That What I See is 'Right'?

This course does not have one set of correct answers. Everyone experiences the innerworlds according to their capacity, experience and background. However, that experience is broadly variable within certain confines. If you are meditating and arrive at a place where a character gives you something, accept the first thing you see, even if it seems trivial or ludicrous. Learn to ask questions, when in doubt. If you are given a feather, for example, ask what symbolic value a feather has for *you*: does it imply 'a white feather', indicating cowardice; does it mean flight; does it mean something else for you? There is no point looking up symbols in a dictionary or table of correspondences since *your* own symbolic values will be different from others'. There are a few sample diary entries to help show you different kinds of response: these are for guidance, not for you to slavishly reproduce.

Meditation courses like this one are written to restore the meditator's personal authority and to wean her off total reliance on sources that supply scenarios for all occasions. The innerworlds are within you, as well as within me and the High Priestess of a Great Goddess-You've-Never-Heard-Of! *Your own experience* is your own pathway; your personal encounters with innerworld inhabitants are your own teaching scenarios. Learn from *them*, not from books that pretend to reveal all.

## 9. What Relevance Does This Course Have to My Ordinary Life?

It is up to each of us to find the relevance of all our esoteric work, including our meditations, to our daily life. It is very easy to lose touch with reality when we let esoteric concerns rule us. By examining each archetype of the Arthurian Tarot and meditating on our connections with the patterns and characteristics revealed therein, we enliven and reawaken those same archetypal strengths within us, as well as realizing which archetypes are weaker and need development. The range of archetypes in the tarot reveals every colour of the emotional, mental and spiritual spectrum. Quite apart from this, there are the mythic levels of the Arthurian Tarot which present us with certain patterns which have eternal verity, whether they happen in Celtic, medieval or modern time. Always correlate what you learn with daily life, but remember that not every piece of teaching or wisdom is pragmatically applicable: but it may have a creative or spiritual application.

## 10. Is Anything on this Course Contrary to My Spirituality?

Used with common sense, the Arthurian Tarot has nothing contrary to your spirituality. If you suddenly decided to make the tarot into a kind of super-deity to grant your wishes, of course, that would be unbalanced. The intention of this course is to help you find and understand yourself so that you can be a more effective and compassionate human being, better able to fulfil your spiritual vocation: this is a primal duty in *all* spiritualities. Many New Age methods seem to stress self-knowledge at the expense of universal integration. But while knowing yourself better is not an end in itself, if you learn to respect yourself you will be better able to respect other living beings. Nourish your body, your psyche and your soul in balanced ways and you will be better able to serve the Spirit also. Test your own motivation by asking: am I co-operating with the universe or am I manipulating it?

## PART ONE

# Preparing for the Quest

*Thou shalt receive the boon whatsoever thy tongue may name, as far as the wind dries, and the rain moistens, and the sun revolves, and the sea encircles, and the earth extends.*

Culhwch and Olwen

Before we set off on our quest, we need to spend a little time in preparation. Efficient travel is based upon well-researched itineraries, on well-packed luggage and nourishing provisions. Lessons 1–5 give us guidelines for meditation, study and practical work, and provide a grounding as well as a personal map for the ensuing quest. Give plenty of time to this preliminary section before you go on to Part Two. Each lesson needs a minimum of a week's work.

---

# LESSON 1

---

## Meditation and Diary-Keeping

You may have had considerable experience of meditation in many forms, or you may have had none. Whatever your experience please read what follows. There is more information about meditation in Chapter 8 of *Hallowquest.*

It helps to sit in an upright posture on a straight-backed chair with, if necessary, a cushion under your feet to raise your knees level to your hips. There is no great mystique about this posture: it merely ensures that you remain wakeful, alert and fully relaxed. It is a meditation posture that is traditionally used in the West. If you lie down to meditate you will invariably fall asleep. If you want to sit cross-legged on the floor, that's fine, if you're comfortable and can keep a straight spine.

Many people assume that meditation is performed in a trance-like state. The whole point of meditation in The Arthurian Tarot Course is your clear perception and remembrance of non-ordinary reality; for this you need to be alert but receptive. You will also need to learn to distinguish between ordinary and non-ordinary reality, and accept that they exist side by side. We normally only access non-ordinary reality through dreams, when we are creative, and at times of heightened emotion, but meditation *purposefully* accesses non-ordinary reality. This is not frightening or sinister. The innerworlds will reveal themselves to you through the simple means of stories unfolding, characters whom you meet, situations in which you engage, and through the images upon the cards that you hold.

By means of meditation you will discover your personal inner landscape. This course is designed to help give your observations a shape and pattern. You may choose to stay within this framework or go beyond it when you have finished the course. The extent to which you flesh out and inhabit this landscape is down to your hard work.

Distractions will, inevitably, arise. Treat them sternly and concentrate more deeply. If your visualization is poor, then distractions will intervene more frequently. If you are emotionally fraught or stressed, your problems will feature more prominently than the subject of your meditation.

Most of the meditation required on this course requires you to 'enter' the card you are studying. This is the reason why the Arthurian Tarot cards are bordered by a black doorway cutout: it is an invitation for you to step within and explore. Once you step within, you will find that the scene is not a static one: it moves, changes and often hides other scenes, characters, animals and impressions.

Allow yourself to use the first images that occur to you when you enter a card. To be truly present within a card, use all your senses. If your impressions are unclear, ask yourself about the temperature of the season, time of day, textures, sounds, colours, and the nature of the ground beneath your feet when you enter the card. Make it as real to yourself as you know how.

You will be instructed to meet with and talk with the subjects of the cards. This conversation may be verbal, silent or symbolic. If you are shown symbols or images, relate your experience directly to the question or point you have raised. Each lesson starts with a brief statement spoken by the subject of each card. These statements can be used as meditation subjects for those who find visualization and inter-relationship with the cards difficult.

You will be given gifts by the Greater Power cards and by others on these quests. These are important and significant. Accept the first thing you are given, even if it seems unlikely, farcical or out of context. Ask the one who gave you the gift to explain its qualities and significance.

Above all, remember to be flexible and adaptable to your own experience. If your meditation goes along other lines than those given here, you are not doing it wrong or disobeying. Your inner journey will unfold *in its own ways*, ways that I cannot predict or allow for. The scenarios given in this course are intended to help you learn, no more.

If the Green Knight leads you to another part of his domain, go with him and see what he wants to show you. If Guinevere gives you a crown, or the unrewarding landscape of Stone Five suddenly becomes full of Spring flowers, investigate it for yourself and ask your teachers, guides and guardians what it means.

# Breathing

Breathing is perhaps the most important factor in meditation. It is the energy that fuels our meditation and clarifies our consciousness. When the quality of our breathing is poor, our mind feels sluggish, our body feels limp and unwilling, inclined to sleepiness and lethargy. Deep, rhythmic breathing is a basic exercise which will always enliven your meditation sessions. You can perform it whenever your direction in life needs clarification.

Because breathing is an involuntary function, we seldom think about it: when we do, it becomes peculiarly difficult! Sitting upright, place one hand on your diaphragm; feel how it rises and falls naturally with each breath. It is displaced every time your lungs expand with air. Now take a deep breath in and feel the difference: it went out further, didn't it? Now, try breathing in deeply until your lungs are full. Steadily breathe out again. Spend at least 2–3 minutes prior to each meditation session 'breathing yourself in'. First of all breathe at least five full breaths in and out, allowing them to cleanse your whole body. Visualize this precious air penetrating every limb, artery and blood vessel; visualize all your worries and difficulties leaving your system as you breathe out. If you breathe too vigorously, you may find yourself over-oxygenating, which may cause you to feel a bit high. If this happens, breathe more regularly. During meditation itself, let the breath look after itself and only refer to it again if you become agitated or distracted. Don't strain after your breath, but let it become steady and slower until you can feel yourself relaxing.

*Note:* If you suffer from a disability that makes performing these instructions difficult or impossible, please do not hesitate to adapt these exercises according to your own capabilities.

# Earthing and Grounding

It may seem an odd instruction to meditators who are not yet 'airborne' to talk about grounding, but this is an important instruction which is often omitted from practical esoteric work. In order to meditate, we need briefly to remove our attention from our daily lives and to concentrate on the subject in hand: you will find many instructions to enable you to do this. However, you also need to return to your daily life again after your meditation. This is just as important. You can formally mark the boundaries of your time of meditation by creating an opening and closing formula that you recite or a gesture that you make to indicate your meditation's beginning or ending (see below, Lessons 2 and 3). Earthing, or returning to ordinary reality, is performed by sealing off the meditative faculties with a clear act of intention and by resuming ordinary activities, or by eating or drinking.

People who are not well grounded have difficulty living efficiently. If you are prone to live with your head in the clouds, if you consider mundane activities with contempt, if you are focused only upon spiritual matters, then you are a person who is badly earthed. You can help yourself by gently encouraging the performance of mundane tasks *with intention and commitment*. Afford the information of your senses and the wisdom of your body the same respect that you show for spiritual concerns. This course is not a mountain-face for you to scale: it is a well-paced and rhythmic method of self-discovery which prepares you to be of service to the universe. If you cannot implement what you learn here in everyday life, then you delude yourself.

## Diary Record

For this course, you will need to keep a meditation diary of your findings. Many esoteric training schemes ask students to keep such a diary. The word 'esoteric' means 'into the within'. Our daily lives are usually lived in outer reality or in the external world. When we turn within, we find another kind of reality, just as real. It is this innerworld reality that has always underlain our outer lives. Esoteric or non-ordinary reality is the inner landscape that underlies the mundane landscape of our physical world and is known throughout the world by initiates of many spiritual paths. The word 'initiate' means 'one who has gone within'. You are going to become an initiate of this inner landscape, using the Arthurian Tarot to help you begin travelling.

If all this sounds bizarre, consider that this procedure is exactly what John and I did to bring *The Arthurian Tarot* to birth. All its images already existed in non-ordinary reality. We meditated and went within to see what each card actually looked like, keeping a daily record of our observations for several months until we could correlate our findings, and draw pictures to pass on to Miranda Gray, who finally anchored their images in reality in the form you now hold. All creative work is done in this way: without a vision of non-ordinary reality, nothing can come into being with intention.

You will need to keep your own daily meditation diary in which to record your progress. This should contain your realizations, which should be noted down *at the time*, however vestigially, or like dreams they will fade before supper. The following is an example, but please regard this as a guide, not a dictate.

| **1. Date** | **2. Time** | **3. Moon Phase** | **4. Weather** |
| --- | --- | --- | --- |
| *25.9.90* | *18.33* | *6th day, waxing* | *Bright, breezy, dry* |

## 5. Meditation Subject
*Gawain*

## 6. Report
*Gawain holds an upraised sword in his right hand and a shield in his left. This reminds me that the warrior is not always on the attack, but also on the defensive. To balance these qualities within myself is very important – not to carp at people when I feel depressed, but to show neutrality to all unless I am actually threatened. Gawain appears to me in the form of a hawk and says: 'It takes a steady eye to gaze into the midday sun. Become acquainted with your weaknesses.' There was another scene which I can't recall now.*

## 7. Card Chosen Today
*Grail Two. Can't think how today's events resonate with this one. Superficially, I suppose there was a pigeon that landed right in front of me on the way home. This might also indicate the way that B. is trying to interest me in the new project at work. It's been going so long I hardly feel any enthusiasm. (Later) reading the meaning, I see that this card also stands for the imminence of the Grail's achieving, so perhaps B. is on to something after all!*

## 8. Reading
*Didn't have time to do one today.*

## 9. Special/Important/Noteworthy Event Today
*M. announced her engagement at work. Petrol went up. I managed not to eat any chocolate all day!*

1. & 2. Date and time record when you had your meditation period. Undated records afterwards prove useless and difficult to correlate.
3. & 4. Moon phase and weather are optional, but they may remind you of the day and also mark your moods or feelings, so that you can establish any cyclic patterns of behaviour.

5. Meditation subject is essential when you look over your record again: you may be unable to work out what on earth you were meditating on!
6. The report should note your findings or lack of them, however trivial they may seem at the time. If meditation results throw up further work or research, take note of this and schedule it as part of future meditation work.
7. Card of the day is optional, but you may find it very useful in familiarizing yourself with the pack. Drawing one card or doing a three-card spread can be very illuminating: draw your card/s the night before or in the morning and then examine them later that night, before sleeping. The Tarot Companions Reading (below) is a useful, short spread of this kind.
8. A divinatory or story-telling reading is also optional, but good for practice.
9. Special events often help remembrance of what you were experiencing at the time; you may also note correlations between readings and events.

Your diary will become an important record of your spiritual growth and personal understanding. Treat it as a friend to which you can return when you feel discouraged; read over past entries and take heart. Add pictures, drawings, doodles or whatever stimulates your work.

## Tasks

1. Sit down and look at this book thoroughly. Flip through the pages and read what you like. What mental and practical preparations do you need to make? What changes to your routine will the course entail? When you have answered these questions and made whatever preparations are necessary, take out your tarot and shuffle it, asking the question: 'What is the most important factor in this course for me?' Spread the cards in any suitable way or merely draw three at random. Record the reading in your diary, noting down any expectations, doubts or internal questions you have about the course.
2. Practice your breathing. Note how you feel afterwards.
3. Choose one tarot image or a sentence from the book to meditate on for at least 10 minutes. Record your findings.
4. Begin your daily diary record.

## Daily Tarot Companions Reading

This is a short exercise using a three-card spread which you can do daily before sleeping or on rising: it will bring you greater familiarity with using the cards. Divide the pack into three sets: Lesser Powers, Greater Powers and Court Cards. Shuffle each pack separately until it is well mixed. You will be asking these questions as you shuffle:

1. The Lesser Powers: What will I learn from my experience tomorrow/ today?
2. The Greater Powers: Who will be my teacher tomorrow/today?
3. The Court Cards: Who will be my guide tomorrow/today?

Draw one card from each pack to find your Tarot Companions for that day. The object is to help you discover the hidden patterns within your life and to understand them better. Here is an example:

**Diary Example:**          **Reading:**
*27.9.91*                   *Tarot Companions*

**Experience**
*Stone Six*

**Guide**
*Stone Queen*

**Teacher**
*Grail Hermit*
   *I feel that these reflect my situation very well, since I want to share so many of my realizations right now. Meditation provides such a rich seam to mine and I sometimes feel a bit overwhelmed by thoughts and feelings. The Stone Queen is a card I've always resonated with: her mirror held up to the snowy landscape is like me forever trying to make sense of the uncharted inner landscape of myself. The Grail Hermit has come up four evenings running now, and must be significant. I will meditate on him tomorrow, maybe.*

**28.9.91**
*Yesterday's Tarot Companions reading was borne out in some part today. I met with my meditation group and got bold enough to share some of my deeper realizations. After that there was a great deal of sharing and much better closeness between us all. I realize that my guide for the day, the Stone Queen, was trying to tell me that I hold on to things too much and need to be more generous. The Grail Hermit reveals to me that I spend perhaps too much time analysing myself and that, though I can profitably benefit from solitude, I seek it too often as an escape.*

**Meditation Subject** *Grail Hermit.*
*I entered his clearing and found him seemingly asleep. When I went to lift the door-curtain of the hut, he coughed gently and I drew back guiltily. He said he had a song for me and sang it: 'The Grail will conquer fear, my dear', which he sang three times, followed by 'All on this day.' The other verses went:*

> *The Grail will bring you strength, my friend,*
> *All on this day.*
> *The Grail will bring you light, my love,*
> *All on this day.*

*There was a sense of self-sufficiency about him that made me envious, for I long for a bit of peace and quiet from the children. He perceived this and began singing quietly to himself again. I didn't receive any clear message from him.*

**Later**
*So I thought! The song had a soft, gentle tune which I've been singing ever since as I walk or garden. The beautiful simplicity of it brought me peace during a busy day.*

# LESSON 2

## *The Seeker in the Wasteland*

> **The Seeker Speaks** *The world is darkening about me. The feet of dancers are stilled: the voices of singers are silent. Someone must find the soul of the land once more. I travel to restore what has been lost. Oh blackbirds, may your singing be my guide as I step upon the rainbow road of dreams!*

## The Fool's Progress

This course is based on the unfolding of your own story and its interaction with the larger story of our time. Both the individual and the universal story are important: our quest is to become sufficiently empowered that we might be a more effective actor in the interwoven fabric of life. This is the purpose of the Seeker's Rainbow Pathway, for it leads to the realms within. To become effective in the universal story, we must each seek empowerment. All quests lead to the realms within,

o the seeker

into the unknown ～ we will each find what we seek only if we give ourselves up to the inner journey.

This is tantamount to extreme foolishness, of course, in the eyes of the world, which sees the Rainbow Path as the retreat of an escapist, as a dead-end or as leading to terrible danger. If we counted the cost of our inner journey, none of us would start it. Part of us must be like the Seeker, always listening to the voices of the blackbirds when the way is unclear.

There are myriads of folk-tales about the lazy youngest son ～ usually called Jack ～ who idles all day and yet gets ahead of everyone else by sheer ingenuity. You may know and envy such people in your own experience: the ones who seem to do very little for a living but who have all the time in the world to laze ～ suddenly they have arrived and are successful and you can't help the feelings of envy that arise deep within you.

The Seeker in the Wasteland is still the Fool, and ordinary people cannot guess at the wisdom of fools, who play games seriously and work playfully.

Human beings distrust space. Going forward over the Abyss needs much courage, yet the Seeker takes the Rainbow Path joyfully and with equanimity. We each have our own personal abyss, inhabited by monsters, fears and doubts; most of us don't look into it too often or too closely in case we get bitten. The choices for the Seeker are to remain in the Wasteland, to fall into the Abyss or to leap over it and enter the unknown landscape. Explore the possibilities for yourself:

1. What is the Wasteland for you?
2. What lurks in the Abyss?
3. What (do you hope/think) lies ahead?

## Yourself as Seeker

The Seeker in the Wasteland represents yourself, standing on the threshold of the quest. Self-knowledge is the object of both your searches. During the quests of Part Two, you, as the Seeker, will undergo many experiences and awakenings. Before you begin your quest, it is useful to assess yourself and clarify your direction:

1. Who are you as a person?
2. What is your life's purpose? What would you like it to be, if you are unsure?
3. What are your greatest strengths?
4. What are your skills?
5. What kind of quest are you already on? What do you seek? What do you hope to achieve?
6. What needs most empowerment in your life right now?
7. Are you a deadly earnest seeker, or do you enjoy straying from the path of the quest for a recreative game?

## Tasks

1. Write about an incident from your life when you were presented with alternative choices ‒ one which seemed 'wise' and the other 'foolish'. Write your story as if you had chosen the 'foolish' alternative, whether you did or did not chose this in reality. What might the outcome have been? OR

   Choose an incident from your own experience in which you felt particularly foolish or at a disadvantage. Mythologize it if you like: rather than telling it in the first person, tell it in the third person and set it somewhere else, for example, 'Once upon a time there was a man who couldn't stop smoking . . . .' Allow your story to unfold but, at the moment when the innate foolishness is revealed, turn the story round and bring it to a resolution so that your 'foolish' action becomes a 'wise' one, for example, 'And as she fell into the hole in the ground and everyone laughed, her eyes lit upon the crock of gold coins that everyone had been searching for.'
2. Select the Seeker from your pack, then shuffle the pack and extract a series of cards to create situations that you as the seeker have encountered in your life recently. Use the face value picture or the

divinatory meanings, as you like, consulting the book if you need to. Compose a story in which the Seeker meets with these situations/ places/people, using the cards as story-components. Examples of this method are given on pp.277-93 of the *Hallowquest* book.

3. Create an opening affirmation with which you can start each meditation session, along the lines of the following example:

> A seeker in the Wasteland wide,
> I seek for truth on every side.
> I journey north, south, east and west,
> To find the object of my quest.

OR

> From this world to that world,
> I go to meet [title of the card you are meditating upon].

4. Look at p.121 of *Hallowquest* and see which of the lesser power cards is assigned to your birth-date. Does this card have any relevance to your life purpose, by way of validating it, challenging it or revealing factors that you had not considered?

## Meditation

In this lesson you begin meditating on the cards. You may find it helpful to set up the card in question on a stand at about your own eye-level for, although you are going to be meditating with eyes closed, you may find it helpful to keep the image before you to act as a focus when you start. The following meditations should be spread over a series of days, rather than performed all at once. Write down your answers with a general report of what you experienced at each meditation session. Don't be discouraged if you don't appear to receive a great deal at this stage; accept your experience and record it. Don't feel that apparently irrelevant images or feelings are unrelated to your experience, but refer them back to your meditation subject.

1. Without referring to the hand-book, look at the card of the *Seeker in the Wasteland*. What general response does the card evoke? How do you feel looking at it?
2. Each card is surrounded by a black doorway or window: this time, when you meditate, step through this doorway and *enter* the card. Close your eyes now and enter the Seeker card, answering the following questions: What is it like being in this landscape? What can you see from the cliff top?

3. Stand in the Seeker's place and become the Seeker, who can be of either sex. If you find this difficult, try questioning him when you enter the card. Find the answers to these questions: Where are you going? What do you seek? What are the blackbirds saying to you? What are the uses of the things you carry: the staff, the knife, the helmet and pendant stone? Are you brave enough to step upon the rainbow road? Or you can ask these questions of yourself in the Seeker's place, such as, Where am I going? What am I seeking?
4. The Rainbow Path of the Seeker takes you from your own world to the innerworlds. You can pass between the worlds by this pathway. As you explore the innerworlds, be aware of the Rainbow Path forming a cross-roads which faces in the four directions. You will be taking each of these roads in turn in the next part of the course.

# —————————— LESSON 3 ——————————

## *The Goddess of the Land*

**The Goddess of the Land Speaks** *Behold! I bring you the wisdom of the deep earth and of the distant stars. From the ages past to the ages to come, I guard the empowering Hallows in the Courts of Joy. Who will seek them now and restore joy to the earth?*

## Our Own Native Land

We hear much today about Gaia – the name that James Lovelock, inspired by the novelist William Golding, has given to the planet earth. Gaia was the primordial Greek Goddess of the earth. The earth needs healing and it is the responsibility of us all to find ways of healing and personally implementing them. It can be discouraging to contemplate such a cosmic task, which seems as hopeless as emptying the ocean with a spoon. But we can help, if we begin just where we are, here and now, in our own land.

The Goddess of the earth has many faces. Our own country has its tutelary Goddess of the Land who watches over it and with whom we can all have close relations. This relationship works on many levels and we need to discover which levels are operative in our own experience.

The Goddess of the Land can have many different appearances: no spirituality or religion has the only correct picture. In Tibet, there is a cave wherein a rock-carved relief of Tara, the Goddess of Wisdom, is growing measurably every month. In Medjugorje, in the Balkans, the Blessed Virgin has appeared to a group of young Catholics. Native peoples of many lands, who see their Mother in natural land-forms, maintain vigilance over her sacred sites, which may be threatened by industrial exploitation and pollution. Worldwide, people are being moved by the plight of the earth which has become personified for them as Gaia, Goddess of Our Common Life. Wherever the energy of the Goddess moves, so people become pilgrims and questers after better solutions.

Some people realize the Goddess in political ways, while others are moved to spiritual action. Many combine their spiritual and political paths, so that one informs the other in a well-balanced way. Whether ecology or worship is your natural response to the Goddess of the Land, your sensitivity and response is going to mean a lot to the land in which you live.

The tutelary spirit of the land may often have other forms: male deities usually appear as heroic protectors; animals may appear as heraldic totems who support the armorial shield of the land; plants, trees or abstract devices may also symbolize the land and appear on the land's coinage. Explore your own land's heraldry, coinage and emblems to get a sense of this. In the Arthurian Tarot, the Goddess of the Land appears on the back of each card to remind us of our responsibility to the earth.

## Questions

1. How do you feel about being a citizen of your country? Are you proud, ashamed, dissatisfied?
2. If you could visualize your land as a person, what would it look like? Meditate and write a short description. Draw a picture.
3. What national characteristics are particular to your country? Choose cards from the Hallowquest pack to represent these qualities.
4. Look honestly at your country and see its failings. What kind of healing does it need? Choose cards from the Hallowquest pack that might represent the healing of this situation.
5. What is your country's romantic or poetic name? This name may be its original, ancient title or else express some deeply perceived quality, for example, England is sometimes called 'Albion', and the United States of America is sometimes called 'the Land of the Free'. You may find that by utilizing such titles in your meditations you access a much deeper and more cohesive sense of your land.

# Tasks

1. As you go about daily in your locality, feel the different energies of the streets, green places, buildings etc. Which areas make you confident, unsure, distressed or uplifted?

2. Choose an area in your locality which, in your opinion, is in need of healing. If you are able to remedy anything by way of local council or committee, or by physical cleansing (e.g. clearing rubbish from a stream), then do what you can by way of campaigning. If you are unable physically to do anything, set aside a period every day when you actively mediate healing, that is, beseeching spiritual help and sending it to that area. You may wish to choose cards to help focus your mediation.

3. Choose an area of your locality which, in your opinion, feels unsafe. Dedicate that area to a specific deity, archetype, healing energy or power and invoke its help by prayer, ritual or meditation. If you are used to thinking of it by its local 'bad-mouth' name, make up a name that inspires more confidence in you, so that Gasworks Alley might become The Track of the Flower Bride, or Perceval's Valley.

4. Create a closing affirmation with which to end each meditation, such as:

> *A seeker in the Wasteland wide,*
> *I sought for truth on every side.*
> *From all points north, south, east and west,*
> *From journeys far, I now seek rest.*

OR

> *From that world to this world,*
> *I return from (title of the card upon which you meditated).*

# Meditation

This course is keyed into the landscape of the *gwyddbwyll* board. *Gwyddbwyll* or 'wood-wisdom' was a game, similar to chess, which was played by the Britons in the time of Arthur. The magical *gwyddbwyll* board whose pieces play by themselves is prominently included in the medieval Welsh list of the Thirteen Treasures of Britain and also appears in many British and Arthurian legends. Here, the board betokens the land itself upon which the mighty figures of the Greater- and Lesser Powers are arranged.

Familiarize yourself with the diagram, for this image is going to become very clear to you in the next year. It is the landscape that you will be walking in imagination. In the quests of Part Two, you will encounter the many faces of the Goddess of the Land in the landscapes of the Lesser Powers through which you'll be travelling.

You will see that at each corner, the cards of each Hallow suit are gathered together: these are the Hallow Courts. The Hallows themselves are hidden at the heart of the land and guarded by Arthur, Guinevere, Merlin and the Lady of the Lake. The figures in Roman numerals represent each of the Greater Powers whom you will encounter on your seasonal quest.

To make the Hallowquest real to yourself, take out your cards and spread them out in this configuration, preferably on the floor, or on a table if you can't manage to sit on the floor. This will give you a better sense of the landscape of your quest. You have spread before you the entire pack of the Arthurian Tarot.

You may be wondering why two cards are not actually part of the board but act as supporters to the diagram. These two cards are XXI The

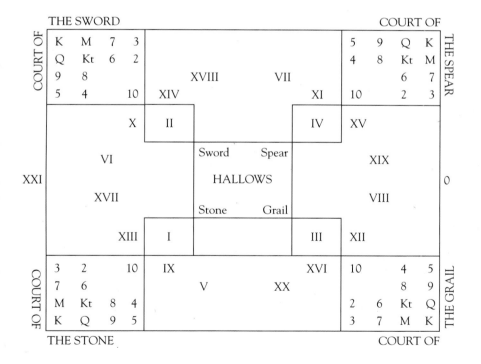

Fig. 1: _The Landscape of the Hallowquest_

Flowering of Logres and 0 The Seeker in the Wasteland. They form the end and the beginning of the Hallowquest: the points of reconciliation or restoration and of loss or seeking. They are very important cards for they represent yourself (the Seeker) and the achieving of your quest (the Flowering of Logres).

Logres is the ancient Welsh name for England. It was used by C.S. Lewis in his marvellous novel *That Hideous Strength* to exemplify the *inner* Britain – the part that is true and perfect.[6] I have used the word to stand for the inner correlative of *any* country and we hope that you will substitute your own country's name in your consciousness every time you read 'Logres'. The quest is not about being patriotic about things British; it is about the abiding Mysteries whose internal correlatives are universal. In order to show forth these Mysteries, we must set them in their proper place – in the archetypal landscape of their mythic origins.

There remains one more thing to add to your spread. Take one of the spare cards which you will find in your tarot box and reverse it so that the Goddess of the Land, complete with the Four Hallows is set centrally on your tarot mandala. You may wish to cut out a small map of your own land and place it on this card, or else substitute a picture card of your own creation showing the Goddess of the Land.

You now symbolically stand facing your own Goddess of the Land and looking towards the fulfilment of your hopes and desires, ready to start the Hallowquest in earnest.

Sit now in front of your tarot mandala, which is the gaming board of your quest, and contemplate it quietly, without pushing your consciousness to have an exciting realization. Gaze at it with half-closed eyes. At the same time, feel the earth beneath you as a sustaining and stabilizing influence, a presence which makes you feel safe and loved. Listen for the voice of the earth. Allow any realizations, visions or insights quietly to percolate to the surface. Write down your impressions for your report.

We take much from the land, but we seldom give anything in return. When you sat in front of your tarot mandala you probably experienced the warmth and nurture of the earth beneath you, helped perhaps by the inviting image of the empowering Goddess of the Land with her Four Hallows. Did you consider thanking the earth or the Goddess at that point? The Hallowquest is about giving and receiving, about losing and finding, for the quest is a continual reciprocation of energy: never forget to thank your helpers and teachers.

# ————— LESSON 4 —————

## *The Flowering of Logres*

xxi the flowering of logres

**The Land of Logres Speaks** *I am the promise of the land that will be restored. Behold! The waters run once more, each bough is in bud or blossom, the sacred grain is ripening. You who dance out the seedtime of your soul's journey upon my broad meadows, I bid you find the rainbow's end and your true treasury.*

## The Wasteland and the Coming of the Hallows

Every age has to solve the problem of evil and find within its people those who are willing to go on a quest, putting themselves at the service of the Grail. For the Grail does not just appear in medieval and Celtic story, it is an ongoing cycle. To help us see the current pattern of events and find the Grail-bearer for this age, we can examine the pattern of the Grail's manifestation, as follows:

1. The Dolorous Blow afflicts the land – this is usually caused by a person supposedly acting in the public interest who in fact acts for his own self-interest. It can also happen when one of the Hallows is misused, as when Balin strikes Pelles with the Spear by way of self-defence.[9] The

ancient analogue of this blow is shown in the incident where Gwenhwyfar has a cup of wine thrown into her lap: an insult to the representative of Sovereignty.[8]

2. The Dolorous Blow afflicts both King and Land with infertility and wasting disease. The land becomes overrun with opportunist foes who waste remaining resources and terrorize the weak. The kingdom becomes anarchistic as the structure of society breaks down.

3. The Grail becomes active, appearing symbolically or actually to those who have dedicated themselves to restoring the Sovereign and the Wasteland to rights again.

4. The healing grace of the Grail is sought by way of chivalric quest, a journey of personal danger, by prayer and seership, and by the formation of a network of dedicated followers of seekers. These form the Grail Family.

5. Of the many seekers, one has a greater affinity with the Grail than others. He or she is often weaker, less able, ill-educated or 'foolish'. This foolishness actually is the result of the non-duality of innocent perception, so that it is the youngest son or maiden who is able to perceive and attain the Grail.

6. The Grail-winner heals the wounds of Land and King by being sufficiently open to the Grail's grace. The land becomes fertile again, the old king dies or retires, the Grail-Winner and companions become the new guardians of the Grail, which no longer appears in symbolic form but is manifest everywhere.

This mythological template can be used in all times and by all traditions and cultures. If you examine the history of your land and age, you will find this pattern endlessly repeated. It can be an act of real seership to recognize the unfolding patterns and protagonists of the Grail in your own time and place. This is true alchemy, where the Great Work is the perfecting of the times.[20]

## Restoring the Likeness

The Flowering of Logres depicts the restoration of all things to their essential perfection. But there may lurk the uneasy suspicion in your mind that life isn't like that, we cannot keep perfection safe and inviolate, for 'things falls apart, the centre cannot hold'. You are, of course, quite right.

We may indeed find what we have lost, achieve our quest and enjoy fulfilment for a little space only. The hard-won knowledge that we arduously acquired deserts us. The Grail-vision is erased from our hearts. What does this mean and what can we do about it?

One of things that we need to be told early in our esoteric training is that loss of our realizations and empowerments is a regular feature of life. It may occur when we change our inner myth, or as the seasonal esoteric tides change (see p.44) What once gave us happiness and fulfilment suddenly seems as empty as a beached sea-shell. It is normal and natural for this to occur. We should be aware that we will pick up our contacts again in a while.

Most esoteric training upholds a holistic viewpoint. Unfortunately, we live in dualistic world where things are judged otherly: good and bad, right and wrong, correct and incorrect are the little lights that go on and off in our heads all day. The Piscean perspective held that our spiritual lives should be aimed at some final, perfected end. The Aquarian perspective holds that we discover our spiritual trajectory by encountering the challenges and rewards of life with equanimity.

One of the initiatic sayings of the Orphic mysteries was 'I have flown out of the weary wheel', meaning that the initiate was no longer subject to the cyclic and mutable nature of life. Most of us do not attain to this mystical awareness, except in brief flashes of comprehension when we see into the heart of things and know ourselves to be part of them. Most of us walk the path with alternate bouts of carefree abandon or anxious suspicion. The Flowering of Logres bids us find a more balanced way of living.

It may be helpful to look upon life as a spiral rather than as a fixed, unchanging wheel. As Winter comes round every year we may have a sense of 'Oh, it's Christmas - nothing achieved again'. When we were 5 years old, Christmas was a good time; our experience of it as a 15, 25, 45 or 85-year-old will be different. Yes, the wheel of the year has spun round, but *we* are different from the people we were last year. Other experiences are available to us in successive cycles. The Wheel of the Year is really a spiral which moves us through the cycles of the seasons and to which we will react differently every year.

This is why keeping a journal, day-book or meditation diary record is so valuable, for as time passes we can look back and recall once more the insights of earlier years.

The perfection that is sought in this card is the restoration of the holy likeness, the rediscovery of the intrinsic sacred quality of all that is created. This is not something that we can achieve alone and unaided but, if we take the Rainbow Path in perfect love and trust, the grace of the Divine Spirit (by whatever name we call It) will lead us to the end of our quest. Worlds may fall, wars may overwhelm us, loved ones may die, but this experience of the restoration of the Hallows can never be taken from us. This vision sustains and strengthens each human heart, but few even begin the quest, out of feelings of unworthiness or hopelessness.

The quest is not for the faint-hearted, nor yet is it a selfish quest on which we find our salvation and ignore the plight of others. It needs to be said that the quest is a rigorous method of self-training that simultaneously creates new opportunities for encouraging and benefiting others. Those who set out with selfish intentions generally do not progress far along the path.

The one who follows the Rainbow Path is impelled by the Grail vision to restore what is lost, whatever the personal cost. In every generation and regardless of their gifts or inadequacies, new seekers arise who know they have to follow that path: you stand now at its very beginning. In Parts Two and Three you will be trying to achieve the Flowering of Logres, the restoration to wholeness of your self, of your own land and of the earth.

## Tasks

1. Make a list of things you would like to achieve: tomorrow, next week, month, year, and in two and three years' time.
2. Look at ideals and hopes you have long cherished. Are you still as resolved to fulfil or actualize them as you once were? Have your ideals become stale and without motion? If you still cherish them, how are you actually going to fulfil them?
3. Do a Mabon's Gate Spread (see p.120 of *The Arthurian Tarot: A Hallowquest Handbook*) for a cherished project of yours which is not coming to fruition. Record it in your diary.

## Questions

1. How does the Wasteland manifest in your personal life and surroundings? What are you doing/can be done about it?
2. What is your secret dream?

## Meditation

1. Set the Flowering of Logres before you and study it. Without looking at the meaning, what impression do you receive when you look at it?
2. When you are ready, enter the scene as an observer and answer this question: What is it like to be in this landscape? Describe what you see, hear, smell and feel.
3. Enter the card and stand in the place of either the Seeker or one of the children. Answer this question: What made the Wasteland flower? What legacy of wisdom would you like to leave to the children? What do the bee and butterfly say? What are the uses of the Hallows?

# Visualization of the Grail Quest

This visualization is intended to give you a sense of over-view of the Quest for the Hallows. You can read this on to a tape yourself or send for the tape that accompanies this book (see p.259).

_Note:_ ★ means a pause.

_Let us enter the realms of the Grail by exploring the landscape within. Close your eyes and see the scenes described. As the pictures form before you, enter them and be a part of the scene as an active participant._

_It is day-time and you are approaching a castle. It is a large and busy place and no one notices you. You enter and find your way to the Great Hall. Here is a Round Table at which many people can sit. You walk around the table and see that there are names written upon the back of each chair. Walk round and find a chair with your name written on it._ ★

_You find it and sit down. Then you see many people come in and sit down. You realize that you are seated at the Round Table in Camelot, that the court has met to discuss matters of importance and that you are here to represent your own country. Each person reports their news. Soon it will be your turn. You turn your mind to your own country and the events of the world: what is happening there right now ~ what is the world's need?_ ★

_You tell your own news to those seated at the table._ ★ _Now everyone has spoken. Suddenly a shaft of light comes through a high window on to the table. You see the Grail shimmering within the light. Its beauty speaks to your heart ~ you know that if the Grail can be found, all the problems of your world will be eased. Make your own dedication now to find the Grail and help heal the world's pain._ ★

_From this moment you are called to the Quest. You rise and get ready to search. You leave the Castle of Camelot and pass out into the countryside on your quest. You may go on foot or take a horse from the stables._

_You follow the path before you and soon find yourself in a dense forest. Your quest does not seem so important, now that the vision has begun to fade. You come to a place where the path splits into four ~ which one shall you follow?_ ★

_As you think, a White Stag appears on one of the paths and you follow it. It occurs to you that you are in the Forest of Adventure where many extraordinary things can happen if you are true to your quest. The White Stag leads you into a clearing ~ a place of tranquillity where you can sit and think about your quest. You had set out in high hopes and with strong ideals, but a part of you is lazy and wants to rest ~ you ask yourself the question: What aspect of myself prevents me finding the Grail?_ ★

_You know the answer deep inside yourself. The birds sing encouragingly to you in the Forest and you continue your quest._

_Still following the path, you emerge from the Forest and see before you a Castle which would look better if it were not situated next to a dank and_ stagnant lake. Still, the sight of habitation cheers you and you approach it. Within, there is a fire and a table spread with food. You recognize some of the people here: they are those who despise or look down on you, the people who weaken and disempower you. They do not understand your quest and they mock your determination with questions which raise doubts in you: 'Why are you so special that you think you are good enough to go on quest? What do you think you will gain, one person alone?' ★

But even as you consider the answers to these questions, you hear the harsh cry of the White Stag. You suddenly become aware that you have accidentally come to the Castle of Case, which is dangerous to questers who are not firmly resolved. You face your challengers and tell them just who you are and what you intend to do. ★

Without more argument, you turn and leave.

You see before you the White Stag once again. It wants to lead you over a hillside and down into a valley. You follow, still feeling angry with yourself for being lured into a confrontation. The land about you is idyllic and you are reminded of a place you knew when you were a child. The air is very pure and colours are bright and clear. Your spirits lift and you continue your quest. You cannot see the White Stag any more, but it doesn't matter. Ahead of you is a fair maiden. She stops you and asks whether you would like to drink from the well. She tells you that it will provide whatever food or drink you desire the most – that it can give you spiritual nourishment from the depths of the earth, before the beginning of time. She draws up a bucket from the well and pours the waters into a cup and dish. Whatever food and drink you desire is within these vessels and you eat your fill. As you do so, you feel great strength and encouragement. ★

Thank the maiden now and pass on your way. She will indicate which road you should take. ★

Strengthened by the draught of the well, you go along your way until you come to a low green mound, set in the side of a hill. Seated at the entrance to the mound is a tall, green figure, dressed in leaves. He tells you that this is the Green Chapel, the place of ancient traditions. He asks if you would like to meet one of your ancestors and receive a token of help on your quest, for you may need this on the way. ★

If you wish to do this, you go deep inside the mound and wait. As your eyes become accustomed to the dim light you see a figure – it may be an ancestor whom you knew, or it may be someone of whom you have no knowledge. ★

Ask your ancestor what is the greatest strength of your family. ★

Now your ancestor gives you a symbol or token to take upon your way. You emerge from the mound and the Green Man sets you on your road with a blessing.

As you proceed, you wonder if the Green Man directed you wrongly. The further you go the more desolate the land becomes. It is obvious now that you are in the Wasteland. You see a place that is desacralized, where no birds sing, where no trees or plants grow, where no fish swim in the waters. The lone figure of a gaunt woman in rags approaches you, asking, 'Once I was the richest woman alive and the most blessed. Why have you made my land like this?' Maybe there is no answer in your heart. Here there is only yourself and the Queen of the Wasteland. Ask her what you can do to heal the land and make it flower again. ★

The blessing of the Grail is needed here very badly. You try to call to mind the grace and beauty of the sacred vessel to inspire you, but your whole being lacks concentration. Bearing the words of the Queen of the Wasteland in your heart, you go on.

You travel until it is nearly dark. Even the sky is without stars. On the horizon you see one pin-point of light and go towards it. As you get nearer you see that here is a tiny hut built out of old and broken things, skilfully made of recycled rubbish. There is a friendly light coming from within and the door opens as you approach. Inside there is a old man, huddled in a long robe. He bids you welcome to his hermitage and invites you within. He tells you that he lives here to welcome and guide all Grail-seekers to the end of their quest. You sit down and relate your journey to him thus far. ★

The Hermit listens and gives you council, advising you and clarifying what you have experienced. Then he brings out a crystal mirror for you to look into. As you sit in front of it, the mirror becomes very clear and scenes begin to form within it. You see a city by the sea and many little boats arriving. It becomes clear to you that this is Sarras, the Grail city and that all the boats contain different Grail-seekers, all arriving together. You see them assemble at a round table, like the one in Camelot, only this table is made of star-light. You see the strength and determination of the seekers and you understand that many have come through pain and great trouble to come here. The seekers all sit and join hands. As they form a circle of fellowship, they begin to sing of their individual quests, their voices raising in a many-layered chant. As their voices blend together, the Grail gradually forms over the crystal table and dispenses its glory upon each person seated there. ★

The beauty of the sound and the brightness of the vision strike your heart deeply. You see each seeker rise with cupped hands, like people taking water from a fountain. They finally leave the city of Sarras to return to their own lands. Your vision begins to fade as the mirror clouds over.

The Hermit tells you that this is a vision of what may be, that in every age of the world this quest is reenacted and that you have a part within it. 'Go now', he says, 'return to your world and seek whatever things are good and beautiful. Remember your vision everyday, even when the Wasteland seems to close about you.' Then he strikes the wall so that a doorway of light opens within his hut. You step through back to your own world, to your own time and place where your quest will continue. There is a blessing on all who serve.

Write down your experiences in your diary.

# LESSON 5

## The Four Realms

### Tides and Seasons

This lesson looks at the inner patterns that determine and demarcate our lives. Although we are exploring inner space on this course, our life's journey is lived out in time and space, coloured by a multitude of moods and qualities which the seasons weave about us.

The seasonal nature of this course may be puzzling to you. Why are the cards split up among the seasons in this way, with no seeming order or progression? The esoteric reason for this seemingly arbitrary apportioning of the Greater and Lesser Powers is that each season brings its own insights which only you can experience *at the time*. The esoteric tides run whether we will or not. You are probably aware of many of them without ever giving them a thought. Let us look at some of the seasonal patterns which weave the tapestry against which our lives are lived.

Fig. 2: *The Cycle of the Day*

The sun governs this cycle and marks the phases of the day. This cycle is the one we respond to most immediately, for it governs our daily lives: when we go to work, when we have lunch, come home or go to bed. Each time of the day has its intrinsic quality. Very few people get up to catch the dawn, but we are aware then of the day's freshness and innocence stretching ahead of us. At midday, usually the busiest time of day, we experience a respite in our work. At twilight, the magical hour, we remember the day's work and see into the heart of things briefly. By midnight we are already asleep or going to bed. Each complete revolution of the day and night is a microcosm of the seasons of growth.

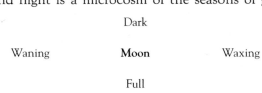

Fig. 3: *The Cycle of the Month*

This monthly cycle is one we appreciate less frequently. Very few people are aware of moon phases, except to notice them briefly as they flick through their diaries. People who live near seas or tidal rivers, people who work at night, gardeners and women all notice the moon more often. The irregularity of the moon means that sometimes there are 12 full moons a year, and sometimes 13. Our present calendar months take little notice of moon phases, although the Christian year is determined by the fall of Easter after the first full moon following the Spring Equinox. In Celtic tradition the major festivals were calculated by them and the months followed the irregular moon cycle which takes 19 years to pass through a complete lunar circuit.

Winter

Autumn          **Stars**          Spring

Summer

Fig. 4: *The Cycle of the Year*

The yearly cycle is based on the circuit of the earth around the sun, which determines the equinoxes and solstices. But the real rulers of the seasonal year are the stars, which have distinct constellations in each season (see The Cycle of the Hallows, below, for a description of the influence of stellar energy). These are different according to whether you live in the northern or southern hemisphere. Dwellers in the southern hemisphere also experience their seasons at the opposite poles of the year so that, although in December Europe may be celebrating Midwinter, inhabitants of the Antipodes and South Africa will actually be experiencing the weather that goes with Midsummer.

Most people in the southern hemisphere who are geared into the mood of the seasons celebrate the seasonal festivals at the appropriate time of year rather than attempting to celebrate them in contradiction to the season, celebrating Spring festivals, for example, in September when the growing season has begun rather than in March when harvest has been gathered in. I have spoken with many people from the southern hemisphere who find the national trend of celebrating Christmas, complete with northern hemisphere Winter Solstice customs of snow, reindeer and warmly clad Santa Claus, exceedingly trying when their land is baking in a Midsummer heat!

Each of these cycles overlays the other in wider and wider spirals. We can even express our own life-cycle upon such a wheel:

Fig. 5: *The Cycle of Life*

As we live through this cycle, the preceding cycles are superimposed to form a great extending or deepening spiral whereby we understand with greater clarity the cosmic patterns of time and space. When all material concerns are laid aside, it is this spiral of our life's experience that is left, as in the Spiral Tower card, where the earthly edifice is struck by lightning, leaving only the crystalline tower behind. Our awareness of these cycles brings us into contact with more subtle tides and seasonal opportunities, and directs us into a deeper understanding of the Hallows themselves.

Fig. 6: *The Cycle of the Hallows*

Here the Hallows have been associated with the Four Directions and with the Four Seasons. You will need to reverse this diagram if you live in the southern hemisphere. The Hallows may be sought at any part of our life cycle: each person who does this follows the quest on behalf of their own generation and land. In terms of the land's own cycle, the Hallows have distinct times of manifestation and withdrawal during the year. These are triggered by the esoteric tides which we can recognize and work with.

The esoteric tides are vast influxes of stellar energy which turn at the solstices and equinoxes. All people who work in an esoteric, magical or spiritual way are sensitive to these tides; they know that it is as difficult to work against them as to row against the prevailing current. If we are aware of the tides we will stand a better chance of achieving what we have planned. Esotericists know that these tidal changes herald upheaval and change in the earthly realm and tailor their work accordingly. [3]

The Spring tide comes in at the Spring Equinox, bringing many new influences and ruthlessly clearing away any outworn concepts. It is a good time to instigate projects, to grip the Sword of Light with justice and young strength.

The Summer tide comes in at the Summer Solstice, bringing expansion and confidence. It is a good time to stretch our boundaries and widen our horizons to let in burgeoning life. We cast the Spear of Life and await the outcome of our throw.

The Autumn tide comes in at the Autumn Equinox, bringing the time of assimilation and gathering in. It is the time to assess our projects and to monitor results. We drink deeply from the nourishment of the Grail of Love and turn generously to share what we have gained.

The Winter tide comes in at the Winter Solstice, bringing with it a time of contraction and contemplation. It is a good time to conceive new projects and to finish off old ones. We take up the Stone of Wisdom and read therein the book of our life.

## The Elements

The four elements underlie the four Hallow suits of the Arthurian Tarot. These have their physical effect in our everyday world which we understand in seasonal and weather patterns; most of us understand them as the physical elements. But they have their inner correlatives: the subtle elements. These subtle elements are the basis of the Otherworldly powers. It is to these subtle elements that we are seeking to align and attune ourselves.

The teachings on the elements have been long understood in the West, though they are mostly now forgotten. The Classical and medieval world understood the human body to be influenced by the 'humours' - the powers of the physical elements which go to make up our constitution. People were understood to possess one of the following kinds of nature and were medically treated accordingly:

| | | |
|---|---|---|
| Sanguine | Airy | hot and moist |
| Choleric | Fiery | hot and dry |
| Phlegmatic | Watery | cold and moist |
| Melancholic | Earthy | cold and dry |

Indian Ayurvedic medicine still operates by similar principles, as does Taoist practice. It is a system that views human beings as microcosms of creation, each part of the cosmic whole in a special way:

> *Man is called a little world not because he is composed of the four elements . . . but because he possesses all the faculties of the universe. For in the universe there are gods, the four elements, the dumb beasts, and the plants. Of all these man possesses the faculties: for he possesses the godlike faculty of reason: and the nature of the elements, which consists in nourishment, growth and reproduction. In each of these faculties he is deficient . . .for we possess the faculty of reason less eminently than the gods; in the same way the elements are less abundant in us than in the elements themselves; our energies and desires are less than the beasts'; our powers of nurture and of growth are less than the plants.* [32]

We each of us consist of 'elements of the elements'. The physical elements that shape the world about us – the winds, sunlight, waters and land features – also influence our constitution. More importantly, the presence or absence of the subtle elements in the realm of our psyche is critical to our smooth operation in daily life.

These subtle elements are the archetypal powers of Life, Light, Love and Law. The realm of the physical elements is that of the created world in which humanity lives with animals, plants and minerals. The elements are pathways into other realms. The pollution of our physical elements has meant fewer opportunities for us to interact with the otherworld: we have muddied the pathways. The subtle elements themselves suffer pollution within us and need aligning. Fortunately this is something we can adjust with perfect practice.

## Questions

1. Review the seasons of the year in relation to your life: which season is easiest for you, which is most difficult?
2. What kinds of weather are best for you, which are more difficult?
3. What is your best time of day? When does your energy become lowest?
4. Which is your natural element?

## Meditation: The Cleansing of the Caers

This is a practical meditation which you can incorporate into your daily practice. It comes in five handy compartments which can be performed separately. It involves breathing, visualization and a sensitivity to your own inner landscape and the elemental balance within you. Note that the colours and directions may be changed by students who are used to different traditional ascriptions and correspondences, or by those who live in the southern hemisphere. You can record this on to a tape for yourself or get the tape that has been produced to accompany this book (see p.259). Each ★ denotes a pause.

★

*Wherever you are sitting, sense the four directions about you, with yourself at the centre of your inner land. You are going into that inner land now. Visualize about you the four elemental caers on the horizons of your inner country. A caer is the British word for a tower; it also means 'a place of establishment'. You start by facing East: you may choose to sit where you are or you can actually turn to face the East.*

*Before you in the East, you are aware of the wind and clouds. What kind of weather is prevalent in your land as you look into the East: stormy/ calm/windy? What kind of clouds are overhead?★*

*Whatever is happening, you can purify and realign the eastern lands by breathing in the yellow breath of the Eastern Caer, which will purify the physical elements into subtle ones. Take the yellow breath of elemental air into your body, hold it in a short while to pass into every part of you. Let the purposeful power of the Eastern Caer come into you.★*

*Now you turn to the southern part of your land. Before you there is a fire burning. What is the quality of the fire ~ is it a small camp fire, a great conflagration or merely smouldering? What is the quality of the sun in the sky? Is it bright, overcast or dull?★*

*Now you may purify and realign the southern lands by breathing in the red breath of the Southern Caer. Take the red breath of elemental fire into your body, hold it in a short while to pass into every part of you. Let the energizing power of the Southern Caer come into you.★*

*Now you turn to the western part of your land. Before you there is a body of water ~ is it a lake/stream/river/sea/well? Is the water clear, muddy, dried up? What quality of weather is prevalent in the western lands?★*

*Now you may purify and realign the western lands by breathing in the blue breath of the Western Caer. Take the blue breath of elemental water into your body. Let the enriching power of the Western Caer come into you.★*

*Now you turn to the northern part of your land. Before you the land stretches: are there plains, hills, mountains or other land features? What does the land look like ~ is it fertile, or barren, does it support vegetation? Is the earth stable, or given to subsidence or earth-tremors? What kind of weather is prevalent in this part of the land?★*

*Now you may purify and realign the northern lands by breathing in the green breath of the Northern Caer. Take the green breath of elemental earth into your body. Let the wise power of the Northern Caer come into you.* ★

Now you turn to the centre, the place where you yourself are seated. The power of the four elemental caers is within you. Now be aware of a central tower about you. What is within this tower? How are the rooms arranged? Here are treasuries, dungeons, libraries, feasting-halls – what state are they in? ★

You may visit them all at some other time, now is the time to purify their condition. Take the translucent breath of the spiritual element into your body. Let the inspiration of the spiritual element of ether come into you. ★

You turn now to look in each of the directions to the four caers of your inner landscape. The land about you is shining with new life and glowing above each caer you see the Hallows, etched in light. Salute each Hallow in turn. The vision fades and you become aware of your own country beneath you once again. You repeat the blessing of the elements:

> The blessing of the strong wave be under me!
> The blessing of the mighty winds be over me!
> The blessing of the deep flame be within me!
> The blessing of the patient earth beneath me!
> The blessing of mighty Otherworld be with me!

**Diary Example:**          **Meditation:**
*14.6.91*                        *Cleansing of the Caers*

This meditation was very powerful! I was amazed at how well I sustained it: maybe the breathing helps? In the East there were lots of dead leaves blowing about: a blustery day with starlings racketing about. In the South, there was a beautiful fire, burning at night. In the West, everything was very dry and the plants looked parched. I had to spend a long time breathing in the blue water to change it. A little brook began to flow. In the North, the earth was moulded with little hills and apple trees. The central tower was exciting and reminded me of a dream I'd had a long time back. There was a loom in one of the rooms which made my fingers itch to weave: gorgeous purples, greens and blues in a geometric design with golden geese and lozenges of dark brown. There was someone winding thread in the corner whom I couldn't see properly. Lots of rooms still to explore – I shall be returning tomorrow!

Later: I realize that my watery landscape is a bit dry because my emotional life is the same. I must keep a couple of Grail cards on my mantlepiece to remind me to let the waters flow into my life.

# Self-Assessment

In any course of self-study, it is difficult to assess your progress objectively. It is important to understand that *only the real person you actually are* (not the one you want to be) can study this course. Self-knowledge is painful but necessary. This course sets many questions: answer these as honestly as you can, leave the questions you cannot answer yet and return to them later. This is often a difficult concept to grasp, but your meditations will follow their own unfolding pattern and there is no 'right' result or realization.

How do you sustain your study? You are like a miner who goes down into the darkness with only a little lamp to bring up the riches of the earth. You suffer the same disadvantages as a miner in that you are working in the unknown, in a cramped space (or in one so huge that very much light would terrify you); to add to your uncertainty, the stuff you bring up doesn't look like anything much, despite the odd gleam. Your work must be sustained by trust, by curiosity, by dogged endurance.

How do you assess your realizations? Some of your findings will be unsurprising and will bear out what you know of yourself; others will be shocking, delightful or strange. It will be difficult to assess what these actually signify when you have just finished recording them, so write up your diary and continue working. At the end of each of the Hallow sections in Part Two, look back over your diary and note any significant patterns there; review your life over that period - how have you changed?

Some people mistakenly believe that any work on themselves is wasted or selfish. The spiritual process is like a journey into a unicursal (one-line) maze: all comers must follow the sole path to the centre, gaining a thorough self-knowledge, before turning round again and re-entering the world in service. It is easy to become very involved with our studies, to clutch our realizations like trophies or fixed signposts to the inner worlds. While you will indeed be subjectively entering the inner landscape and finding many helpful signposts to your life, be aware that nothing is permanent. As the seasons turn, so your focus will change. Sometimes you will be full of knowledge, at other times empty - this is normal.

The tarot has survived as a game which transforms and illuminates things, so be playful as you walk this way. Take signs of incipient self-importance very seriously and bring them down to size; it is no blasphemy to laugh at your own mistakes and misapprehensions. You may wish to study with a friend, so that you can share your insights and help and encourage each other.

## PART TWO

# The Quest for the Hallows

*Then Ceridwen began to boil the cauldron, which from the beginning of its boiling might not cease to boil for a year and a day, until three blessed drops were obtained of the grace of Inspiration.*

Taliesin

The Quest for the Hallows is the main object of this course. But what is meant by this? We are certainly not going off, armed with metal detectors, to dig up the countryside. Nor are we going to manifest a physical Grail in our living rooms.

The Hallows or 'Holy Things' are the essences of the prime fourfold energies of creation. Each land has its own symbolic representations of the Hallows, which have a presence and power upon which all inhabitants of that land can call. But the Hallows are often withdrawn or inoperative due to various factors.

The object of your fourfold quest is to seek these primal energies, by means of entering the inner landscape portrayed on the Arthurian Tarot, and to clear the way to help make their influence manifest in the world. Manifesting the Hallows is the responsibility of us all.

The following four seasonal sections can be worked in order from the time the reader decides to follow the course. Thus, for example, if a reader bought the book in January and worked through the introductory material of Part One, she would be ready to start at Spring (Lessons 6–18), working through to Summer, Autumn, and Winter in turn. If a reader bought the book in April, he would work through the introduction and start Part 2 from Summer (Lessons 19–31), going on to Autumn (Lessons 32–44), Winter (Lessons 44–57) and Spring (Lessons 6–18). It doesn't matter where you start your year's study. The purpose of this part is to explore the Wheel of the Year as a personal quest, relating the Arthurian Tarot to our deep selves, and to take a series of journeys which will build up an inner landscape wherein the Hallows can be found.

*Alternatively*, you can follow the quest by starting from Lesson 6 and working through, in your own time, to Lesson 53. This method may be preferred by busy people who cannot maintain their regular daily practice. They may still want to celebrate the quarterly festivals at the appropriate seasons and these are found on the following pages:

The guidelines for celebrating these rituals are given on p.63. Each of the Hallows becomes operative and available in a deeper way at the quarter days of the year: it is this energy that will be harnessed and distributed through the ritual.

The seasonal study units which form Part Two are primarily intended to attune the student more strongly with the elemental powers of the Hallows and their gifts, and to enable her to mediate the power of each Hallow to our own world by personal service.

| Element | Hallow | Season | Guardian |
|---|---|---|---|
| AIR | Sword | Spring Equinox | Lady of the Lake |
| FIRE | Spear | Summer Solstice | Arthur |
| WATER | Grail | Autumn Equinox | Guinevere |
| EARTH | Stone | Winter Solstice | Merlin |

## Meditational Format

Each seasonal section in Part Two deals with 19 cards which form a cumulative meditational journey. The four seasons through which you will work next are ruled by the guardians of Llys Arthur, the Inner Court of Arthur - Merlin, Lady of the Lake, Guinevere, Arthur - who are the inner guardians of the Hallows in this course. Each is accompanied by other Tarot companions who guide the seeker further into the inner landscape.

| Court: | Hallow Guardian: | Companion: | In Lands Adventurous: | In Otherworld: | Experience: |
|---|---|---|---|---|---|
| Sword | Lady of Lake | White Hart | Round Table | Cauldron | Moon |
| Spear | Arthur | Prydwen | Sovereighty | Green Knight | Sun |
| Grail | Guinevere | Gawain | Wounded King | Spiral Tower | Sleeping Lord |
| Stone | Merlin | Taliesin | Grail Hermit | Washer | Star |

The Lands Adventurous are the inner landscape which borders our own reality: the Greater Powers which we encounter here are often the first experience that we have of the inner realms. After we have passed these causal realms, we enter into the Otherworld where we will meet the Otherworldly Greater Powers and receive the deepening experience of the celestial Greater Powers. Your quest is pursued in the landscape of each of the Hallow realms in turn. These are the itineraries and signposts of your quests:

## Spring
21 March–20 June (southern hemisphere 21 September–20 December).
   Explores the Sword Realm with Greater Powers of the Sword: nos II, VI, X, XIV, XVIII, and Sword Family.

## Summer
21 June–20 September (southern hemisphere 21 December–20 March).
   Explores the Spear Realm with Greater Powers of the Spear: nos IV, VII, XI, XV, XIX, and Spear Family.

## Autumn
21 September–20 December (southern hemisphere 21 March–20 June).
   Explores the Grail Realm with Greater Powers of the Grail: nos III, VIII, XII,XVI, XX, and Grail Family.

## Winter
21 December–20 March (southern hemisphere 21 June–20 September).
   Explores the Stone Realm with Greater Powers of the Stone: nos I, V, IX, XIII, XVII, and Stone Family.

Whether you study this course in seasonal order or by numerical order of lessons, work through each section completely before passing on to another one. If you want to set yourself a strictly scheduled study programme, a suggested format is given on p.251.
   The starting point for all four quests is the same: the Rainbow Path of the Seeker in the Wasteland (which is depicted on this card). Follow this path into your own inner landscape, which you began to explore in Lesson 5; at the horizon of your inner landscape stand the four caers or towers. At its centre the Rainbow Path divides into a cross-roads – you will take one of these roads for each quest. If you haven't managed to get a clear impression of the Rainbow Path and your own inner landscape, do continue meditating on Lessons 1–5 before you pass on to the quests in Lessons 6–53.
   The meditation instructions which accompany your study of each card in the following pages may seem very minimal to you. This course encourages you to go within the landscape of each card and find what is there for yourself; it doesn't *tell* you what to see. Only your personal meditation can inform you. When you 'enter' each card, you may find helpers, challengers, animals, buildings etc. which aren't depicted on that card. You may find certain cards very difficult to enter: record your

findings carefully and review why this should be so. If you encounter difficulties at any point, refer these to the Greater Power guide appointed to that quest for clarification and help.

# A Word on Divination

In Part Two, you will find many new tarot spreads which will help you discover more about your quest. You have probably used the tarot to do fairly general readings for yourself. Some of these spreads are read within the context of your meditation. With the insights gained in your meditations, you will be able to home in upon more specific issues. This will bring you into contact with the deeper levels of the tarot as an oracle.

The tarot is not a totalitarian destiny device. Be sensitive to the impressions or 'story-lines' that begin to run when you lay down a spread. Without focusing on the given attributes of each card, look the spread over and relate the first impressions to your original question. Accept these impressions and let them stimulate remembrance, interconnection and association within you. Spend time allowing these impressions to deepen, as though you were sinking an artesian well. You can enter each card and commence a dialogue with its subject or move within its landscape, asking for light to be thrown upon your question. By doing this, you will find your reading becomes a meditation, and the cards will become a true oracle for you.

If you have trouble beginning this level of tarot-reading, make a clear statement of intention and set aside your mental reservations. But don't limit your experience by being deadly determined to succeed: it may help to approach the cards in a more playful and light-hearted spirit. Let the story-line of the spread unfold gently, allowing your imagination to be led along the path that it evokes. The following questions can be applied to help unlock difficult readings:

1. Who/what is the subject of this reading?
2. Which card holds the most power? How?
3. Which card/s indicate blockage? Why?
4. Which card/s indicate free flow of movement? What kind?
5. What practical action does this reading suggest? How do you implement this?
6. What mental attitude surrounds this question?
7. What would be your ideal outcome to this situation? What outcome is indicated in this reading?
8. Enter the Greater Power Cards in this reading. What do they tell you about this question?

# Bach Flower Remedies

On p.255 you will find correlations between the Arthurian Tarot and the Bach Flower Remedies. This may seem a surprising combination, but the list is given to help and encourage the lone student to transform, challenge and transcend difficulty by balanced understanding. The non-addictive Bach Flower Remedies act as transformers of the emotional and confused states to which all individuals fall prey over a long period of study. Use them creatively to help yourself. See also Resources on p.259.

# SPRING:
## The Quest for the Sword

*And Galahad unsheathed the Sword, and when he saw the blade, whose brilliance was a mirror to the face, he prized it more than any thing on earth was ever prized.*

Quest of the Holy Grail

We begin our Spring quest within the Realm of the Sword at the Sword Castle. Our guides here are the Sword Family. Companioned by the White Hart, we learn from the Round Table, we encounter the wisdom of the Cauldron and experience the illumination of the Moon. The Sword itself is guarded by the Lady of Lake. You will need the following cards for study:

The entire Sword Suit
The Lady of the Lake
The White Hart
The Round Table
The Cauldron
The Moon

# The Realm of the Sword

SWORD TEN

**Sword Ten Speaks** *Who crosses the sword-bridge is impelled by necessity or love. Great remedies require great deeds.*

The Sword Castle is a difficult place to find, and only a few have ever been within its precincts. Like the fortified lake-islands and moated castles of old, it keeps strangers at bay by its inaccessibility. This is a feature of all the castles, except the Grail Castle, which is surrounded by other protections. The Sword Ten seems to represent the enormity of our quest. There is no way into the castle save by the bridge. The castle resolutely keeps outsiders out. Our quest is stimulated both by personal need and by impersonal love of creation. There is no easy way to begin our quest, save by a personal dedication of service which clears the way. Our dedication must become our bridge.

All tarot tens potentially represent great gifts, although divinatory meanings tend to stress the responsibilities of these gifts. Sword Ten expresses a cumulation of repressed Sword gifts: championship becomes oppression, power becomes affliction, incisive clarity becomes pain. Our quest is to reverse these tendencies and discover our inner championship, wielding the Sword with compassionate clarity and loving strength.

When we finally enter the Sword Castle, we will find what kind of gifts lie in its treasury for us to discover. As we journey out from the castle in search of the Sword Hallow, we may find parts of our life that have dictated our response and perhaps distorted our focus. We begin to understand our life's direction by means of the Greater Powers whom we encounter in this landscape and we welcome the guidance of the Hallow Family whose qualities reflect the aspirations of our quest. The Sword Hallow itself is a true mirror, showing our life's direction with unswerving truth.

## Questions

1. What crises surround you at present – as a person, as a citizen of your land, as a human being upon planet earth?
2. What opportunities for total change lie in your grasp?
3. If you were supremely daring and courageous, what actions would you take now to remedy the problems of the first question?

## Meditation

1. Take the Rainbow Path of the Seeker and enter the innerworlds until you come to a cross-roads. Take the eastern road and travel until you come to the Sword Ten, following the Rainbow Path.
2. Enter the Sword Ten card and go inside the Sword Castle. Describe what you find inside. Who is within? Explore it.
3. Within the Sword Castle there is a locked room that is rarely opened. Find the key and go inside. There is a book in which the deeds of your *present* incarnation are detailed. Take two sheets of paper. On the left-hand one list the deeds that have upset the lives and circumstances of others, bringing imbalance or disharmony into the world. Do not indulge in guilt, but look at your list dispassionately. On the right-hand page, write down what you are currently doing to keep your existence harmonious within creation. You may also want to write down the ways in which you wish to bring restitution or harmony to situations that you have helped unbalance. Destroy the left-hand page and put the right-hand one into your book of life.
4. Fly aloft with the hawk and look down over the Realm of the Sword – what do you see? What does the land look like? Which areas look healthy, which need attention?

## Spring Ceremony of the Sword Hallow

This should be performed on the Spring Equinox (21 March in the northern hemisphere, 21 September in the southern hemisphere).

The Spring tide comes in at the Spring Equinox, 21 March. This tide is usually heralded by the gusty March winds. Both the Spring and Autumn Equinoxes suffer particularly choppy seas and it is usually unwise to take a sea-journey at this time. The Spring Equinox can be a particularly rough time on the psychic and emotional levels; you may find that you need to exercise great calmness and patience at this time. The Spring warmth causes the flowers suddenly to shoot up, but only after their exposure to the germinating chill of Winter. Trees come into new leaf and blossom. The Zodiacal sign of Aries starts at this time and is the initiator of a tide of new beginnings. This is the moment to start new works which you have conceived over the period of Winter. The Sword of will is grasped firmly in hand, imbuing us with confidence and purpose.

The four seasonal rituals in this book are intended to help you focus upon your quest for the Hallows and to prepare the inner way. Each can be performed simply with the minimum of equipment. If you have not enacted a ritual before, you may feel tempted the first time just to read it through quietly to yourself and leave it at that. But ritual has to be personally enacted: so get up out of your chair and do it! Written courses can easily become introverted exercises in ego-stroking unless the student really intends to interact with the cosmos and help focus the potencies of the Hallows for the benefit of all creation. You may wish to adapt this ritual for use in a small group.

Rituals are not just made up of words. Suggestions are given to help you concentrate on what you are doing and why. Your intention is the dynamo of the ritual vehicle: the words, gestures and movements are the fuel. Don't be afraid of long moments of silence: it is in the sacred silence that the Spirit speaks to your soul.

# General Notes for Performance of the Quarterly Rituals

Each ritual comes in seven parts.

1. The Making Sacred: this is where mundane space is ritually demarcated, becoming sacred space. This is done by invoking the four elements, and by asking the help of all inner helpers. The elemental qualities are visualized by feeling their action within your own body, within the earth and their archetypal action.
2. Meditation on the Mystery of the Festival: here you attune to the season in a deeper way and bring to mind the needs of the world which the Hallow in question can alleviate.

3. Invocation and Visualization of the Hallow Guardian:
   The Sword is under the guardianship of the Lady of the Lake
   The Spear is under the guardianship of Arthur
   The Grail is under the guardianship of Guinevere
   The Stone is under the guardianship of Merlin.
Each is asked to preside over the ritual and act as an initiator.
4. The Epiphany of the Hallow: an epiphany is 'a showing forth' or
   'manifestation'. This is the mystical heart of the ritual where the
   Hallow comes into operation in our world.
5. Communion: here you share the gifts of the season in a simple
   celebratory meal.
6. Establishing the Hallow Shrine: your quest is an ongoing one. By
   making a simple shrine, you will remember your purpose and the oath
   you made at it. If you cannot maintain an elaborate or obvious shrine,
   then sain (make holy) the place where it is to be and merely prop up
   your symbolic Hallow token each time you sit to meditate. This token
   can be a drawing on paper or painted stone which depicts the Hallow
   in question. The following might be used without calling overt
   attention to your shrine:
   Sword: a small knife
   Spear: a sharpened twig
   Grail: a small bowl/dish
   Stone: a pebble
7. The Return: this concludes the ritual and must never be left out. Your
   sacred space returns to its mundane state again.

Parts 1 and 7 of the Hallow rituals only appear here. You will need to
turn back to these pages when you perform the seasonal rituals of the
Spear, Grail and Stone.

Before you begin, you will need appropriate seasonal flowers, some
incense for air, a candle for fire, a cup or chalice for water, a bowl of earth,
and something to symbolize the Hallow. You will also need bread/
biscuit/wafer and wine/milk/water to make a ritual meal.

Although a full ritual format is given here, feel free to use your own
form of words, or add those given. The words in italic are spoken. Readers
in the southern hemisphere should note that your ritual action will be
anticlockwise: this is not a sinister instruction but a dictation of necessity,
since your magnetic 'north' is the South Pole. Please reverse the
instructions accordingly, moving East, North, West and South in turn.

### 1. The Making Sacred
Standing centrally, facing East,
   *In the season of Spring, I dedicate myself to the quest for the Sword
   of Light.*

Taking up the incense, face East and say,

*In the East, I call upon the power of the element of Air.* (Become aware of the element by breathing deeply and oxygenating your whole body. Perceive the air which wreathes our planet. Envisage the primal, unpolluted air of creation.) *Blessed be the precious and preserving air which gives us life and inspiration.*

Offer (by symbolically holding up) the incense in turn to the South, West, and North (always going clockwise in the northern hemisphere).

Taking the candle, face South and say,

*In the South, I call upon the power of the element of Fire.* (Become aware of the element by feeling the blood coursing through your veins and the beating of your pulses. Perceive the heat of the sun and the warmth held within the earth's centre. Envisage the primal, unpolluted fires of creation.) *Blessed be the precious and preserving fire which gives us warmth and energy.*

Offer the candle in turn to the West, North and East.

Taking the cup of water, face West and say,

*In the West, I call upon the power of the element of Water.* (Become aware of this element by sensing the essential moisture of your own body. Perceive the sweet waters of the planet. Envisage the primal, unpolluted waters of creation.) *Blessed be the precious and preserving waters which cleanse us and give us vision.*

Offer the water in turn to the North, East and South.

Taking the bowl of earth, face North and say,

*In the North, I call upon the power of the element of Earth.* (Become aware of the substance of your own body, its skin, muscles and bones. Perceive the density and endurance of the planet. Envisage the primal, unpolluted earth of creation.) *Blessed be the precious and preserving earth which gives us nourishment and stability.*

Offer the earth in turn to the East, South and West.

Now stand centrally and raise your heart and mind upwards to the realms of the Divine. *I call upon the powers of the Divine Spirit (or of named deities or helpers).*( Be aware of spirits, spiritual teachers and guides, saints and inspirers and the influence they have had upon you.) *Blessed be your precious and preserving knowledge that illuminates our path.*

Turn clockwise to acknowledge the influence of the Spirit within the physical realm.

Now still standing centrally, direct your heart and mind downwards to the realms of the Ancestors. *I call upon the powers of the Ancestors.* (Be aware of specific family members, of the many teachers of your tradition in past ages, of totemic guides of all species.) *Blessed be your precious and preserving wisdom that guides our footsteps.*

With both hands crossed over your own breast, be aware of the soul within your body. *I call upon the powers of the soul within me.* (Recall the nature of the soul, which is a bridge between the Divine and Ancestral realms and which undergoes the experiences of incarnation in ordinary reality.) *Blessed be the precious and preserving gift that confers eternal compassion.*

## 2. Meditation on the Mystery of the Spring Equinox

*I stand at the gate of the year new-born and welcome the dawning of the light. It cuts through the darkness and doubt of Winter and releases the Hallow of the Sword. From this portal stream forth the gifts of truth, innocence and justice. May all that is false, oppressive, unjust and illusory be cut away that all creation may benefit from the gifts of this Hallow!*

Sit and enter into silent meditation upon the nature of the season in your land. Contemplate the powers of the Sword as you understand them. Bring to mind the needs of creation: your own circle of family and friends, your land, troubled places in the world, and other global issues. Spend at least ten minutes doing this.

## 3. Invocation and Visualization of the Sword Guardian

Stand facing East:

*I call upon the Lady of Lake, guardian of the Sword Hallow, to help and assist me. Lady, you are the mistress who initiates and arms the sovereign. You stand ready to guide the seeker through dream and vision, into the greater mystery of the Otherworld. I seek the empowerment of the Sword Hallow for the benefit of all beings.* (Visualize the Lady of the Lake bearing the Sword in her hand. Here you may ask her any question and listen to her words.)

Chant/sing the following (tune on p.254):

> *Lady of this ancient land,*
> *Take us gently by the hand.*
> *Show us your wisdom, show us your power,*
> *Show us the sword within your bower,*
> *Keep faith with the Seeker.*

See a ray of clear light emanating from her heart to your feet, forming a path between you. Breathe in that light, breathing it up until it reaches your heart. Now call to mind the great need for the Sword of Light in the world, holding that clear light at your heart. When the urgency of the need becomes too difficult to hold in your heart any longer, return a ray of light from your own heart until it touches the Sword. Only need of great magnitude, directed by the earnest seeker, can call forth the Sword.

## 4. The Epiphany of the Sword Hallow

Welcome the Sword in your own words, and see the light from your heart streaming into it. The Sword begins to glow with a great, piercing light that is refracted into every direction. When this happens, be aware of its light streaming impartially through the world to all who need its power. Be aware of the mediation of power. At this point, you may wish to speak aloud the people, issues or needs that are known to you, turning in a circle, so that the light of the Sword is mediated to all.

## 5. Communion

Take the food for your ritual meal and bless it in your own words. Be aware of the land where the ingredients were grown, the elements that went into growing them, and the necessity for spiritual nourishment. As you eat it, make conscious attunement with the Realm of the Sword which you are going to explore in the coming season. A suitable seasonal song can be sung to welcome the Spring.

## 6. Establishing the Sword Hallow Shrine

Bless your empty shrine with the elements and adorn it with Spring flowers. Take your chosen symbol of the Sword Hallow: *Let this token represent the power of the Sword Hallow in this place. May it be blessed by the powers of the Great Above and the Great Below, the inhabitants of the ages before the ages. This shrine is established for the restoration of all the worlds.*

Now take your symbol to each of the quarters, starting in the South, finishing East, and say: *Behold the Sword Hallow! May the gifts of truth, innocence and justice be operative in this quarter.* Place it on your shrine with: *May the power of the Sword Hallow be the indwelling presence of this shrine.* Make a gesture of homage or service and place your hand on your symbol. *On this day of the Spring Equinox, I dedicate myself to the quest for the Sword Hallow.* Make your own promise or dedication to the principles of the Sword.

## 7. The Return

The powers are thanked in the reverse order of their invocation. As you do so, bring them consciously to your mind and heart.

In the centre, with both hands crossed over your breast, *I give thanks for the gift of my ever-living soul: may I never forget my sacred quest.*

Still in the centre, direct your heart and mind to the realms of the Ancestors. *I give thanks for the powers of the Ancestors: may we ever listen for their ancient song. And may they bless my quest.*

Now raise your heart and mind to the realms of the Divine. *I give thanks for the powers of the Divine Spirit (or of named deities or helpers); may we ever live in spiritual joy. And may they bless my quest.*

Face North: *I give thanks to the element of Earth; may the power of Earth be maintained with loving service.* Touch the bowl of earth.

Face West: *I give thanks to the element of Water: may the power of Water be purified with loving service.* Touch the water within the cup.

Face South: *I give thanks to the element of Fire: may the power of Fire be fuelled with loving service.* Touch the warmth of the candle flame.

Face East: *I give thanks to the element of Air: may the power of Air be inspired with loving service.* Touch the air from the incense.

During this Spring season you can reaffirm your purpose and quest at your shrine each time you sit to meditate. You may wish to reaffirm your aspirations by a simple prayer or invocation.

# LESSON 7

# *The Sword Maiden, Sword Two and Three*

SWORD MAIDEN

**The Sword Maiden Speaks** *I sew the scabbard of the Sword: that the blade of justice may be guarded by integrity of service. I weave the belt of mercy from the hair of my head, that the bearer of the Sword may be girdled with humility and compassion.*

The Sword Maiden is a messenger and an awakener. She is that part of you that is ready to start the Sword quest with a willingness and humility that does not flinch from service, that envisages and prophesies change, even though we may not act on that vision at the time.

Each of the maidens is a virgin in the original sense of 'one who is pure to her purpose'. True virginity is about spiritual purity or integrity and is emblematically represented in Celtic tradition by crystal. Crystal enhances and amplifies, acting as a mirror in which no distortion is possible. Each of the maidens can also act as a mirror in the course of our quest. The Sword Maiden is the seer of the Sword. She has rightly intuited that it will be wielded only by a worthy champion of justice and she sets to work to awaken those in whom the qualities of the Sword lie dormant. She prepares a scabbard in which the Sword can be carried. The significance of the scabbard is related in Malory, where Arthur receives Excalibur and its sheath:

> *Whether liketh you better, said Merlin, the sword or the scabbard? Me liketh better the sword, said Arthur. Ye are more unwise, said Merlin, for the scabbard is worth ten of the swords, for whiles ye have the scabbard upon you, ye shall never lose no blood, be ye never so sore wounded; therefore keep well the scabbard always with you.* [9]

During the Grail quest, Dindraine – who is depicted on this card – presents Galahad with the sword of King David, whose girdle she has fashioned from her own hair. The scabbard of this sword is called 'Mover of Blood', made of serpent's skin and of the wood from the Tree of Life, and called so because no mortal might look upon it without being reminded of the death of Abel – the very first spilling of blood, a forerunner of the Dolorous Blow. It also has the property of preserving from bloodshed the one who wears it.

Both instances bring us back to the function of the Sword Maiden, who prepares the way for the wielder of the Sword, using her skills as seer. We note the symbolism of blood, which is safe-guarded by the scabbard or shed by the sword. The preservative virtue of the scabbard is only efficacious if the bearer lives a clean life. It is this virtue of personal integrity that the Sword Maiden upholds. Blood symbolizes the vital essence of our lives; the integrity of the body preserves it as the scabbard does the sword; our incisive acts are the strokes of the sword.

The Sword Maiden maintains the temple of the body and invests the sword-bearer with virtue. This ancient word has the original meaning of 'strength': a definition that overturns the connotation of 'a pious or narrow weakness' which it has recently accrued. The Sword Maiden corresponds to the archetype of the 'Daughter of Life'. In the quest that follows, ask her help, or that of any of the Sword Family or Greater Powers if you need clarification.

**Sword Two Speaks** *Mine is the path of amnesty. Make allies of your doubts and fears, that they may bring you into the fair land where the light of justice shines.*

Sword Two bids us bring our warring thoughts and opinions to a temporary truce. The seeker who sets out on the path of self-discovery finds that travelling in innerworlds requires a similar suspension of disbelief. We all travel 'as if' these realms were real. Their actual reality is something only you can prove to yourself by travelling thither. This important realization enables the seeker to begin the quest. In terms of the spiritual path, the seeker can spend a lot of time deliberating in this card and never starting this journey. This is a factor within all the tarot 'twos', for we can be so bound up in life issues that we endlessly delay our departure.

SWORD THREE

**Sword Three Speaks** *This is the bridge of loss. Yet not all is lost. This necessary separation leads you to a domain wherein the lost will be found, where sorrow will be assuaged by deepest joy.*

Sword Three brings us to a critical part of our path. All esoteric training changes our lives. This card, like that of the Seeker in the Wasteland, presents us with an abyss. On this side of the bridge, we know what life is like; the other side is unknown to us and therefore frightening. After we have crossed it, we may have to change and be unable to draw upon our resources, whispers a little voice. Sword Three challenges us to count the cost of our training. This is often the time when our outer lives present challenges and when we feel that to continue in this way will be to the detriment of our well-being. This critical time of decision comes to us all.

## Questions

1. Are you looking after your body, the vehicle of your soul?
2. What are you giving up to walk this path? Focus on these aspects of your life now and allow the energies that inhabit them to be released. See them pour forth freely down the path that lies before you.
3. What either/or decisions face you right now? Choose one such and list the pros and cons of either side.
4. When you meditate, do you push aside the first image that you see

as inappropriate? In future, trust the first thing you see/experience.
5. What are you desperately holding on to that needs to leave your life?
6. Who or what has been most formative in your life to date?

## Task

You can keep connection with the Sword by making a rising dedication each morning. Before you get out of bed, bring to mind your most deeply held principles, for example, 'I maintain that all life is sacred.' Visualize the Sword in the Stone and draw it forth. Whatever your hand touches during the day will be freshly energized by these principles which will then manifest in your life.

## Meditation

1. Leave the Sword Castle and find the Sword Maiden. She sits on a hill overlooking the Sword Realm where you can look down on the road ahead. The Sword Maiden is embroidering the scabbard for the Sword you hope to win. Every step of your journey is embroidered on the cloth. You may ask the Sword Maiden about any aspect of the journey ahead on your inner or outer path, for she is clear-sighted. When you are ready she will lead you into the landscape of Sword Two.
2. Follow the path that leads to the landscape of Sword Two. Consider both sides of the path, both forests. What message does your rational side give you? What message does your intuitional side give you? What is the message of the path under your feet? Ask the adder if you need guidance.
3. Follow the path to Sword Three. Bring to mind whatever makes your quest problematic. When you have crossed the bridge, cast down into the abyss anything that is unnecessary to your quest.

## ———————— LESSON 8 ————————

# *The White Hart*

**The White Hart Speaks** *Follow me: I will lead you to the fields of delight. Long ago I was crowned and caparisoned as the messenger of the lists of love. I am the desire that impels your feet to follow. I am the fleeting glimpse of paradise. The collar about my neck is linked with the gold of loving service, the fealty of friendship on your quest.*

*ʋi the white hart*

The White Hart is the Otherwordly messenger of spiritual adventure and purity of love. It is the symbol of the hunt on all levels, denoting the vision of inner beauty. *Amor* or pure love, *eros* or erotic love, desire and duty are some of the ways it manifests. Emotional ties and trust in our quest form the golden chain that leads us onwards. It represents the ways in which unequal affections can be balanced by compassionate dedication.

The White Hart is the messenger to bring us into the heart of our quest. It helps us rediscover our youthful desire, which can be honed from naive enthusiasm into a sword of true power. Ask the White Hart to help you turn the sword into a weapon of love's service that your vision may be kept bright.

The White Hart is one of the prime animals of Celto-Arthurian tradition. Its appearance betokens a thinning of the veil of reality between the worlds. Like the Unicorn, which is rarely seen, the White Hart usually leads the quester into the Otherworld. It represents the quarry of our desire. If we pursue it long enough, we will learn dedication and commitment, respect and grace. It bestows rich gifts with great simplicity and openness of heart.

## Meditation

1. Follow the path from Sword Three until you come to the woods wherein you find the White Hart. Commune with it and learn its

nature. The White Hart will be your guide upon this Sword quest and you can ask it for help or advice.

2. Become one of the lovers in the picture. Standing opposite you in this wood is your best beloved. What is the greatest thing you can offer him/her?

3. Before you pass onwards, ask a gift of the White Hart. This gift may appear as a symbolic object. If you don't understand what the gift signifies, ask.

## Task

Create a reading that uses 10-15 cards, including the Sword Maiden, Sword Two and Three, The White Hart and Sword Ten, drawing upon the pack at random to make up the number of cards required. Use some of the themes you have explored to stand as position-meanings. OR Create a story, in which you yourself are a character and in which these cards appear, using other cards at random or by choice, as needed.

---

# LESSON 9

# *The Sword Knight, Sword Four and Five*

sword knight

**The Sword Knight Speaks** *I rise like hope with the dawning, in the service of the Sword. I listen to its voice and follow wherever it leads me, that injustice may be vanquished and the oppressed set free of torment.*

The Sword Knight is a fearless companion on the quest. He is that part of you that learns through the journey of the quest, taking forthright action whatever the time of day or night in the fearless defence of the innocent. He accompanies us, reminding us to remain wakeful.

Each of the knights is a prime-mover in whom the strengths and weaknesses of their Hallow quality is evident. Knights are mounted warriors who can move where they will in the service of the chivalric code. In Celtic tradition, warriors are emblematically associated with bronze, the alloy of copper and tin. Bronze is strong and yielding at the same time, like the Hallow knights, who are resolute but vulnerable. Their adaptability is a factor in their defence of the Hallow. Each of the knights exemplifies the mood of different times of day when they are particularly strong.

The Sword Knight is the Way-Shower of the Sword. He rises early, opening the gates of dawn to reveal a pathway through which the Sword can be manifest. Dawn has ever been the traditional time when the fears that gather in darkness and the oppressions of evil are overthrown. The cold light of morning brings its own hard-edged reality which banishes phantoms.

This card is based on the figure of Lleminawc the Irishman, 'the Fated Deliverer', whose flashing sword is the signal for Arthur to steal the cauldron of Diwrnach or Pen Annwn from the Underworld of Annwn in ancient British tradition. The cauldron was that which would not boil the food of cowards; food for one person could be put into it and food for one hundred brought out again. In *Culhwch and Olwen*, Lleminawc seizes Arthur's sword Caledfwlch (Excalibur), causing it to flash brightly: this feature also appears in *The Dream of Rhonabwy* where Arthur's sword is fashioned of two serpents which burst into flame whenever it is drawn from its scabbard.[8] Lleminawc has been associated by scholars with the later figure of Lancelot, who himself performs the spectacular feat of crossing a sword-bridge in his attempt to rescue Guinevere from imprisonment.

We note that the courage of the sword's wielder causes the Sword to emit light. The action of the Sword also releases treasures which are being hidden away or held inoperative in the inner worlds. This is one of the damning features of our society: that we each use very little of our inner resourcefulness but depend on public or corporate figures to act on our behalf. The sudden lightening flash of the Sword can help bring us to awareness of our gifts and wake us from our sleep of dependency or forgetfulness of our duty. The incisive stroke of the Sword can also liberate us from the chains of stale custom or oppressive bondage.

The function of the Sword Knight is to restore what is lost and to awaken that which is sleeping. One of the inner titles of this archetype is 'the Son of Life'.

SWORD FOUR

**Sword Four Speaks** *At twilight, the seeker rests. Sink deeply into the peace of the spirit and wake refreshed for the quest.*

Sword Four bids us take time to nourish ourselves. We need many kinds of nourishment to keep us healthy: food and rest for our bodies, daily meditation and prayer for our spirits. When we start our esoteric training, we are impatient of any period of seeming passivity. These times of fallowness should be welcomed as necessary stopping places on the quest.

**Sword Five Speaks** *One misplaced spark causes conflagration. No amount of self-justification will replant a forest.*

Sword Five reminds us that every action we make has its effect somewhere. The Swords represent light but, just as when someone maliciously focuses the light of the sun through a burning glass on to flammable materials, it can be misused, becoming an agent of destruction. The tarot fives represent the kinds of major obstacles that

stand in the path of our quest. As Swords represent life patterns, so the Sword Five shows how we are when we run from our quest. Swords draw their prime impetus from justice: the distortion of this is justification, one of its weakest and most cowardly substitutes.

## Questions

1. Which deeply seated fears need the fearless action of the Sword Knight?
2. In which areas of your life do you need to be more adaptable?
3. What lies imprisoned within you?
4. Which part of yourself is undernourished?
5. How are you sabotaging your own life right now? Look at areas of untidy or sloppy thinking/planning/organization. How can you sharpen up your act?
6. Who or what do you blame when things go wrong? Objectively assess why you blame and what lies at the root of troubles you may be currently facing.

## Task

Spend one morning/afternoon/evening this week in complete rest. Make sure you prepare everything you need for this special time of rest and recovery from your quest.

## Meditation

1. You now pass from your own inner landscape into the Lands Adventurous, which border upon it. The Lands Adventurous are where you encounter challenges and testings. Leaving the White Hart, you follow the path and encounter the Sword Knight at morning. He will guard your way on this part of your quest. You accompany him to the distant sacred hill where you dedicate your quest at the shrine that is there.
2. In the company of the Sword Knight you travel to Sword Four. Here the Sword Knight prepares you for the vigil that you must make in this chapel. What happens during your vigil?
3. You follow the path to Sword Five. What has happened here? What can you do to set things straight?

---

# LESSON 10

## *The Round Table*

> **The Round Table Speaks** *I am the mirror of the cyclic tides. The spinning earth, the season's circle, the wheeling stars: all answer to the*

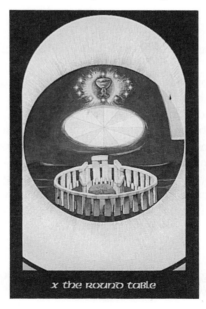

x the ROUNO taBLe

*natural law of life. I see the fulfilment of the tides of time, the incarnational patterns that spiral out from the still point of every soul. I hold the centre in every age, welcoming each living soul to the perilous siege of service.*

The Round Table represents the stability of eternal laws. Whoever sits at it is subject to those laws and learns the way in which our lives must adapt in order to be true to them. The place of ancient assembly where the ancestral tribes met is here formalized into a meeting table. But above all images is the eternal starry council which oversees the fate of those upon earth. This card is about our incarnational field of service.

The Round Table is one of the three reavings of the Pendragon line: Ambrosius took the Stones of Mount Killarus to form the monument of the dead; Uther stole the wife of Gorlois to be his own; while Arthur reaved the cauldron of Diwrnach for eternal life, which he has won. The story of Merlin's magical transposition of Stonehenge from Ireland to England is told by Geoffrey of Monmouth in his *History of the Kings of Britain*. It is a parable about the transmission of tradition, for the stones of Killarus in this story may have curative properties and their talismanic power is brought to Britain by Merlin.

We seek to come to this table and dedicate ourselves to the quest in true earnest, as the knights dedicated themselves to the service of Arthur's kingdom. The Round Table was made in the likeness of the earth's roundness. It is for us to discover the universal applications of our spiritual service, that the ripples of our actions may spread wider throughout the world. The gift of the Round Table is in helping us to live in harmony with the cosmic laws.

## Meditation

1. Leaving the devastation of Sword Five, you come to a hillside overlooking an open plain where you see the Stone Circle of the Round Table card. Stand at the Stone Circle's centre and turn to each trilithon doorway. See the cycles of your life ·so far through each opening.
2. Be aware of the Stone Circle fading and being replaced by a Round Table. Who sits there? What is the most urgent wrong to be righted?
3. Be aware of the Round Table transmuting into a starry circle. Listen to the singing of the Grail. What is its message for you?
4. Be once more aware of the Stone Circle. On the central stone lies a gift for you, left there by the merlin who sees all.

# Task

Look back upon the three circles of your experience: the circle of your culture, land and society; the circle of your family; the circle of your education. What are the best things that you have gathered at these points of interrelation?

# ─── LESSON 11 ───

## *The Sword Queen, Sword Six and Seven*

SWORD QUEEN

**The Sword Queen Speaks** *I am she who burnishes the Sword when it is dull from combat. I guard the watchful rest and oversee the skilful preparation for the fray. Mine is the equity of just deliverance, the unswerving light that cleaves injustice in twain.*

The Sword Queen is one who inculcates a love of life. She is that part of us that has found the object of the quest, the part that is dedicated to the eradication of ignorance by effective action.

Each queen is the bearer or mother of her Hallow. The position of queen is often depicted as a passive one, yet it is critically important in upholding and maintaining the focus of sovereignty. The principles of the land are also hers. In Celtic tradition, queens are emblematically depicted within a field of silver to denote their grace and insight. Each queen is the powerhouse of each quest and invests all her fosterlings with a cloak of empowerment.

The Sword Queen is the empowerer of the Sword. By her often harsh words, we are driven to strive harder and to win our own sword by grappling with her in combat. She burnishes the Sword to keep it bright, encouraging us also to keep our integrity bright by its constant application in our lives.

The archetype of the woman warrior is a common one in Celtic tradition. Many Celtic heroes, including both Fionn MacCumail and Cuchulainn, have female instructors in arms. In the Arthurian tradition, it is Peredur, the early Perceval, who receives this kind of tuition. He is defending the castle of a maiden from the nine witches of Gloucester, when he hears an outcry in the middle of the night. He rushes out and wounds one of the witches and she asks mercy of him by name:

> 'How knowest thou, hag, that I am Peredur?'
> 'By destiny and the foreknowledge that I should suffer harm from thee. And thou shalt take a horse and armour of me; and with me thou shalt go to learn chivalry and the use of thy arms.'[8]

Peredur goes with her and becomes accomplished in arms. It may seem odd that one of Arthur's knights should need such tuition, but Peredur was raised by his mother in ignorance of arms in the depths of a forest, since she wished him to live peacefully and not die in battle like her husband and other sons. The woman warrior of Gloucester and her sisters are called witches or sorceresses in the story, but they are more likely remembrances of a circle of priestesses whose specialist skills serviced the ancient Celtic world. We may wonder also at the prophetic insight of the woman warrior who foretells her own death at Peredur's hands.

This brings us back to the function of the Sword Queen, which is to inculcate practical understanding to her fosterlings. Her desire to train and send out into the world one whose skills surpass even her own: this is the ambition of any good teacher who sees that the best way of redeeming their own debt of thanks to their tutor is to pass on what she has learned to others. If only one student surpasses her own skills, she can be proud.

The Sword Queen is thus a stern teacher who teaches us every stroke of the blade, how to parry and how to attack. Not only with her sword, but also with her tongue, she can lash out and expose our flank so that we will know how best to defend ourselves next time. One of her many titles is 'the Mother of the Life', for she fosters the life within us by her strong defence.

**Sword Six Speaks** *I bear you safely away from trouble. Take heart and find joy in the winding way that lies before you.*

Sword Six is like a haven of harmony along a difficult road. The sudden appearance of the boat at this point takes you from the road to the river. All the even-numbered Sword cards represent some kind of rest or respite from the quest, from the stagnation of Sword Eight to the joyful release of this card. When our quest has seemed particularly arduous it is sometimes disorientating to find that suddenly there are no obstacles: the journey must proceed by a different, easier means. The ease that is won by hard work sometimes surprises the student. Accept it as a free gift, a bonus or reward for your labour, and enjoy the sensation of being carried along while this phase lasts. It is a time marked by synchronous events, by insights in meditation that come as if by second nature, by luminous dreams and happy coincidences that give life a charmed quality.

**Sword Seven Speaks** *I flow, I flood, I fail. Draw forth the sword that the quest may be achieved.*

Sword Seven represents the first signs of oscillation that indicate the quest is losing impetus. All students wobble from time to time, especially when the free ride of Sword Six comes to its end. The need to grasp the sword and draw it forth is not immediately recognized after the holiday euphoria of easy realization has evaporated. Refocusing is hard work. It seems easier

SWORD SEVEN

to leave the quest to others. Only by systematically reapplying our
rhythmic meditational pattern will the way become easier again.

## Questions

1. What training do you most need to be effective in your life?
2. How would you describe yourself to others?
3. Are you a defensive or forthright person?
4. What is passing away from your life right now?
5. If you could holiday anywhere at all, where would it be? In
   visualization, go to that place now. In non-ordinary reality, who is the
   guardian spirit of that place? What does that guardian say to you?

## Meditation

1. Leaving the Round Table, you journey deeper into the Otherworld.
   Here you come to a clearing in which you meet the Sword Queen.
   You may ask her to help you overcome any disempowerment which
   is troubling you.
2. In her company, travel to Sword Six and take the little boat. Where
   does it take you?
3. Leaving the boat, proceed on foot until you find the floating stone
   of Sword Seven. Take a branch from the bank of the river and stop
   the floating stone. Can you pull the sword from it?

# The Cauldron

xiv the cauldron

**The Cauldron Speaks** *Who seeks rebirth must enter the transforming vessel. I am the womb of transmutation. I am the agent of regeneration, wherein the elements of life are remade. I am the witness of all initiations and my brew is blent of every experience upon earth. Drink from me and be remade.*

The Cauldron represents the regeneration of all things created. This process may take many years, and no amount of impatience will speed it up. In the alchemical work, as on the esoteric path, the elements within the alchemical *vas*, within the cauldron or within the womb, must be truly mixed in order to manifest. A draught of the cauldron will bring us to memory of our true selves and to spiritual empowerment.

The Adder is the totem beast of this card and it appears twice in the Sword Realm: here and within Sword Two. It signifies the transformation that is undergone at this point in the journey. There comes a point when the knowledge that we hold in separate vessels boils over and recombines, bringing us a new set of understandings. This tends to overset our fixed notions to such an extent that we need a goodly period to assimilate our findings.

The Cauldron is usually administered by nine sisters, represented here by three of their number (see Matthews, *Ladies of the Lake*). Like the nine muses, they represent the manifold gifts of the arts which recreate our world. Each of the ninefold breathes upon the brew of the cauldron and endows it with her own quality. The gift of the Cauldron is the healing of change.

## Meditation

1. Leaving the landscape of Sword Seven, you follow the river into its underground cavern, finding the Cauldron.
2. One of the Cauldron guardians takes you to a nearby cavern to meet one of your distant ancestors. You may ask the ancestor questions.
3. If you wish, you may place any quality, situation or thing into the cauldron to be transformed.
4. Ask the Cauldron guardians for a gift that will transform your life, but be aware that if you ask for this, you *will* change.

## Ninefold Sisters Reading

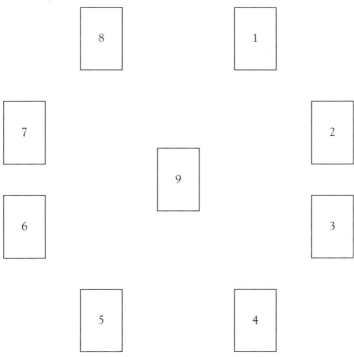

Fig. 7: *Ninefold Sisters Spread*

Each card in this reading represents one of the sisterhood of the cauldron. You can read about their roles in more detail in *Ladies of the Lake*. Use this reading to clarify your ideas about projects you are working on. As you shuffle the cards, visualize the cauldron before you.

## Meaning of Positions

1. The Energizer: what needs more energy in the situation?
2. The Measurer: what are the limitations of the matter?
3. The Protector: how does the matter need protection?
4. The Initiator: what will lead you deeper into the matter?
5. The Challenger: what challenges will hone and shape it?
6. The Deliverer: what needs liberating in the matter?
7. The Weaver: what creative aspects are still lacking?
8. The Preserver: what will sustain this?
9. The Empowerer: what gives it final empowerment?

# —————————— LESSON 13 ——————————

# *The Sword King, Sword Eight and Nine*

sword king

**The Sword King Speaks** *Many come to this mound demanding justice, wanting one word of mine to change their lives. But my answers come from the earth itself and accord with natural justice first. The land is patient and waits long: my judgements come from its deep heart. The service of the Sword is the path of justice. Whoever walks that path must walk the sword-bridge of balanced truth.*

The Sword King is an insightful counsellor and judge. He is that part of you that is committed to understanding the qualities and functions of the Hallow he guards. This requires the deep analytical insights of concentrated meditation.

Each king is the guardian of his Hallow's power, exemplifying it. In Celtic tradition, kings are emblematically depicted within a field of gold, betokening their steadfast nature. Each king is thus a touchstone of truth.

The Sword King is the guardian of the Sword. He wields its power impartially, for none may presume upon executive use of its qualities, least of all the King himself. Whoever takes the Sword unworthily for selfish ends is usually destroyed by it. This explains the dynamic tension in this card, for the King listens well to the voice of the Sword. In many traditions, swords sing to proclaim their inner nature when they are drawn. The Sword King is the voice of the Sword and speaks as a judge.

In Celtic lore, as in other North European traditions, law-giving and judgement often took place on a mound. This tradition may be traced to the reverence for certain sacred sites, which were the nexus points between the Otherworld and our own. The kingly judge was set up on a high place, above the people who came to be judged, but not as high as the Gods themselves. In medieval tradition both kings and judges made circuits of the land so that all people could receive the blessings of good sovereignty and justice. This was an important progress which kept people and sovereign in contact with each other, mindful of the sacred contract that both subject and sovereign owed to each other and the land. A noble king would always create opportunities for justice to be done.

In this subtle relationship, the importance of listening was paramount. The king or judge listened to the 'hearings' in full court; the people also listened and heeded what was said. All evidences were weighed against a deeper voice: that of the justice of Sovereignty, the Goddess of the Land herself.

Arthur's establishment of the Round Table is in accordance with this tradition, for not only does it send forth knights to act as a chivalric militia against oppression, it also acts as a focus of justice.

The Sword King is the just and discerning maintainer of the Sword. Like Solomon's, his sword can cut both ways. Those who appeal to him for justice do well to also ask for mercy, for the blade is sharp and his judgement may be severe and exacting. Yet, he can show us the way to keep our lives on their rightful course by means of self-clarification, for he is the 'Father of Life' who accords respect to all.

sword eight

**Sword Eight Speaks** *Energy follows thought. Why have you imprisoned yourself in this place?*

Sword Eight represents the kinds of self-made mind-traps into which we can fall if we don't maintain an open mind. This is a particularly pernicious trap for esoteric students, who can become obsessively wound up with their system of study. By following it by rote, they may suddenly find themselves plodding endlessly round in a treadmill. It is only when we allow the light of our own originality to shine that such stagnation is illuminated and kindled to fresh activity. Even the most basic questioning can agitate the prison-bars sufficiently to dislodge a few of them. It is often a question of passing beyond the narrow definitions of others: we are all unique human beings with a capacity and resourcefulness that can take us to the heart of our quest. Another person's path may not be yours.

**Sword Nine Speaks** *I challenge you to the combat within; let the barrier between your world and this be dissolved and may peace reign between us.*

If Sword Eight represented self-made prisons, then Sword Nine represents the mental anguish endured within those prisons. In our time there are more cases of mental torment than at any other era in history, it seems. From everyday human paranoias through to the worst criminal mentalities, we see the horrific defeat that humankind has brought upon itself. Our species has imprisoned every other species in its own conceptual frameworks, which are alien to the natural order. The existential anguish of humankind is certainly in proportion to its need for the Sword's liberation.

## Questions

1. Which actions violate your sense of integrity? You may find the perusal of a daily newspaper will help focus your sense of justice.
2. What are the best ways of listening to the messages of the earth?
3. Which areas of your life are unmoving and stagnant?
4. What are your worst fears?

## Tasks

1. Spend one day this week really listening to what people say to you; concentrate on listening rather than responding. What did you hear?
2. Choose one area of personal responsibility and determine to take positive action on it this week.

3. Pick out a recurring nightmare or a bad dream you have recently had. Write it down. What is most fearful to you in this dream and why? Now rewrite your dream, bringing it to a satisfactory resolution using the imagery and power of the Sword cards.

## Meditation

1. Leaving the underground cavern where the Cauldron is, follow the way upwards until you meet the Sword King. He is the guardian of the deep Otherworld who will bring you to the illumination of the Moon. Sit beside him and witness his judgement as people are brought before him. If you are brave enough, you may also submit any matter before him for impartial assessment.
2. The Sword King guides you to the moor of Sword Eight and here leaves you alone for a period. Meditate upon the things that hem you in, the way that others' opinions circumscribe your life, and your own stale patterns of thought which restrict you. What are the most effective ways of by-passing or overcoming these restrictions?
3. You follow the path until you arrive at night outside the stockade of Sword Nine, with severed heads aligned upon the fence. As you gaze on the sword in the ditch, bring to mind the times when you have succumbed to grave doubts, to depression or despair, the times when you've thrown in the towel. With fresh resolve, take the sword out of the ditch and make your own vow of disciplined commitment.

─────────────── **LESSON 14** ───────────────

# *The Moon*

**The Moon Speaks** *The experience that you seek comes from a time when I was part of the earth. I appear in your sky to show that things grow, change and die and are born again – nothing is complete for eternity. What do you need to lose? What skill do you rejoice in? What is striving to be born within you? What lies dead and is awaiting transformation? As the sword Excalibur was taken from the waiting earth, so too was I.*

The experience of this card is the rediscovery of potential and the necessary fallowness that we must live through in order to gain new understanding. The fiction of progress makes us all wish to make haste

xviii the moon

to gain wisdom. The truth is that we cannot force growth. We may indeed intellectually comprehend certain aspects of esoteric wisdom, but they remain meaningless until we receive personal experience of them. The Moon is endlessly patient, waiting for us to grow, allowing us to undergo the painful process of self-discovery that will help us manifest the wisdom we so desperately seek to be ennobled by. The Sword is forged in secret: the skill to wield it becomes ours only after painful and ardent practice. These are the stark initiations that we receive bare-breasted under the Moon, when we cry, 'Why me?'

Our society has lost its children and its childhood. The story of Mabon which underlies this card, his loss and finding, is essentially personal to our own experience. We often lose our childhood's vision, delight and wonder when we grow up. Mabon helps us regain these qualities but only if we value all phases of life and respect all species. The imbalance of our society is shown in the received pecking order of importance: male adults at the top, followed by women a little lower down, then children, animals, plants, minerals etc. This hierarchical view is the legacy of our culture and one which is still intrusive and persuasive in our society.

Many commentators on the Tarot speak of the Moon as unchancy, because of its mutability, full of psychic spooks and frightening fantasies. This dualistic view plays upon our fear of the unknown. The experience of the Moon's illumination is under the aegis of the Lady who is our fosterer – she knows the wisdom we need to gain and she will put us in the way of the necessary experience when the time comes. We are prepared for our life journey in her womb, where our potential qualities are also nurtured. The gift of the Moon is the realization that we are the sword awaiting to be drawn from the stone.

## Meditation

1. The Sword King leads you away from the sorry scene of Sword Nine until you enter the landscape of the Moon card where your vision is cleansed of the troubles of your quest. Alone, you climb upon the back of the salmon and swim to the furthest horizon of your own potential. What lies in that country to be discovered?
2. Return from your excursion with the salmon, who leaves you at the doorway to one of the two towers. Go within and release whatever/whoever lies imprisoned within.
3. When you return from the Tower, you see the salmon bearing a gift in its mouth. It will help you come to spiritual rebirth.

---

# LESSON 15

# *The Lady of the Lake*

ıı the laоy of the lake

**The Lady of the Lake Speaks** *I am the Fosterer of all knowledge. The flight of my cranes writes my wisdom on the winds, and in the depths of the lake are the far memories wakened. You seek me in the rustling of the reeds and in the empty places of your soul. I will help you find the empowerment that you seek and give you the Sword of my authority. Fosterling, come to the secret places and learn of me!*

She is our foster mother, our teacher, the true wisdom who loves us enough to let us be. She is not a mother in the way that Guinevere can be, full of gifts for her children; the Lady is secret and remote in order to help us learn. Every time we take the inner road – by meditation or dream – to her realm, we are aware of how very special the Lady of Lake can be to us. She is the initiator of the Sword, of justice through inner wisdom.

The Lady keeps the ancient places. Within her book all the secrets of esoteric wisdom are written. We cannot read this book for ourselves, because we live on the wrong side of the veil. For us these secrets are written on the wind, in the water, in the portent of fire and the casting of the stones or twigs. We do not need to read countless esoteric books in order to find the ancient wisdom of the Lady of the Lake. We only have to enter the stillness of creation and listen well.

The Lady does not walk abroad in our world, unless she is veiled. But she may appear to us in unexpected ways as a guide and instructor. She allows us brief glimpses of knowledge, like a mother weaning her child, until we can bear the full illumination of enlightenment. By the time we have become readers of her book, we ourselves understand the impossibility of divulging what we have learned to others: not because of esoteric secrecy, but because the experience we receive defies language. The gift of the Lady is the healing empowerment of knowledge.

# Meditation

Go down-river from the Moon card and follow the cranes' flight. They direct you until you arrive at the lake where you meet the Lady of the Lake. You are already written into her book and she greets you. She asks you what wisdom you are currently fostering. You answer. She invites you to lay it, in a symbolic form, in the basket floating at her feet. It will then grow under her watchful eye. She then gives you a gift.

# The Sword Hallow

sword hallow

**The Sword Hallow Speaks** *Who wields me, wields victory. Who comes against me, shall not rise again. I am the Bright One who illumines the dark places of the soul. I give hope to the oppressed. I bring help to the powerless. Mine is the deep deliverance that sings of Spring.*

The Sword Hallow which is sought on this quest affirms the incisive energy of life. It dispels illusion, bringing light to dark places. It is the champion of innocence, truth, justice. Although swords are thought of as instruments of destruction, this Sword is one of the ancient gifts and empowerers of the land. When it is manifest, it overthrows injustice and oppression. It cuts through obstacles like the cutting winds of March, dispelling Winter and bringing the renewal of Spring to the land.

Swords are associated in our society with violent death, skilful combat, ceremonial processions and military or sovereign investiture. Swords are rarely used in daily life today and even when they were commonly in use, they were usually worn only by gentlemen or knights, not by commoners. On this course it is the appropriate symbol of one who is setting out on a quest for the first time, because the quester seeks to discipline his or her will under service. To wield the Sword, the quester must possess great integrity.

## Meditation

You ask the Lady for sight of the Sword Hallow. She asks by what right you make this request, and you make your reply. But no mortal can have sight of it. With a touch of her hand, she transforms you into one of her cranes and you fly aloft in their company. You fly high until you come to a summit where the winds meet. Here you find a deep fissure in the rock from which issues a great cloud of steam. From it arises the Sword.

Look along the burnished metal of the Sword and see a pathway leading from it ahead of you. This pathway is the augury or mystical foretelling of the Sword, for you personally. Follow that pathway and see where it leads. Record all that you see and experience. What relevance does it have for your life and spiritual progress?

You return from the mountain and the Lady touches you once again, so that you resume your shape. Her book has become the Arthurian Tarot, which she hands to you. Now you make the following reading:

## The Augury of the Sword of Life

For this augury, remove the Sword Hallow and all the Greater Powers. Set the Sword Hallow card at position 5. As you shuffle the remainder of the pack, strongly visualize or gaze at the Sword, and put your trust in its inspiration. Ask it: 'How can the Sword be manifest within me?' Then draw four cards from the main pack and lay these on positions 1-4. Shuffle the Greater Powers separately and ask for the augury (or prophecy) of the Sword Hallow. Draw one card and lay it on position 5, covering the Sword Hallow. Each of the positions in this augury represents some aspect of the Light which the Sword symbolizes.

1. Represents your power, the cutting edge of your will. Unless it is balanced by loving service, it can be oppressive to others. The challenge of this card is, 'How do I discriminate?'
2. Represents the illusions that the Sword can dispel for you. We are each englamoured by various illusions which restrict us; the Sword will overcome these. Illusions arise in our minds and can rule us insidiously. The challenge here is, 'What am I holding on to?'
3. Represents the area in your life where the Sword can champion you. This may be an area where you are disempowered, oppressed or not free to act. The challenge here is, 'What freedom do I need?'
4. Represents your integrity. Things go wrong when the truth is not

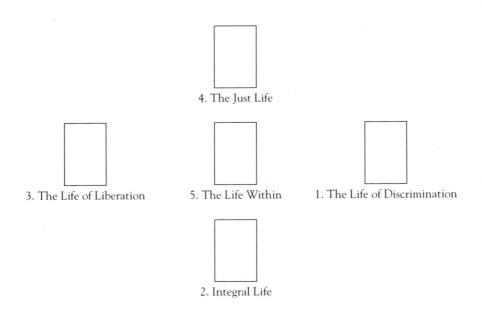

Fig. 8: *The Augury of the Sword*

   upheld. The challenge here is, 'How do I serve justice?'
5. Represents the inner integrity that illumines your way. This Greater
   Power card represents the nature of your inner life. It challenges you
   to answer, 'How am I serving the universe?'

After you've laid and interpreted your reading briefly, look down at it
and ask the Sword Hallow to speak to you through it. You can take the
central card as a guide and travel through your spread in meditation.

**Diary Example:**      **Reading:**
5.6.91              *The Augury of the Sword*

1. *Sword Five. When I saw this I nearly gave up! What a terrible card to draw!*
   *Unethical and sloppy! Is this really how I discriminate?*
2. *Spear Knight. This is a hard one. I suppose I am like this: rushing off to*
   *have inner adventures without a moment's thought. I've learned that*
   *meditation is made of far more than this.*
3. *Spear Eight. This suggests that I need to go into full spate and not be*
   *restrained by circumstance. My present stop-go-stop pattern is becoming very*
   *frustrating.*

4. *Spear King. I must serve the justice of the Sword by being like the Spear King: open to ways of healing. This includes listening to others more, which I'm very bad at.*
5. *Green Knight. I need him as a teacher and Way-Shower of Light, to help me conquer my inflexibility and to help move me out of stagnation into a wider creative pattern.*

After I wrote this down, I asked the Sword Hallow to speak to me through the reading. Here's what it said: 'You have laboured long without resting. Go now with the Green Knight and visit the scenes and people of this augury.' The Sword Hallow authorized the Green Knight to take my hand and we set off. 'I am the sword that was broken because it wasn't equal to the fight', said Sword Five. 'You must leave me behind you and find another.' 'You want adventures, but they come too thick and fast for you. Learn to find your own centre by considering the noon-day sun', said the Spear Knight. 'No one stops the spate of my inspiration. Go with the flow and find the place of your renewal', said Spear Eight. 'You've come to the right place', said the Spear King. 'Plunge into the fire of my forge and be remade.' Before I knew what I was doing, I was inside the fire, which didn't burn me. I had become molten metal. Each stroke of the hammer was another knock on the anvil of life itself. The Green Knight drew me out and breathed on me saying, 'Be a soul new-made, a blade keen in the struggle, a weapon against the darkness.' All the while I had the sensation of the Sword very close to the back of my neck. I heard the sound of a blade being sharpened and the distinct chime of its singing, like great sheets of gold foil twisting in the breeze. (Later I remembered that Gawain hears the Green Knight whetting his axe-blade with sounds like these! Very eerie!)

# ———————— LESSON 17 ————————

## *The Investiture of the Sword*

*Lay the cards of this Sword Quest about you, either on the floor or about your room, in the following way:*

This is the inner court of the Sword which you have explored upon this quest. Here the Lady of the Lake sits surrounded by the quest's inner figures of inspiration. The time has come for the investiture of the Sword.

Fig. 9: *The Inner Court of the Sword*

## Meditation

Visualize the eastern part of your inner landscape that you worked with in Lesson 5. Now see the inner court of the Sword superimposed upon it. Seeing the Rainbow Path of the Seeker at the centre of your inner landscape, you now enter this airy Sword quarter, passing through it without fear or difficulty. You may wish to meditate upon this over several sessions.

As you approach each new scene or character, briefly enter into communion with it. Start meditating at the Sword Maiden and continue in clockwise order. The Sword Family gives you gifts: the Maiden gives you a scrying crystal that is tuned to the Sword Hallow; the Knight gives you an emblem of the dawn; the Queen gives you a healing herb; the King gives you a gold coin with your own image upon one side and the Sword on the other. These gifts will prove useful in your future journeys in the Sword Realm. Each of the landscape cards gives you a different coloured ribbon with which to weave a scabbard for the Sword. Each of the Greater Powers imparts a special blessing.

Continue meditating on each of the cards in order until you reach the centre where the Lady of the Lake sits in the Sword Castle (Sword Ten) with the Sword Hallow in front of her. You may not enter here until you have shown her the gifts you have gained from the Greater Powers during your meditations of this season. The combined energy of these gifts forms a strong bridge between the place where she sits and the Sword Castle. You kneel before her and make your personal dedication to the Sword. Then you enshrine the Sword in the Sword Castle, which is the same as the Eastern Caer of your own inner landscape.

Slowly allow this image to fade and to be replaced by that of your own Sword shrine. Open your eyes and formally repeat your inner dedication to the Sword, that its energy may be once more operative in the outer world.

# Assimilation and Examination of Lessons 6-17

You have concluded the Sword Quest, but please do not pass over this last section. Following any intense period of meditation, it is important to allow a time of assimilation. The questions and tasks in this section will help you earth your realizations in an appropriate way. The following section can be studied in relation to each of the Hallow suits in turn.

## Tasks

1. Draw a map of your journey or create a cartoon strip that depicts your experiences. It doesn't matter whether you can draw or not. This can then be placed upon your Sword shrine.
2. Write a blessing of the Sword to benefit all living beings.
3. Make a meal in celebration of your Sword quest with the food and drink that you consider most suitable. This could be a ritual meal, a small dinner for friends, a party, or a solitary meal in communion with all your inner friends.

## The Sword Family

The Sword Court are an incisive family. They are attuned to the element of air and to the earth's Spring face. Answer these questions about them:

1. Who does this card remind me of? (A living friend, enemy, acquaintance, relative etc.)
2. Which historical/mythological character does this remind me of?
3. What features/characteristics do I share with the Sword Family?

## Greater Powers

1. What gifts have you gained in the Sword Realm? What qualities do they convey? How will you use them?
2. What blessings can you mediate from this realm to the world about you?

## Sword

The Spring Sword cards speak to us of burgeoning new growth. Here we discover the elements of the Sword in our own story. Answer the following questions about each of the Sword cards numbered 2-10.

1. What part of my life does this card represent?
2. How did I feel at that moment?
3. If I could change this experience, which Arthurian Tarot Card would I set next to it, to mitigate, complement, improve or lessen its effect?
4. What have I learned from this quest?

You can now pass on to the next quest or to Part Three, if you have completed all your quests.

# SUMMER:
## The Quest for the Spear

*When thou wast in the court of the Lame King and didst see the youth bearing the streaming spear, from which were drops of blood flowing in streams . . .thou didst not inquire their meaning nor their cause. Hadst thou done so, the king would have been restored to health, and his dominions to peace.*

Peredur ap Efrawc

We begin our quest in the Realm of the Spear, starting from the Spear Castle, with the Spear Family acting as our guides throughout the land they know so well. In the ship Prydwen, we learn from Sovereignty, encounter the Green Knight and receive the initiation of the Sun. The Spear Hallow itself is guarded by Arthur. You will need the following cards to study:

The entire Spear Suit
Arthur
Prydwen
Sovereignty
The Green Knight
The Sun

# LESSON 18

## The Spear Realm

spear ten

**Spear Ten Speaks** *None gain entrance to me unless they bend their backs with effort. None can live within me who do not know how to bear their responsibilities with a light step.*

The Spear Castle is inaccessible save to those willing to make the long climb upward. It crowns the hillside and surveys the whole land. Spear Ten expresses the cumulative powers of the spear cards, representing burdens and struggles which must be coped with somehow. The skills of the spear are to make light of this, just as a professional subsumes the efforts of training in the practice of his or her craft.

The cumulative focus of Midsummer often brings things to crisis, so that we feel over-burdened by many cares. If we can find the indwelling strength of this season and work with it, we may find that we are able to carry our burdens effortlessly. Such are the testings of this quest that we often steel ourselves to continue climbing an apparently limitless slope when in fact we have reached the plateau several feet back!

The Spear Castle has many rooms within it enclosing mysterious treasures. The Spear quest puts us on our metal to manifest these upon our road. We have to beware how we apply our efforts and that we don't fall into the extremes that often typify this path. We must balance resolution with the subtle messages of our intuition. To enter this high place, we must raise our aspirations and learn to draw upon our power.

## Questions

1. What are the nature of the responsibilities that fall on you at this time?
2. Which of your duties can be delegated to others? Which duties can only you perform? Which duties are best shared?
3. How can joy and service be best combined in your life this Midsummer?

## Meditation

1. Following the Rainbow Path of the Seeker, you arrive at a cross-roads. Northern hemisphere readers take the southern road, southern hemisphere readers take the northern road. Set out in search of the Spear Realm. The Spear Castle, depicted on Spear Ten, is hard to reach and seems to have been built in the era of giants. It takes all your efforts to reach this place.
2. Enter the Spear Castle and explore. Describe what you find. Who is within it?
3. Sunk in the depths of the Spear Castle there is a dark hall wherein day-light never comes. Taking a candle you explore it. Pull down the dark hangings that you find there, the once royal banners, the moth-eaten tapestries of past greatness. Everything in this hall is mouldering away, its purpose lost. Hanging here also are faded photographs of your own life, depicting the moments of achievement that were full of promise, to which you have not been faithful. Take these down also and add them to your heap of rubbish, unless you really intend to fulfil the promise depicted within them. Now set fire to the heap and see the smoke rise upwards through the flues set in the ceiling, drawn upwards by a great draught. By the light of the great conflagration, you now see the original hall walls. They are painted with tall trees like columns and between them are beautiful scenes. You find paints and brushes. If you wish, you can paint successive scenes, continuations of the moments held in the photographs of your life, or other moments yet to be. (You may wish to draw or paint these scenes on paper after you finish meditating.)
4. To explore the Spear Realm, you can stand on the Castle walls and look beyond. If you wish, you can fly over it in the shape of a raven.

# Summer Ceremony of the Spear Hallow

Celebrate this on the Summer Solstice (21 June in the northern hemisphere, 21 December in the southern hemisphere)

The Summer tide comes in at the Summer Solstice. The longest day is Midsummer Day, when many people rise early to catch the first rays of the sun. The weather is usually sunny and calm. It is traditionally a magical time of changings – a tradition exemplified by Shakespeare's *A Midsummer Night's Dream*. It is a time of joy and expansion. The trees are in their young green. The Zodiacal watery sign of Cancer heralds this tidal change. This tide is one to celebrate and expand. This is the time to widen our horizons, to take time off and enjoy the easy flow of life. We are able to open ourselves to this expansive tide and find true fulfilment at Midsummer. This is often the time of educational examinations in which the breadth of our knowledge is tested. The Spear of purpose is cast and we wait to reap the results of our throw. For this ritual you will need Summer flowers. See the general notes on p.63 for performance of this ritual.

### 1. The Making Sacred
Standing centrally, facing South,

*In the season of Summer, I dedicate myself to the quest for the Spear of Healing.* For the standard opening ritual see p.64.

### 2. Meditation on the Mystery of the Summer Solstice
*I stand at the gate of the year well-grown and welcome the fullness of the light. It illuminates the obscurity and· banishes doubt, releasing the Hallow of the Spear. From this portal stream forth the gifts of creativity, innovation and energy. May all that is stale and lifeless be pierced by the light, that all creation may benefit from the gifts of this Hallow!*

Sit and enter into silent meditation upon the nature of the season in your land. Contemplate the powers of the Spear as you understand them. Bring to mind the needs of creation: your own circle of family and friends, your land, troubled places in the world, and other global issues. Spend at least ten minutes doing this.

### 3. Invocation and Visualization of the Spear Guardian
Stand facing South:

*I call upon King Arthur, guardian of the Spear Hallow, to help and assist me. Sovereign Lord, you are the one who wields the weapons that protect the land. You stand ready to guide the seeker through courage and responsibility into the greater mystery of the Otherworld. I seek the empowerment of the Spear Hallow for the benefit of all beings.* Visualize

Arthur bearing the Spear in his hands. Here you may ask him any question and listen to her words.

Chant/sing the following (tune on p.254):

> *King who was and yet shall be,*
> *Clear our vision, help us see:*
> *Show us your courage, show us your power,*
> *Show us the Spear this very hour,*
> *Keep faith with the Seeker.*

See a ray of clear light emanating from his heart to your feet, forming a path between you. Breathe in that light, breathing it up until it reaches your heart. Now call to mind the great need for the Spear of Life in the world, holding that clear light at your heart. When the urgency of the need becomes too difficult to hold in your heart any longer, return a ray of light from your own heart until it touches the Spear. Only need of great magnitude, directed by the earnest seeker, can call forth the Spear.

## 4. The Epiphany of the Spear Hallow

Welcome the Spear in your own words, and see the light from your heart streaming into it. It begins to glow with a great, piercing light that is refracted into every direction. When this happens, be aware of its light streaming impartially through the world to all who need its power. Be aware of the mediation of power. At this point, you may wish to speak aloud the people, issues or needs that are known to you, turning in a circle, so that the light of the Spear is mediated to all.

## 5. Communion

Take the food for your ritual meal and bless it in your own words. Be aware of the land where the ingredients were grown, the elements that went into growing them, and the necessity for spiritual nourishment. As you eat it, make conscious attunement with the Realm of the Spear which you are going to explore in the coming season. A suitable seasonal song can be sung to welcome the Summer.

## 6. Establishing the Spear Hallow Shrine

Bless your empty shrine with the elements and adorn it with Summer flowers. Take your chosen symbol of the Spear Hallow: *Let this token represent the power of the Spear Hallow in this place. May it be blessed by the powers of the Great Above and the Great Below,* the inhabitants of the ages before the ages. This shrine is established for the restoration of all the worlds.

Now take your symbol to each of the quarters, starting in the West, finishing South, and say: *Behold the Spear Hallow! May the gifts of creativity, innovation and energy be operative in this quarter.* Place it on your shrine with the words: *May the power of the Spear Hallow be the indwelling presence of this shrine.* Make a gesture of homage or service and place your hand on your symbol. *On this day of the Summer Solstice, I dedicate myself to the quest for the Sword Spear.* Make your own promise or dedication to the principles of the Spear.

## 7. The Return
For the closing ritual see p.67.

---

# LESSON 19

## *The Spear Maiden, Spear Two and Three*

**The Spear Maiden Speaks** *I follow the running of the deer on swift feet. I am the freedom of the forest, the opener of its ways. Loose your jesses and fly free!*

The Spear Maiden is one of the great messengers of the Arthurian tradition. She is that part of you that is direct and immediate in response to need. Within each of us is a deep resourcefulness that can often only be accessed by extreme conditions. As the seer of the Spear, she goes directly to her prey or goal. She can immediately distinguish one within whom the qualities of the Spear lie dormant and sets to work to awaken them.

In the story of *The Lady of the Fountain*[8] we find the prototype of the Spear Maiden in Luned, the servant of the Lady. After the hero Owain has won through to the Otherworld to challenge the Knight of the Fountain, and killed him, he finds himself in a terrible predicament: trapped between the inner and outer gates of the dead knight's castle. As he awaits discovery and certain death, Luned notices him,

> *It is very sad that thou canst not be released, and every woman ought to succour thee, for I never saw one more faithful in the service of ladies than thou. As a friend thou art the most sincere, and as a lover the most devoted. Therefore, whatever is in my power to do for thy release, I will do it. Take this ring and put it on thy finger, with the stone inside thy hand; and close thy hand upon the stone. As long as thou concealest it, it will conceal thee.*[8]

With the discernment of an Otherworldly woman, Luned immediately perceives Owain's nature and assists him to become the new Knight of the Fountain and the Lady's husband.

However, the Spear can often exhibit its fiery, almost searing, quality through the forthright sharpness of the Spear Maiden's tongue, as Owain discovers. Beguiled back to Arthur's court, he forgets all about the Lady of the Fountain, his wife, until Luned rides into Arthur's hall to rebuke his unfaithfulness and take back the ring: 'Thus shall be treated the deceiver, the traitor, the faithless, the disgraced, and the beardless.' Sudden remembrance returns to Owain and he wanders disconsolately in the wilderness, becoming weak and half-mad until he resumes his former service.

The Spear Maiden is able to cut through seemingly tangled situations to the heart of the matter by the shortest means. The Spear Maiden upholds the virtue of one-pointed concentration. She is the 'Daughter of Light' who maintains the vital energies within the body, keeping vigilant watch over their use. In the quest that follows, ask her help or that of any of the Spear Family if you need clarification.

**Spear Two Speaks** *The land lies open before you. Take up your pack, armed with the many skills that life has given you. Come, you are called to the path!*

spear two .

Spear Two shows us the way of self-determination. Usually the seeker sets out having first surveyed the terrain ahead and matching her skills and talents with the likely challenges ahead. It is our way to set ourselves tasks we can reasonably achieve. This view gives us confidence in our own resources and enables us to proceed with surety, even though some finer details may be missing yet.

spear three

**Spear Three Speaks** *We are the guardians of the pathway, tall keepers of the beech wood. You may pass beneath our branches with the blessing of self-confidence and of sweet strength.*

Spear Three builds upon this initial mastery and organization, and shows us a broad, easy way wherein we are open to many new ideas and opportunities. This is the broad pathway upon which our meditations have creative space to branch out and develop. This easiness enables us to exercise our intuitions with confidence, so that we are less liable to go down the wrong road on our spiritual pathway.

# Questions

1. Which areas of your life are seriously devitalized? Bring your findings to the Spear Maiden and ask for her guidance.
2. Focus on one factor in your life that requires unblocking: what personal resources can you bring to this task?
3. How can you bring your personal skills together in a dynamic synthesis?
4. What do you find easiest about meditation?

# Tasks

1. During this quest you can reconnect with the Spear throughout the day by making a noon-day dedication. This can be performed anywhere and takes only a minute. At midday, enter into stillness wherever you are and bring to mind your highest aspirations, for example, 'May the earth be healed!' Visualize these as indwelling the Spear and cast it high into the heart of the sun. As the sun's rays radiate upon the earth, so will your aspirations filter into manifestation.
2. Sit down this week and plan the coming week efficiently, allotting time for meditation, recreation and socializing as well as for the things that must be done. Be prepared for the unexpected also.

# Meditation

1. Leave the Spear Castle and journey to find the Spear Maiden. She is your initiator into the Spear Realm. You can ask her anything about it or about your Spear quest, for she is a seer. She and her spear are at one: when she casts it for you, she knows where it falls and will advise about resourceful ways of coping with dangers or difficulties ahead.

2. She accompanies you to Spear Two where you look over the landscape below you. You may chose to shapeshift and fly with the falcon and look down the path ahead. Ask why it sits upon its perch hooded in this card.
3. Pass down into the valley below and enter Spear Three. From behind the beech trees two figures emerge. Who are they? They challenge you to discover the sources of your strength and the integrity of your intentions. You must spend at least one night under these trees, seeking for a true dream.

## LESSON 20

# *Prydwen*

vii pRyoωen

**Prydwen Speaks** *Wherever the path leads, I am the vessel of the deepest way. No scathe comes to those within me if they keep the bright song in their hearts. I have been to the roots of the world and returned. Through dangers I pass to the heart of Hallows, to the fair land. Your soul shall be restored and you shall sing of wonders yet to see. Be not afraid, for I will bear you up!*

The ship Prydwen bears us into the depths of the Underworld of Annwn or 'the In-World', as it called. The plunging into deeper areas of the unknown after knowledge or empowerment is always fraught with risks, but we should not draw back from lack of courage. The vessel of our journey is normally comprised of the frameworks and ideological structures of whatever spiritual path we follow. The ancient concept of the 'ship of souls' is relevant here. The way between the worlds is often by means of water: the Odyssey, the Charon's ferryboat, the voyage stories of Celtic tradition all tell of the soul's journey.[12] Prydwen shows us how to stay 'on course' and to trust in both our own determination and courage as well as in the current that impels our journey.

Discovering the self-confidence to begin our journey is often a problem because so much of our society disempowers us. Those who know us often concentrate upon our worst propensities and expect little of us; it is so that we speak slightingly of ourselves and our abilities with false modesty. The presence of the White Boar, emblematic both of Arthur's title 'the Boar of Cornwall' and of his battle with the monstrous Underworld boar which ravages the land, reminds us that what we think of as our bad qualities can indeed be used in spiritual service.

Prydwen takes us into the deeper regions where treasures lie to be discovered. The Underworld is not analogous to the Christian Hell; rather, it is a place wherein ancestral guardians preserve the ancient wisdom of the earth. To prove to them that we are worthy bearers of that wisdom, we may be submitted to many challenges on our quest for the Hallows. Such challenge does not imply that the Underworld or its inhabitants are malign in intent. We cannot hope to stroll into the treasuries of the innerworld and filch what we will. Wisdom must be earned by the dedication of our abilities.

## Meditation

1. Night falls as you lie down under the beech trees of Spear Three to sleep. In your dreaming, the Spear Maiden brings you to the seashore and sets you in the ship of Prydwen, which will become the vessel of your journey through this part of the quest. You descend with Prydwen into the Underworld in order to bring back seven lost parts of your life from each of the towers upon the cliff-tops. (You may meditate on one tower in any one session.) Take the long path from the ship up the steep cliffs to each tower in turn. The towers mentioned here are translations of the original seven caers or towers mentioned in the early British text *Preiddeu Annwn*. You may have very different experiences in each tower: you may meet people, animals, spiritual beings, or ancestors. Follow your experience at each tower

like a story and note it down afterwards.

2. Tower of the Sea: enter and ask for the return of your true voice. This is the tongue that cannot lie, the part of you that cannot be influenced by anyone else but which must speak the truth. When you experience this, speak aloud the things that you have not been openly admitting.

3. Tower of Hospitality: enter and ask for the joy of your childhood. The steady erosion of this joy in our adult life leaves us tense, mean-spirited and closed to opportunity. Retrace your personal road to childhood and find this joy, drinking its draught again.

4. Tower of Riches: enter and ask for the sum of the insights that you have had in your life. Each insight is like a flash of lightning or a period of daylight; we cannot hope to be always in the light of knowledge, but we may illumine the darkness of our own ignorance with the lamp that is fed by our revelations.

5. Tower of Trees: enter and ask for the table of your destiny. Made of many woods, inlaid and carved, this wooden board depicts the broad pattern of your life path. What do the symbols upon it mean to you?

6. Tower of the Four Corners: enter and ask for your lost and wasted opportunities to be returned to you. Each wall of the four-sided tower represents the four seasons: as you go up each floor, you enter a new year. Reflect on the ages of your life in turn, and gather up your opportunities.

7. Tower of Carousel: enter and ask for the inner childhood friend who once accompanied you. You may have put this friend behind you as a childish fancy, but as you grew up, so did your inner friend and guide. What does s/he look like now?

8. Tower of Glass: enter and ask for the key of initiation. This key has been many times in your hands, perhaps, and you have mislaid it. Now it returns to you, to be used as you go through your quest.

9. When you return from your sevenfold retrieval, you see that upon the deck of Prydwen lies a gift for you. Accept whatever you see first. If you don't understand it, ask the council of Prydwen or the Spear Maiden.

## Reading of the Seven Caers

This reading can be done separately from the meditation retrieval above or as a part of it. If you decide to do the latter, then draw one card *after* you've meditated and record it in your diary, reading all seven at the end of all the sessions. While you are shuffling, ask that what is hidden be revealed to you.

Fig. 10: *The Reading of the Seven Caers*

1. Represents your true voice: what you are really saying within.
2. Represents the joy of your childhood: what you need to regain now.
3. Represents the sum of your life's insights: what is most true for you.
4. Represents your destiny: your true direction.
5. Represents your lost opportunities: regrets which impede your progress.
6. Represents your childhood or inner friend: your creative instinct.
7. Represents the key to initiation: the challenge which faces you next.

# —————————— LESSON 21 ——————————

# *The Spear Knight, Spear Four and Five*

spear knight

**The Spear Knight Speaks** *I cast into the eye of the sun itself. My sight is keen to spy danger on the horizon and to come against it. My spear flies fast upon the wind and maintains its trajectory whatever the odds.*

The Spear Knight is an energetic companion on the quest. He is that part of you that maintains the velocity and enthusiasm of the quest, letting nothing stand in his way. This forthright concentration is as unremitting as the rays of the midday sun, and can be quite intimidating to those who do not share the same enthusiasm.

He is the Way-Shower of the Spear, and so his speed and confidence reflect the unswerving cast of the lance. The Spear aims at the heart of the goal or problem. Midday is a time of surety and confidence, when there are no shadows to confuse us. This is when we implement the visions of the dawn and when things have their own momentum.

This card is based on the figure of Bedwyr, who is described as swifter than all others.

> *Although he was one-handed, three warriors could not shed blood faster than he on the field of battle . . . his lance would produce a wound equal to those of nine opposing lances . . . The head of his lance (would) leave its shaft and draw blood from the wind, and (would) descend upon its shaft again.* [8]

Bedwyr is the earliest appearance of Bedevere, the last companion of Arthur who takes Excalibur back to the Lady of the Lake in later medieval legend. We see that the lance or spear of Bedwyr has its own life and that its effect is devastating.

The wielding of any kind of power in our own society is fraught with abuse. A too hasty head of power can boil over and scald the wielder and hurt anyone else nearby. While energy and inspiration are to be applauded, a good rein of control is required also. An ability to move effectively and swiftly is also needed when abuses threaten, as when Bedwyr pierces the knee of Yspadadden the Giant in the story of *Culhwch and Olwen*. [8]

The function of the Spear Knight is to guide the trajectory of our life's purpose and to awaken us to action. One of his titles is the 'Son of Light' and he may be seen as bearing a torch above his head in meditation.

**Spear Four Speaks** *I am the heart of the festival, come and rejoice! Bring the harvest of your achievement to the hearth of your home that all might share it, then take bread for the road.*

spear four

Spear Four shows us the gratification of our enterprises which often comes shortly after we have set foot on the path to self-knowledge. It is tempting to consider this stage of the quest as our appointed goal, while we should really regard it as a point of refreshment only. This early success usually indicates that the seeker has concluded some piece of work which was begun *before* consciously travelling the path. Once a soul has set foot upon the path, there is little space for other concerns, some of which come to a speedy resolution. We should take heart if this is the case with us, for this perhaps indicates that we have begun the karmic adjustment by our renewed commitment in this lifetime.

> **Spear Five Speaks** *In life there are many struggles, many obstacles to be overcome. Do combat with me and you will find the road ahead easier to travel. I will show you your true motives.*

Spear Five reminds us that the path does not run on smoothly. Sometimes we must turn aside along it to deal with challenges. Modern life is full of many such combats which seem to steal time from our 'spiritual' pursuits; we should consider all strife as a teacher that challenges our motivations and desires. One of the subtle traps into which we may be tempted is spiritual competitiveness: each student travels his own road and is responsible for his own journey. To pit ourselves against other travellers is foolish: rather let our inner teachers

be our tuitional combatants – they will give us the challenges that we need.

## Questions

1. In what kinds of situations are you inclined to be hasty and unconsidered?
2. In which instances do you need the swift dispatch of the Spear Knight?
3. What have you achieved in the last year? (Look at inner achievements as well as outer ones.)
4. What harmonious conclusions or happy culminations have you experienced recently?
5. When you are challenged, do you give in, walk away or fight back?
6. What have your challengers taught you about yourself?

## Task

Spend one morning/afternoon/evening this week in celebration of your life so far. You might look through old photographs, diaries or other records for ideas. What has been the consistent golden thread of your life? Which people, places and things have supported you on your journey? You may choose to celebrate alone quietly, or else have an 'unbirthday' party and share your celebration with friends.

## Meditation

1. When you travel through the land, the essence of Prydwen shapeshifts into the shape of a white pig, which is your guide and companion. On whatever part of your quest you are, you may ask its advice. It leads you now to the verge of the Lands Adventurous where you meet the Spear Knight at midday. He will guard your Spear quest.

   Look around the plain on which you are standing. The long grasses wave lazily in the midday heat. The Spear Knight looks for pathways in the grasses. When he sees what he's looking for, he casts his spear and follows. You mount up with him.

2. You ride into Spear Four and find the village in festival. They invite you to join them and say that you may invite whichever guest from your own life with whom you'd most want to celebrate. Enjoy yourselves.

3. The Spear Knight is in a hurry to be gone, for there is a combat to be fought. He takes you to Spear Five as the sun is going down. Near the monolith stands the person with whom you agree the least. The Spear Knight arbitrates and referees your combat, the aim of which is to find the best creative channel for the energies of you and your opponent. Not all differences can be reconciled, but it is possible to learn respect for an opponent and so learn wisdom.

# LESSON 22

## *Sovereignty*

> **Sovereignty Speaks** *I offer the cup of truth to all who will drink from it. I am the deep abiding well of justice, whose springs nourish this land. None may enter into rule and enjoyment of this land without a draught from my cup. The drink is sharp and bitter, but it illumines the recipient with the flame of integrity.*

The Goddess of Sovereignty is in deep communion with the land: whatever injures the land, injures her. She is the integrity of the earth which remembers all wrongs and all good deeds. It does not matter in which land we live, for Sovereignty has her local manifestation wherever we go. Her domain is all around us and sustains us, so it behoves us to maintain her natural laws along our path. She is the touchstone of truth against which we can measure any motive about which we are unsure.

xi sovereignty

The oracle of the earth cannot lie; it is maintained by countless written and unwritten laws which govern our lives.

Sovereignty is often interpreted in a narrow political sense to indicate the dominance of one racial or political group. Issues of sovereignty are particularly prominent near disputed borders where national interests have been confused. Such disputes inculcate nationalist paranoia and often racial hatred. This is not true service to the Goddess of Sovereignty, nor is it true patriotism. The Goddess of the Land accepts those who show respect for the land when they enter a country. Those without respect, she repels or causes her defenders to repel them. At this time, all people need to learn respect for the Goddess of the Earth, our home, regardless of nationality or religion.

The encounter with the Goddess of the Land is really the testing of justice. She and her laws must be consulted whenever questions or disputes about the land arise. She can help us perceive our true motives and promote a more equitable relationship between ourselves and the land.

## Meditation

1. You leave Spear Five and come to the centre of the Lands Adventurous. Here sits Sovereignty with her cup. You may drink one of three draughts from it: the white, the red or the black. Which wells up within the cup? If you see a white liquid, Sovereignty becomes a

young girl. If you see a red liquid, she becomes a mighty queen. If you see a black liquid, she becomes an ancient grandmother. Take the hand of whichever aspect of Sovereignty is appropriate and let her lead you through the land. She will show you what needs to be done in your inner landscape.

2. On your return from your circuit of the land, Sovereignty assumes her original guise and gives you a gift.

# LESSON 23

## *The Spear Queen, Spear Six and Seven*

spear queen

**The Spear Queen Speaks** *Behold, I weep for the wounding of the earth! I keep watch through the night of the aeon and see the forests cut down, the earth washed away. I taste the poisons within the waters. I feel the harsh unseasonal winds. Come, enter into the service of the earth for its healing.*

The Spear Queen is one who exemplifies the struggle to shed light on the path of life. She is that part of ourselves that clearly perceives the need and loss which provoke the quest. She communicates the urgency of the need for healing, becoming the empowerer of the Spear. The depth of her grief remains unassuaged while there is any species upon earth that still suffers. Her continual supplication for new protectors to come forward and serve is sometimes seen as an onerous plaint, but that is her function: to maintain the vigil for the earth and let no-one forget.

There are many guardian queens in Celtic tradition. This card is attuned to the Lady of the Fountain who inhabits the deep Otherworld. Her husband, the Knight of the Fountain, defends the Otherworld against all comers and is slain in combat by Owain, one of Arthur's knights. The Lady's grief at her loss is terrible:

> And Owain . . . beheld a lady with yellow hair falling over her shoulders and stained with blood . . . and it was a marvel that the ends of her fingers were not bruised from the violence with which she smote her hands together. Her cry was louder than the shout of the men or the clamour of the trumpets. No sooner had he beheld the lady than he became inflamed with her love.[8]

With the help of Luned, Owain pays his court to her and justly recompenses her for the loss of her husband and defender of her realm by fulfilling this role himself. He defends the realm well until he goes back to Arthur's court. The Lady has to send Luned to remind him of her service once again, for the land and fountain are undefended.

One of her titles is 'the Mother of Light', for she keeps vigil for all sentient beings. She teaches the duty of the Spear in such a way that we are bound to understand for ourselves how we can best serve. She sensitizes our personal vulnerability until we can also discover the wells of compassion within us.

> **Spear Six Speaks** *Who goes there? Pass, Seeker of the Spear! Behold, the banner of victory is spread and the enemy is subdued. Advance with confidence and seek a test worthy of your strength.*

Spear Six brings a self-confidence and satisfaction from service which is deeper than that gained from Spear Four. The severity of challenge meted out by Spear Five has been overcome and the inner landscape lies open for the student to proceed. The validations of success come only by good preparation and steady progress. In this world, no formal honours are given to successful esoteric students by way of medals or certificates; success is validated by the student being requested to help or serve in some more challenging way. No victor's laurel is proffered, only the new awareness that one has advanced sufficiently to tackle the next task.

spear six spear seven

**Spear Seven Speaks** *I defend the gap with tenacity. None may enter the walls of the place I love if they come against it with destruction in their hearts. I am strong to maintain my beliefs.*

Spear Seven shows the way in which the student is often challenged after the successful validations of Spear Six. When we profess our adamant belief in something, the universe often provides us with an immediate opportunity to implement our words by putting our deeds foremost in their defence. Such a challenge puts us on our metal and evokes our most tenacious courage in opposing or defending.

# Questions

1. What steps are you following in the service of the earth?
2. What hidden sorrow within you still drips blood? Ask the Spear to staunch your grief at its source.
3. Which of your strongly held beliefs is challenged by the society in which you live? How is it best defended?

# Meditation

1. The Sword Queen greets you on the borders of the Otherworld. She is veiled. You may speak to her about any lack of confidence or disempowerment which is troubling you at this time. She will give

advice. Ask her to tell you why the spear she holds drips blood. Write down her story.

2. The Spear Queen leads you to Spear Six. Climb the spiral pathway up the hill and raise the standard of your quest. What is on the banner that represents your quest?

3. Enter the fortress of Spear Seven. Who are those you are set to defend at this place? From what or whom are they hiding?

---

# LESSON 24

## The Green Knight

xv the green knight

**The Green Knight Speaks** *In your world it is Midsummer, but in mine Midwinter. I come in challenge, to seek you out and to test your nerve when you least expect me. Stand fearlessly before my axe and you shall pass the test.*

The Green Knight is a threshold guardian, a wise turner of the wheel of experience. He tests all that we would be and he calls our bluff when we boast about our abilities or aptitudes. He is the one who sets us riddles and dream nets about our own self-limitations: when we break our dreams open and see what they are saying, we often find the images of a mighty joke or pun upon our lifestyle.

The tradition of the riddling Otherworldly champion is strong in Celtic lore. He is sometimes called the Knight of the Riddles, or the False Knight Upon the Road. To meet with him, we need our wits about us. Many people are threatened and downcast by challenges of any kind, perceiving all challengers as evil enemies. In dualistic spiritual models, this card is represented by the Devil. But the Green Knight is not the Devil. He keeps just and often humorous account of our quest, turning the wheel of our progress so that we never attain a fixed, unmoving attitude. It is perhaps for this reason that he, as King of Midwinter, makes his unexpected appearance in this hallow-suit of Spears, the rulers of Summer!

The Green Knight is good at reaching behind what we are missing and showing us positive paths of change. Those who attempt to take him on alone, secure in their own abilities, live to regret it, for he leads them a merry dance to discover their true inadequacy and natural humility.

## Meditation

As you stand at the gate defending Spear Seven, the Green Knight approaches you as the guardian of the Otherworld. He challenges you and touches you with his holly axe and you are transformed into the likeness of a wren to fly up to his shoulder to perch there. He leads you into your own shuttered life and shows how things must change. Only you can direct him to strike with his axe whatever is limiting you or which needs liberating from stale patterns. The energy that is trapped within these things will now be released and your subsequent road should be easier. When you have completed your task, return to your place at the doorway of Spear Seven and there find a gift left for you by the Green Knight.

---

# LESSON 25

# *The Spear King, Spear Eight and Nine*

**The Spear King Speaks** *If you would hit the mark, let it be with the sharpest metal! To bring healing takes courage and a steady hand. Let the poison be extracted by the flame of healing.*

The Spear King is the passionate guardian of the Spear. He is that part of you that is deeply committed to healing that which has been wounded.

spear king

His guardianship is often hard-won and he has to fight to maintain it: it is evident that whoever wields the drastic energies of the Spear may also have a short career. Bran the Blessed suffers a wound caused by a poisoned spear-head in the appalling combat between the British and Irish in *Branwen, Daughter of Llyr*, becoming a prototype of the Wounded King. But perhaps the most famous exemplar of this role is King Pelles. Attacked by Pelles' brother, the invisible knight Garlon, Balin enters the room where the Hallows are guarded and takes up the Spear in self-defence. He wounds Pelles in the thigh with it and thus causes the Wasteland. [9]

The forge, wherein the Spear King stands, is a common theme in Celtic legend. The smithy is seen as the place where souls, not just weapons, are honed to sharpness. The training schools of Irish poet-craft were called 'the forges of song'. In Irish story, the Spear is fashioned by Goibniu, the great smith of the Tuatha de Danann as the ultimate weapon which will defeat their enemy, the giant Balor.

In the hands of the unworthy, the Spear can be an instrument of terrible destruction, which is why the King is willing to accept his own sacrifice rather than have it fall into the wrong hands. He is the 'earth' of the Spear if its action short-circuits. His counsel comes directly from the Spear: he heeds its words perceptively and obeys them unflinchingly. He is likely to be found at the centre of any action it involves.

spear eight

**Spear Eight Speaks** _I am the perpetrator of prophetic knowledge._
_I speed towards my goal with willing swiftness, stopping for nothing_
_in my headlong career. Come and hear my news!_

Released from the defensive framework of Spear Seven, Spear Eight
hurtles on with certainty towards its goal. This is often the effect after
a period of difficult assimilation: the sudden release gives true aim and
direction. It can also signify too much haste and not enough thought.
Like a bow that is bent for a long time, a student who has laboured
defensively for a long time can find the strain intolerable, or else go
straight to the heart of the matter. Things move fast on the path,
sometimes too fast for us to grasp.

**Spear Nine Speaks** _I am the last defender of the shore. All that is_
_strongest resides in me. I will never be overcome, save by death itself._

Spear Nine shows us in defensive mood, facing the storm, trying to battle
on and through. This is not like the defensiveness of Spear Seven, which
can overcome slight opposition. Spear Nine shows us the reserves of
strength that our quest has built up in us and how they can be best
deployed. When our backs are to the wall, as here, the only defence is
to summon the powers that have assisted us in our quest and to combine
these with our personal powers. To rely totally on our own strength is
useless. The earth-warrior also calls upon the powers of the universe.

## Meditation

1. The Spear King is the guardian of the deep Otherworld. He brings you into his forge and encourages you to help him about his work. You also may forge new concepts which will permeate your life. See your idea come to birth within the molten metal over the fire.
2. Take your newly forged creation to Spear Eight where you set it in the water, to be borne into the future when you will be ready to wield it.
3. Following the river down to the sea, you come to the place of Spear Nine. Here you stand guard, looking out to sea, scanning the horizon. What enemies, challengers or opponents are waiting for you to be less watchful? (Note: these may not be personal or national enemies so much as inner challenges.)

---

# LESSON 26

## *The Sun*

**The Sun Speaks** *I give awareness and growth, but I can also scorch and destroy. Your faculty of concentration is a burning glass for your life. Attend to it, for it brings my energy and strength to all that you*

*xix the sun*

*attempt. My Spear is the shaft of light which pierces the dead places and awakens them once more. I can see into your heart and cause the dormant seeds of your purpose to grow.*

The Sun exhibits the pure enthusiasm of one unfettered by guilt or hatred. We see the Mabon, the youthful protector of Celtic tradition, who upholds innocence and justice. He is shown as a wielder of the Spear at midday: a true upholder of the Hallow. Meeting with the Otherworldly child is an important part of the quest. The child (sometimes children) represents the primordial world of creation and shows the quester that she is near to the heart of all things. The Sun is the Child of Light, allowing no shadow of guilt or uncertainty. Mabon lightly rides the White Mare, the horse of the Sun itself. The White Mare endures and bears all burdens, but never shirks her duty.

The revitalization of the sun is a gift given at each new dawning. Recent popular esoteric tradition has tended to belittle the sun's gifts in preference for the moon's gifts, and has upheld a very strict symbolic gender association of man = sun, woman = moon. To turn towards the sun is not to belittle the inner feminine, which is often symbolized in Celtic tradition by the sun. The following Gaelic chant retains the female gender for the sun, which has always typified the earliest beliefs of North-West Europe:

*Welcome to you, sun of the seasons' turning,*
*In your circuit of the high heavens;*
*Strong are your steps on the unfurled heights,*
*Glad Mother are you to the constellations.*
*You sink down into the ocean of want,*
*Without defeat and without scathe;*
*You rise up on the peaceful wave*
*Like a queen in her maidenhood's flower.*
                                   (Trans. C. Matthews)

The Sun always represents the true image of ourselves as we will or can be, with an unwavering reflection of our potential. Nothing evil, false or unfree can withstand the beams of the midday sun. The Sun's energy is the kindler of life on our planet.

## Meditation

The Sun is the luminary of this quest. The Spear King comes to you in Spear Nine and continues your watch for you. You proceed upstream a little until the midday sun shines above you. A naked youth rides up and greets you, offering you a ride on his white mare. You mount up and ride easily into the golden heart of the Summer Country. All the troubles of your Spear quest drop away from you and you are filled with joy and wholeness of vision. Within the courts of the Sun, for such the youth is, you are given golden nourishment. The Sun gives you a gift from his harp-bag.

## Task

Make a reading or a story that uses the Spear Family and the Sun cards as major characters.

─────────────── **LESSON 27** ───────────────

# Arthur

**Arthur Speaks** *I am the abiding father of the land who keeps watch in every season. I draw upon the resources of my kingdom and weld them into one. I preserve the laws by my loving strength that all may walk abroad in my kingdom without let or hindrance. Keep well my ways!*

IV ARTHUR

Arthur is the primordial leader who galvanizes disparate factions into a strong unified entity. He brings self-worth and definition of our life-task. He stands perfectly poised between the two appearances of reality: administrating the outer world with the principles that he learns from the inner world. His partnership with Sovereignty is the key to his perennial fame and glory, for the earth does not forget those who have served her faithfully. He gives us a model of good government and of self-discipline, which combines loving fatherhood and leadership with courageous authority and dynamic organization.

As the guardian of the Inner Court of the Spear, Arthur is well placed in this season. Each of the greater powers that make up this seasonal court are concerned with his testing: Prydwen sees his descent into the Underworld, his encounter with Sovereignty fits him for kingship, the Green Knight challenges his rule and in the Sun, he sees himself as the youth about to set out on his adventures ~ an ongoing cycle.

The image of the Emperor is often seen as a stern, immovable patriarch and has even been purged from many feminist tarots, but Arthur rather represents the loving and resourceful father. He represents those who have earned their power by responsible living and who are willing to use that strength for the good of all.

*The Arthurian Tarot* derives its impetus from the stories and legends that constellate around Arthur. If we can find how to substitute ourselves for Arthur in any situation, we may learn how to become guardians of the land and true wielders of the Spear.

# Meditation

You begin to climb upwards towards the mountain top above you. There Arthur sits, surveying the realms below. His eyes have been ever upon you as you pursue your quest. He grips your hand and makes you welcome, asking about your journey to this place. You look out over the land together. You see, beneath your feet, the entrance to a maze of many turnings. Arthur bids you enter, before you attempt the Spear.

You may either meditate your way through the maze, or else make one on your floor out of string and walk it. It has an entrance, seven turnings and a central chamber. These are guarded by nine of the cards you have encountered thus far. As you travel through the maze, each guardian questions you. Make answer as best you can. You may wish to draw a card for each of the questions, if you are walking the maze: read these before passing on. The questions are derived from the ancient Celtic duties of a ruler.[1]

At the Entrance, Arthur asks: 'At this entrance to Sovereignty's maze, how will you uphold my justice?'

At the First Turning, the Sun asks: 'The ruler's acts are reflected in the land itself; what kind of weather typifies your actions?'

At the Second Turning, the Spear King asks: 'The ruler is known for great generosity; what gift do you give to all impartially?'

At the Third Turning, the Green Knight asks: 'The ruler maintains the

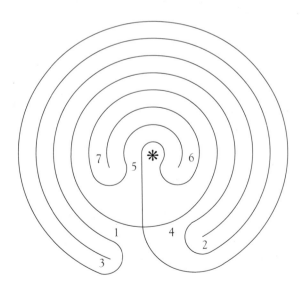

Fig. 11: *The Maze of Sovereignty*

boundaries; how will you defend your land?'

At the Fourth Turning, the Spear Queen asks: 'The ruler shows compassion to the unfortunate; how will you relieve distress?'

At the Fifth Turning, Prydwen asks: 'The ruler looks for a cure for the land's sickness; what disease currently afflicts your land?'

At the Sixth Turning, the Spear Knight asks: 'The ruler maintains the land's honour; how are you attuned to the honour of your land?'

At the Seventh Turning, the Spear Maiden asks: 'The ruler maintains truth in all things; what is the root of your own integrity?'

At the Centre, Sovereignty asks you: 'At the centre of my maze, I ask you, what oath will you make to be worthy of the Spear?'

Sit for a while in meditation at the centre, if you are walking the maze; turn and walk slowly outward, remembering your answers.

As you emerge, Arthur gives you a gift.

# LESSON 28

## *The Spear Hallow*

spear hallow

**The Spear Hallow Speaks** *I bring fire out of the deepest rock. I am the life that dances, the lance that sings. There is a fire within you*

*also, the kindling of creative life. Wherever you are wounded, that is
the place of greatest power. I am your healer and your empowerer.*

The Spear Hallow is one of the deepest symbols of wounding and healing.
This dual role can only be understood if we look to the source of power.
Power itself is neither good nor evil: it is. Power cannot be held in a rigid
way, only wielded creatively. The Spear is a kindler of our own power;
it is a weapon that can strike from afar. We tend to forget that our own
actions are innately governed by the laws of cause and effect: one word
or deed may strike afar, or indeed, return to wound ourselves. To wield
the Spear is to be skilful. The Spear pierces whatever is corrupt, allowing
the poison to drain away. It lets in the fire of life, like the penetrating
beams of the sun.

Once the Spear is used, we often find that the results are not to our
liking; as when we lance a wound, blood and pus well up. We can tell
when the Spear has hit its target because of the intensity of the reaction,
which may manifest in anger, violence, denial or sudden grief. On this
course, the Spear is the appropriate symbol of the seeker who is mature
enough to comprehend the laws of cause and effect yet who has sufficient
dynamism to cast it. The wielder must have a steady nerve.

## Meditation

As you emerge from the maze, you feel empowered to ask Arthur for the
Spear Hallow. He asks by what right you make your request, and you
make reply. He touches you with his hand and you are transformed into
a chough, the black, red-beaked bird that perches beside him.

You fly ever up the mountainside until you come to its fiery summit.
Here the Spear hovers in the flames of the volcanic mountain. Look
deeply into the flames and concentrate upon your highest aspirations.
When you visualize these clearly, take the Spear and aim it into the heart
of your vision, that it may be accomplished. Record all that you
experience.

You return to Arthur who touches you so that you resume your own
shape. He then lays down his own spear upon the ground, so that it forms
the shape of the following reading, which he bids you make.

## The Augury of the Spear of Light

For this reading, remove the Spear Hallow, setting it at position 5, and
all the Greater Power cards. As you shuffle the remainder of the pack,
strongly visualize or gaze at the Spear, and put your trust in its validation.
Ask it, 'How can the Spear be manifest within me?' Then draw four cards

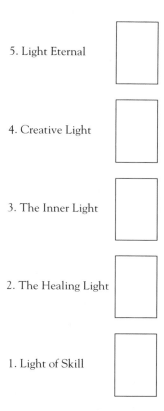

5. Light Eternal

4. Creative Light

3. The Inner Light

2. The Healing Light

1. Light of Skill

Fig. 12: _The Augury of the Spear_

from the main pack and lay these on positions 1-4. Shuffle the Greater Powers separately and ask for the augury (prophecy) of the Spear. Draw one card and lay it on position 5, covering the Spear Hallow card. Each of the positions in this augury represents some aspect of the Life which the Spear represents.

- Position 1. Represents the light of your purpose, your life's direction. Beginnings are important, and many lives go wrong because the initial cast of the Spear is mis-aimed. The challenge here is 'How do I use my skill?'
- Position 2. Represents the many wounds that life deals us. While their vulnerability opens us to compassion, our wounds can also prevent us from having a whole life. The challenge here is 'How can the Spear heal me?'

- Position 3. Represents the doubts which prevent us from fully exploring the wondrous convolutions of life's maze. The challenge is 'What do I need to trust?'
- Position 4. Represents your creativity. Without this potent need within us we become arid and dull. The challenge is 'How do I keep the creative flame burning?'
- Position 5. Represents the quintessential light which is never extinguished. This Greater Power card represents the nature of your soul. It challenges you with 'How do I serve all sentient life?'

---

## LESSON 29

### *The Investiture of the Spear*

Lay the cards of this Spear Quest about you, either on the floor, or about your room, in the following way:

Green Knight

Spear 6 & 7                    Spear King

Spear Queen                    Spear 8 & 9

Sovereignty      Spear Arthur      Sun
                 Spear 10

Spear 4 & 5                    Spear Maiden

Spear Knight                   Spear 2 & 3

Prydwen

Fig. 13: *The Inner Court of the Spear*

This is the inner court of the Spear which you have explored upon this quest. This inner court shows us Arthur at the centre of the major events of his career: his going forth as a young man to claim the kingship (Sun), his descent to Annwn to fetch the cauldron (Prydwen), his meeting with the Goddess of the Land (Sovereignty) and his challenging at the hands of the Green Knight. The time has come for the investiture of the Spear.

## Meditation

Visualize the southern part of your inner landscape that you worked with in Lesson 5. (Readers in the southern hemisphere see the northern part of their inner landscape.) Now see the inner court of the Spear superimposed upon it. Seeing the Rainbow Path of the Seeker at the centre of your inner landscape, you now enter this Spear quarter, passing through it without fear or difficulty. You may wish to spread the following meditation over several sessions.

Starting at Spear Maiden, you will meditate on each card in clockwise order until you reach the Sun. The Spear Family give you the following gifts: the Maiden gives a scrying crystal that is tuned to the Spear Hallow; the Knight gives an emblem of midday; the Queen gives a healing herb; the King gives a golden coin with your own image on one side and the Spear on the other. These gifts will prove useful in your future journeys in the Spear realm. Each of the landscape cards gives you a different colour candle with which to surround the Spear. Each of the Greater Powers imparts a special blessing.

Continue meditating on each of the cards until you reach the centre where Arthur sits, upon the Spear Castle with the Spear Hallow in front of him. You may not enter here until you have shown him the gifts you have gained from the Greater Powers during your meditations over this season. The combined energy of these gifts forms a strong bridge between the place where you stand and the Spear Castle. You kneel before him and make your personal dedication to the Spear. Then you enshrine the Spear in the Spear Castle which is the same as the Southern Caer of your own inner landscape.

Slowly allow this image to fade and to be replaced by that of your own Spear shrine. Open your eyes and formally repeat your inner dedication to the Spear, that its energy may be once more operative in the outer world.

# Assimilation and Examination of Lessons 19-29

You have concluded the Spear Quest. Please turn to p.99 and study the assimilation exercises in relation to the Spear Court. This energetic family is attuned to the element of fire and to the land's Summer. Discover how well you have responded to their creative energy. You can then pass on to the next quest, or to Part Three, if you have completed all your quests.

# AUTUMN:
## The Quest for the Grail

*The Holy Grail appeared covered with a cloth of white samite; and yet no mortal hand was seen to bear it. It entered through the great door, and at once the palace was filled with fragrance as though all the spices of the earth had been spilled abroad.*

Quest of the Holy Grail

Our quest begins in the Realm of the Grail, starting from the Grail Castle, with the Grail Family acting as our guides. Companioned by Gawain, we learn from the Wounded King, enter the Spiral Tower and receive the initiation of the Sleeping Lord. The Grail Hallow itself is guarded by Guinevere. You will need the following cards for study:

The entire Grail Suit
Guinevere
Gawain
The Wounded King
The Spiral Tower
The Sleeping Lord

# The Grail Realm

grail ten

**Grail Ten Speaks** *Behold the place of peace and contentment! All that you ever wished lies within me. This is the holy home and the fulfilment of desire. Enter me, all you whose hearts are full of loving service!*

The Grail Castle, depicted on Grail Ten, looks easy of access, but its protections are nonetheless in place. We must pass between a thorn and an apple tree to enter within: both trees of faery which have their own guardian qualities. Sometimes it is possible to discern this castle from afar, yet when we approach, the sea-mist has swathed it in thick white cloud and it is lost to us. We may even lose sight of it again if we have entered just once.

The Autumn Equinox brings with it the tide of culmination, when our energies are gathered together again after the dissipation of the holidays. We feel empowered to find new and better ways of working things out, how to gather a meaningful harvest of our realizations.

We each discern this castle from afar at least once in our lives. It shines and beckons us nearer; it emits a pure note which calls us home. Within, we find the deep refreshment that perfectly fulfils our expectations. For within is the perfect homecoming that is sought at the heart of each spiritual quest. Whatever we have been seeking for lies within this castle.

## Questions

1. What vision of wholeness and completion calls to you at this time?
2. Call to mind the people who make you feel content and peaceful in your life: what qualities do they intrinsically manifest?
3. What factors make you feel spiritually 'at home?'

## Meditation

1. See the Rainbow Path of the Seeker and travel along it until you come to a cross-roads. Take the western road and set out in search of the Grail Castle. Note if any animals, birds or other significant things help you on your way.
2. Enter the Grail Castle and explore. Describe what you find. Who is within it?
3. Within the middle of the castle is a sacred area or room. It is completely empty and dark except for a lantern burning in the centre of the roof. The pattern of the beams reflects on to the floor, illumining a well set therein. There are steps leading down into the well and a bucket which can be drawn up. Before you draw water, briefly consider your own spiritual path: what is your general direction? Which clues and keys have illumined the way for you? Which things remain unclear? Bearing in mind your last answer particularly, descend the stair and draw up a bucket of water. Using only one bucketful, you are permitted to illuminate the walls of this dark room with the water you've drawn up. Wherever you wish, you may wash the walls with the water to uncover what lies in the darkness; there isn't enough to wash all the walls. As you do so, the darkness retreats where you have washed to reveal clearly illuminated images and patterns. Record what you see.
4. To explore the Grail Realm, you can stand on the castle walls and look across the land. If you wish, you can fly over it in the shape of a sea-gull.

## Autumn Ceremony of the Grail Hallow

Celebrate this seasonal ritual at the Autumn Equinox (21 September in the northern hemisphere, 21 March in the southern hemisphere). Decorate your place of working with Autumn fruits.

The Autumn tide comes in at the Autumn Equinox. This is the beginning of the academic year when we long to go and assimilate a new skill, building upon the resources we have garnered. We are post-harvest, and enjoy the fruits of our labours. Again, the seas and winds are inclined to be rough, in time to blow the old leaves from the trees. The Zodiacal fiery sign of Scorpio comes in now. This tide is one of assimilation and gathering in. It is the time to assess what we have done, to discover where we are really investing our time and energy and whether it is worth it. The Grail of compassion is held to our lips and we must decide whether we are ready to drink or not. See the general notes on p.63 for the performance of this ritual.

## 1. The Making Sacred
Standing centrally, facing West,

*In the season of Autumn, I dedicate myself to the quest for the Grail of Love.* For the opening ritual see p.64.

## 2. Meditation on the Mystery of the Autumn Equinox
*I stand at the gate of the year full-grown and welcome the fading of the light. It brings the gifts of the twilight when the heart is touched by enchantment, releasing the Hallow of the Grail. From this portal stream forth the gifts of fertility, healing and gladness. May all that is barren, failing, full of sickness and sadness be gladdened by the waters of the Grail of compassion, that all creation may benefit from the gifts of this Hallow!*

Sit and enter into silent meditation upon the nature of the season in your land. Contemplate the powers of the Grail as you understand them. Bring to mind the needs of creation: your own circle of family and friends, your land, troubled places in the world, and other global issues. Spend at least ten minutes doing this.

## 3. Invocation and Visualization of the Grail Guardian
Stand facing West:

*I call upon Queen Guinevere, guardian of the Grail Hallow, to help and assist me. Sovereign Lady, you are the one who weaves our hearts into a single duty. You stand ready to guide the seeker through harmony and fulfilment, into the greater mystery of the Otherworld. I seek the empowerment of the Grail Hallow for the benefit of all beings.* (Visualize Guinevere bearing the Grail in her hand. Here you may ask her any question and listen to her words.)

Chant/sing the following (tune on p.254):

> *Queen of love's own heart so deep,*
> *Wake this land from endless sleep,*
> *Show us your beauty, show us your pride,*
> *Bring us the healing that will abide:*
> *Keep faith with the Seeker.*

See a ray of clear light emanating from her heart to your feet, forming a path between you. Breathe in that light, breathing it up until it reaches your heart. Now call to mind the great need for the Grail of Love in the world, holding that clear light at your heart. When the urgency of the need becomes too difficult to hold in your heart any longer, return a ray of light from your own heart until it touches the Grail. Only need of great magnitude, directed by the earnest seeker, can call forth the Grail.

## 4. The Epiphany of the Grail Hallow

Welcome the Grail in your own words, and see the light from your heart streaming into it. The Grail begins to glow with a great, piercing light that is refracted in every direction. When this happens, be aware of its light streaming impartially through the world to all who need its power. Be aware of the mediation of power. At this point, you may wish to speak aloud the people, issues or needs that are known to you, turning in a circle, so that the light of the Grail is mediated to all.

## 5. Communion

Take the food for your ritual meal and bless it in your own words. Be aware of the land where the ingredients were grown, the elements that went into growing them, and the necessity for spiritual nourishment. As you eat it, make conscious attunement with the Realm of the Grail which you are going to explore in the coming season. A suitable seasonal song can be sung to welcome the Autumn.

## 6. Establishing the Grail Hallow Shrine

Bless your empty shrine with the elements and adorn it with Autumn fruits. Take your chosen symbol of the Grail Hallow: *Let this token represent the power of the Grail Hallow in this place. May it be blessed by the powers of the Great Above and the Great Below, the inhabitants of the ages before the ages. This shrine is established for the restoration of all the worlds.*

Now take your symbol to each of the quarters, starting in the West, finishing South, and say, *Behold the Grail Hallow! May the gifts of fertility, healing and gladness be operative in this quarter.* Place it on your shrine with the words, *May the power of the Grail Hallow be the indwelling presence of this shrine.* Make a gesture of homage or service and place your hand on your symbol. *On this day of the Autumn Equinox, I dedicate myself to the quest for the Grail Hallow.* Make your own promise or dedication to the principles of the Grail.

## 7. The Return

For the closing ritual see p.67.

## Task

Write a short report of your ritual, including later notes if you experience any resonances to this ritual during this quarter.

--------------------- **LESSON 31** ---------------------

# *The Grail Maiden, Grail Two and Three*

grail maiden

**The Grail Maiden Speaks** *I am tender and true of heart. I am the vision that greets you at twilight and at the threshold of your dreaming. All who wish to serve must drink of my cup.*

The Grail Maiden is the one who bears the Grail in her hands in Arthurian tradition. She is that part of your imagination that is kindled and ready to serve. As the seer of the Grail, she knows in whom the deep waters are stirring and she brings them visions which will guide and prompt them to greater achievement. Hers is the primal Grail which is envisioned in many scenarios; it is also the one that is closest to hand when we are in need. She offers the hospitality of the spirit to those in trouble, and with her insight finds the ways through the overwhelming currents of life.

This function is clearly demonstrated in the story of the Damsels of the Wells.[11] In the time before Arthur, there were always faery women who served at the wells, offering hospitality to all spiritual travellers. But King Amangons raped one of the maidens and stole her golden cup. After this terrible event the kingdom lost the voices of the wells and the damsels therein.

The maidens ceased their service and the land became a wasteland. In later times, Arthur and his men attempted to right the wrong that had been done, resolving to kill Amangons' descendants. But they discovered that *his* descendants were also the children of the damsels of the wells! The knights strove hard to restore the action of the Grail and eventually the wasteland was healed.

The Grail legends also tell of a series of maidens, some named, some unnamed, who bear the Grail through the hall. Elaine[9] and Repanse de Schoy both uphold the ancient guardianship of the deep, nourishing wells, eventually becoming companion or wife of one of the Grail seekers. The fusion of maiden and Grail is long established in Celto-Arthurian tradition. The maiden is the pure voice who cannot speak falsely. Both maiden and Grail represent the eternal call of the imagination to re-enchant the earth. When we lose touch with that primordial quality, our lives turn into wasteland.

The Grail Maiden bids us listen to the voices of the wells once more, to rediscover our own deep access to the imaginative worlds. She is the 'Daughter of Love' who holds the healing Grail to her breast, inviting us to drink and be healed also. The Grail Family are to be found wherever the sound of water is heard. They are evoked by the light shining on the waters.

> **Grail Two Speaks** *Listen to our song, twin voices in harmony. When one sings, the other listens. Our song is love reciprocated, and the concord of partnership. Learn the way of beauty and listen to the voice of the song.*

The beauty of this card is the active support that our friends and partners bring us when we are upon the path. Although our partner may not walk the path with us, yet the deep accord that is between us is nonetheless a great reserve of strength to draw upon. The greatest love is to extend this support to our loved ones. It is, of course, easier to be in complete accord and partnership upon the path, but this cannot always be so. We have to look to the deepest levels of our relationships to find this comradeship.

**grail two**    **grail three**

**Grail Three Speaks** *Gather round and eat what you will. The table is broad and there is no formality: guests may sit where they please. Take an apple for your journey and share it with all you meet.*

The student who is well supported finds speedy access to comfort and fulfilment. When we are on the path we are seldom aware of our own good fortune at the immense resources of spiritual solace that surround us on every side. This card bids us heed our abundant blessings and receive nourishment as needed. We must learn to draw upon these resources in an efficient way: to enjoy the banquets of spiritual help that come our way and to take with us the apples of joy and gladness for stretches of the path that are less rich in nourishment. Regular spiritual solace sustains us in the bleak times.

## Questions

1. Our society distrusts and shuns the imagination; bring to mind a time when your imaginative or creative life suffered mockery or imprisonment. Ask healing of the Grail Maiden.
2. With which of your close friends/family do you feel greatest concord? Which qualities typify this concord?

3. What is the nature of your spiritual reserves? Where do you go to when you are spiritually dry? (This might be a book, a place, a form of devotion etc.)

## Task

During this quest you can reconnect with the Grail each day by making a dedication at twilight. This can be performed anywhere and takes only a short time. At twilight, enter into stillness wherever you are and bring to mind your dreams and longings. Visualize a pool rippling out into the distance, bringing your dreams out of the still centre into manifestation.

## Meditation

1. Leave the Grail Castle and journey in search of the Grail Maiden. She is your initiator into the Grail Realm. She may not let you drink from her cup unless you first promise to guard the waters ~ keeping both the water we drink and the waters of the imagination free from pollution. Make your own dedication to serve these waters before you drink. Sit with the Grail Maiden and look deeply into the waters. As a seer, she will give answers about any aspect of your quest.
2. She leads you through the forest to Grail Two. Here there is an indescribable feeling of great peace and tranquillity. Sit in the rays of the Autumn sunshine and let some of that peace now enter your soul. As you hear the crooning of the doves, be aware of drawing the sunlight into your body through every pore of your skin, through every breath you make. This is important spiritual nourishment for the quest ahead.
3. You follow the path to Grail Three and find a table laid out for you. As you sit there, a group of maidens come bearing the food that you most desire and serve you. Eat as much as you will and give thanks to the damsels of the wells. Go on your way, full of strength and gladness.

# ———————————— LESSON 32 ————————————

# *Gawain*

**Gawain Speaks** *My strength is greatest at midday, yet the enemies of the kingdom come often by night. I must hone my skills upon the*

*uiii gawain*

*stone of fortitude in all seasons, to pit my body and spirit against the challenges that threaten this land. Have courage, be ready and fight with me.*

Gawain holds the power of the tanaiste, or 'likely-successor' to Arthur. In Arthur's absence, he stands in the place of the king as defender of the passes that the kingdom may not be invaded by anything that would harm it. This position in the orthodox tarot pack is one of Strength, most often represented by a woman. The kind of strength represented by Gawain is that which is evident in any person of integrity. Gawain is also a champion of the Goddess. Throughout his career, he shows a tendency to frequent the company of women, to champion their causes and to have many meetings with the Goddess' representatives. The polarities of male and female guardianship are balanced in him, for he shows an extraordinary balance of strength and compassion, severity and mercy in his nature. Whether as companion or opponent, he shows the same courtesy which stems from his self-discipline and poise. [26] Here he is shown defending the land, in Arthur's absence. Gawain is the companion of the Queen in this court, so he may be seen also as the Queen's Champion – a role that more usually falls to Lancelot. This is his function in the autumnal Grail court, for there are many cards in this set that denote the withdrawn nature of the King in autumn; not only do we have the Wounded King but also the Sleeping Lord.

# Meditation

Gawain is your companion upon this Grail quest. He shows you the strategies of defence and attack. You may call upon him at any point for help or advice on this quest. He asks if you are willing to guard the pass for him. In order to test your aptitude for this quest, he will put you through five feats. He asks you whether you are willing to stand a trial session through the night.

As the light begins to fail, a woman with a child in her arms approaches you for protection. You may not leave your post at the pass. What service can you offer her?

As night falls and the dew rises, a poor and homeless woman approaches you for alms: you have only enough food for yourself. Give what you can, remembering that you are not free to forage for anything more until the dawn following.

At darkest midnight, an old woman approaches you, asking to be ferried across the river which crosses the valley of the pass. She is anxious, crotchety and sharp with you, but she is not an enemy. Call upon what courtesy you can muster and help her across.

At the first pale lightening of the sky, a woman sick of a contagious disease approaches you with bell and clapper. She is friendless and unwanted, needing only your attention and conversation. Show her what compassion you can.

At the first red streaks of sunlight, an angry woman strides towards you. You realize that she has had an argument with someone and is ready to strike out at anyone. Using all your self-discipline, calm and comfort her and prevent her from hurting herself or you.

The sun now rises and Gawain comes to ask how you spent the night. He listens and gives you a shield like his, asking you to represent the five encounters you have undergone, setting one card at each point of the Pentacle. He explains that each point represents the five duties of strength. The inside of the shield should represent your guardianship of the earth. This will be your protection upon the Grail quest.

# Gawain's Shield Reading

For this reading, remove all the female greater power cards to make a separate pile. Shuffling the rest of the pack, lay one card each on positions 1-5. Remove one card, unseen, from the separate deck to lie on position 6.

Just as Gawain inherited the right to wear the magical green girdle or lace as a sign of his own vulnerability, so you may find that one or two of the cards you've drawn may seem to reflect shamefully on you. Through the power of the endless knot of the pentacle and of the

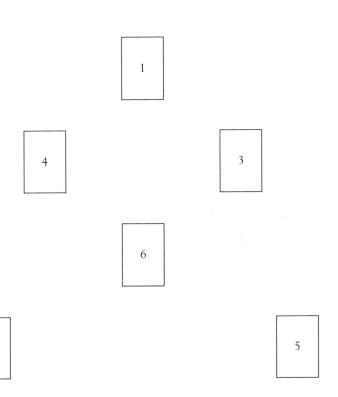

Fig. 14: *Gawain's Shield Spread*

indwelling guidance of the Goddess, you may find that these 'faults' are transformed into powers as you go on your quest. This reading can be done again after the Grail is achieved. Make a careful note of what has changed.

1. Represents the nature of your service.
2. Represents your generosity.
3. Represents your courtesy.
4. Represents your compassion.
5. Represents self-discipline.
6. Represents the aspect of the Goddess who oversees your Grail quest, and denotes the quality of your commitment to it.

When you have finished making your shield, Gawain gives you a personal gift.

# *The Grail Knight, Grail Four and Five*

grail knight

**The Grail Knight Speaks** *I follow the Grail vision wherever it leads, for I am destined to find and wield the holy vessel. They call me 'fool' and 'dreamer', but for this purpose was I born and in the service of the Grail I will die.*

The Grail Knight is the truest guide and companion on the quest, for his eyes are ever set on the Hallow of his heart. He is that part of you that remains ever true to the vision of bliss and fulfilment. As the Way-Shower of the Grail, he can be trusted to follow faithfully its wake through deep waters. For him, the Grail is the vessel of inspiration; its music, poetry and beauty are all hints to its whereabouts. We may also keep sensitive to our quest by means of the true arts which inspire us with irrational urgings and unbidden emotion, for these are similar pathways.

The upbringing of the Grail Knight is always in seclusion from the world. Perceval is brought up in the forest, and Galahad in a convent; both are surrounded by the influence of women. Both have to strive to find a way within the world. Perceval is ignorant and foolish, following his desire rather than his quest. Galahad is both disciplined and dedicated; he chooses not to live an ordinary life, but to keep his eyes ever upon the Grail of his vision. These two knights, prime Grail seekers in the early and later legends respectively, represent the twin poles between which we as seekers may fall.

It is all too easy to drift into a spiritualized kind of life which has no thrust, which becomes wishy-washy and unfocused, sloppy and defused. Yet we must guard against the other extreme, of fanatical dedication which may be both ruthless and lacking in compassion. The Grail comes to rebalance our lives with the vision of one who is attuned to wholeness.

The Grail Knight guards the twilight or between-light times, when vision is near. This is why he is depicted with his harp. The resonance of song and music is the universal language of spiritual desire. The Grail Knight's function is to awaken our hearts with divine longing. His esoteric title is 'the Son of Love', for he awakens our creative *eros*.

grail four

**Grail Four Speaks** *I am wanhope who falls by the wayside. There is no Grail and all is emptiness. After all my efforts I am tired of trying.*

The low times, when energy ceases to flow and ideas seem stagnant, come to all who walk the path. When spiritual nourishment is withdrawn or when we have surfeited on the good things of life – these are both occasions to trigger this experience. A strange reluctance to continue our progress sets in and we find little to stimulate our appetite for learning. At such times, we must gently encourage a return to our spiritual programme and turn attention away from ourselves towards where more pressing needs beckon.

grail five

**Grail Five Speaks** *There is no wind upon the water, my sail is slack. All that I longed for and trusted in has shattered. I drift in search of a meaning for the mistakes I've made.*

This card marks the difficult moment of truth for some students of the path. Our limitations surface and we have to accept that the strengths on which we relied so firmly will not serve for this journey. Our faith can also be severely shaken by the very thing for which we seek, which often has its own integrity and which will not bow to our often hidden self-serving attitudes. It takes great maturity to realize that it is our own mistake that has led us into these waters. Disillusioned by our own powers, we are able to sail on in a better, more humble spirit.

## Questions

1. Do you incline to the dreaminess of Perceval or the fanaticism of Galahad in your spiritual quest?
2. In which areas of your life do you need to be more reflective?
3. When your quest seems boring and pointless, what is the best course of action for you to restimulate your motivation?
4. What are your limitations?

# Task

Spend one morning/afternoon/evening this week doing what you most enjoy. This can be anything at all; the only rule is that you are to give yourself up to your own pleasurable enjoyment. This treat is for the benefit of *you*.

# Meditation

1. Gawain sees you safely through the pass. You travel onwards and towards late afternoon you discover the Grail Knight. He is your guide through the Lands Adventurous. He hands his harp to you and you are able to play upon it, singing. A song or poem for your quest springs up within you as you listen to the music that you make. Allow the thread of your creative self to be unwound and record whatever Grail song comes to you.
2. Leaving the woodland behind, you come to Grail Four. The day is overcast and all looks thoroughly unpromising. You need to drink, but there is only the stagnant lake waters which taste bitter. A terrible lethargy to go no further invades your body. The Grail Knight rescues you from this torment by playing his harp to dispel the illusory boredom that has overcome you.
3. With better heart, you go on until you find the ship of Grail Five waiting for you upon the sea-shore. It is magnificently appointed and you set out to sea, full of pride. Soon the weather becomes misty and the ship suddenly much less attractive. You have no mariner to help you sail: perhaps you should have thought before coming on board? Look upon the shield that you made when you guarded the pass for Gawain, especially noting any points that are weak. Without self-reproach, commit these weaknesses or any other limitations you have to the aspect of the Goddess upon your shield. Looking only at her, hold up your shield and allow the wind to fill it and so propel the ship towards the island close ahead.

—————————————— LESSON 34 ——————————————

# The Wounded King

**The Wounded King Speaks** *Whom does the Grail serve? Will no one ask? My blood runs down and none asks why. I am one with the*

xii the wounded king

*wounded earth whose wisdom abides patiently down the interminable aeons. May I be worthy to serve!*

Here we find the part of ourselves that is wounded. We all suffer from a loss that robs us of decisive or practical action: all we can do is suffer and wait. This can be a time of learning, but it is certainly not one that we should revel in. The notion of the 'nobility' of suffering is attached to the idea of sacrifice: indeed there can be few nobler things than the purposeful voluntary sacrifice of one life for the benefit of others. During the suspension of time and action that attends this experience, we revolve between pain and understanding. Our wounds often prove to be the vulnerable channels for compassion and change.

This card indicates an aspect of Arthur himself as the wounded Grail king, unable to move about his land, dependent on the wise actions of independent questing knights who work without any seeming co-ordination. It may also denote that immobile part of ourselves which is waiting to be restored to active life, a restoration that is dependent upon a set of circumstances which we cannot bring about of our own volition.

The giving up of the will into the greater care of the universe is terribly difficult. Human beings like to manipulate events and to use their own powers to change things; to be totally out of action, dependent upon other creatures or greater archetypal energies brings us new insights into the nature of the Grail and sacrifice.

The Wounded King knows that, despite his regality, he is as powerless as the humblest of his subjects. He is wounded and his healing is in the hands of others. Unlike his subjects, he cannot ask for help: *they* must ask why he is wounded. This Grail question is the healing key to this experience, for the need must be expressed or recognized before help can come.

## Task

Compare the varying patterns of the path leading through the Grail Maiden, Grail Two and Three and Gawain, with the path leading through the Grail Knight, Grail Four and Five and the Wounded King.

## Questions

1. Which areas of your life are most wounded? What have you learned from being vulnerable?
2. What do you think would heal your life to your satisfaction?
3. What are your most urgent needs at this time? Make a prayer of this need and direct it to your own personal spiritual source of help.

## Meditation

You sail towards an island. Step out of the ship and follow the path that leads to a grove in the centre of the island. You find the Wounded King who cannot rise to greet you, nor can he speak, but his experiences weave visions around the grove, which is hung with many banners. The dog scratches your hand and looks questioningly up at you, so that you know you must ask certain questions here. Ask each of these in turn and see what is revealed upon the banners.

> *Why does creation suffer?*
> *Why are you wounded, O King?*
> *What can I do to bring healing?*

Record your visions carefully, especially answers to the last question. The Wounded King wishes to give you a gift, which the dog brings to you.

# The Grail Queen, Grail Six and Seven

grail queen

**The Grail Queen Speaks** *I am the mother of love who pours out her cup for the good of all. My draught is boundless as the sea. May your hearts be open, may your senses be receptive to all experience!*

The Grail Queen exemplifies the path of love. She is that part of yourself that never turns away from the need within another sentient being. As the empowerer of the Grail she maintains a vigilant regard for those who are drawn to the quest. The runnels of wine that stem from her cup pass down the worlds into some unlikely places and stimulate new seekers: by this means she creates new foster-children who follow her compassionate way. She rejects no one who is able to serve in however small a way. Her love brings beauty into the darkest places.

The Grail Queen is nearest in nature to the Goddess of the Celtic Otherworld, called by many names in folklore and legend. Her waters are the fructifying channels of grace which stimulate creativity in all who drink them. She is the mother who keeps nothing back but gives all her care to her children, as does Elaine, mother of Galahad. The Grail Queen guards the lineage of the Grail family throughout all generations: hers is not only a guardianship of the bloodline but also a guardianship of the spiritual lineage which is created between student and teacher, as the sacred teachings are passed down. With the Grail King, she upholds the Grail teachings.

The esoteric title applied to her is 'the Mother of Love', for she awakens a caring attitude within us. She sets our hands around the Grail and teaches us the work of healing with such an understanding and sympathy that we cannot help but learn.

grail six

**Grail Six Speaks** *I am the home of the ancestors, the place of deep memory. I will reconnect you with your roots and bring you the deep delight of recollection.*

After the emptiness and disillusion of Grail Four and Five, Grail Six brings us renewed encouragement from the hidden places within. There is often a sense, when reaching this point, of stepping along a clear path which has been well travelled. There is a sense of continuance and traditional support that give us new strength. Some, who drink too deeply of these ancestral waters, can fall into an unhealthy atavism, whereby they become dependent upon the past and cannot live in the everyday world at all. But for most of us, a judicial drink from the ancestral head-waters will give us new heart for our task.

**Grail Seven Speaks** *Traveller on the way, you are welcome! Here is the land of shifting shapes, of strange reflections. What is reality in the land of veiled appearances?*

grail seven

Grail Seven reveals a danger for all students of the path: the glamour of esoteric work. It is very important for the seeker to know how to read the visions that appear in dream and meditation with a true eye. If inner reality begins to take on greater substance than outer reality, the student's sensibilities are dangerously englamoured. Inner reality is not illusory, but founded on the true nature of the Otherworld. To be able to distinguish one reality from the other is the supreme task. Some may mistake this for the Grail Castle, which may subsequently become an ivory castle - impregnable, unrealizable and vainly sought.

## Questions

1. Where is love absent in your life?
2. Upon which ancient foundations are your own lifelines set? Which ancestral influences beat strongest in your blood?
3. What are your own guidelines for guarding against self-deception? Are these different in spiritual matters from mundane matters?

## Meditation

1. You return from the island in your ship, which sets you back further up the shore from your embarkation point. A series of caves riddles the cliff-face and you enter one. Within is the Grail Queen who stands at the borders of the Otherworld and welcomes you. You may ask her

for any healing that is needed, for yourself, for another or for some other need. Her cup spills forth and pours down into the cracks of the world to have its effect.

2. She leads you deeper into the Otherworld to Grail Six. You have only to bathe in the waters that gush forth from this mound in order to have communion with the deepest levels of ancestral awareness. As you bathe in the stone basin of the spring, you may have a vision or experience of far-memory, of your own continuance in the sacred mysteries. Record these carefully and return to this card if you need to clarify anything you don't understand. Also call upon the Grail Queen for answers.

3. The warm sun dries your body and you put on your clothes and set out again. You come to the vision of Grail Seven. It is late and you wish you could shelter somewhere. The castle looks inviting but something is not quite right. This doesn't feel like journey's end after all. You go in and look around. There is nothing there. You look out through the windows into the waters and see the cause of your unease – the reflection reveals another kind of castle.

## ──────── LESSON 36 ────────

# *The Spiral Tower*

xvi the spiral tower

**The Spiral Tower Speaks** *I spin the whorl of change. I break down what is made to last forever. Feel the oscillation of the aeons and open yourself to changes ahead. I will transfigure your soul if you let me, or I will shatter your limited perceptions with a searing shock.*

The Spiral Tower is the place of changing, where we are broken and rewrought. This is a shocking experience for which nothing can prepare us. It is one of the most essential initiations along our path. The Spiral Tower reminds us that we are not central to the quest, that there are wider, cosmic issues at stake, that we are but puny seekers on the road to a greater truth which is working itself out. The natural cycles often appear destructive to our human perception, for they come suddenly and without concern for personal issues. It is one of the most humbling of experiences to realize that our part within the macrocosmic patterns of the ages may be smaller than we first thought. This is an awakening which all humankind has yet to undergo as another evolutionary phase awaits its time. The Spiral Tower acts as a point of reversal or liberation, to channel our energies into a new phase.

There is a close connection between Grail Seven and the Spiral Tower, which you will have discovered in your meditation. Study the differences between them very carefully so that you will not be confused by their similarities. Remember that, although the physical tower on the Spiral Tower is stricken by lightning, the crystal spire of changing remains eternally. It is the mill of heaven which appears in many North-West European traditions, emblematic of the cosmic axis. Only when we have personally experienced the complete round of its wheeling changes can we say that we have lived our lives to the full.

# Meditation

You look out of the window of Grail Seven and find that another reflection is revealed. You are actually within the Spiral Tower and the waters have become striated hills. Around you the land is spread out like a great amphitheatre.

You ascend the Spiral Tower and come out into a high, central observation room. Into its white emptiness wings an owl bearing a mouse in its beak. As soon as it drops the mouse, the owl becomes a white-clad faery-woman of more than human stature. Her prey has become a sleeping soul which rises and floats up the spiral staircase above. The owl-woman tells you that this is the tower of changing to which she brings souls who need to be liberated from stale patterns. You have come here inadvertently, but you are also welcome to bring change into your life.

Looking out over the land, you see the cycles of cosmic time endlessly

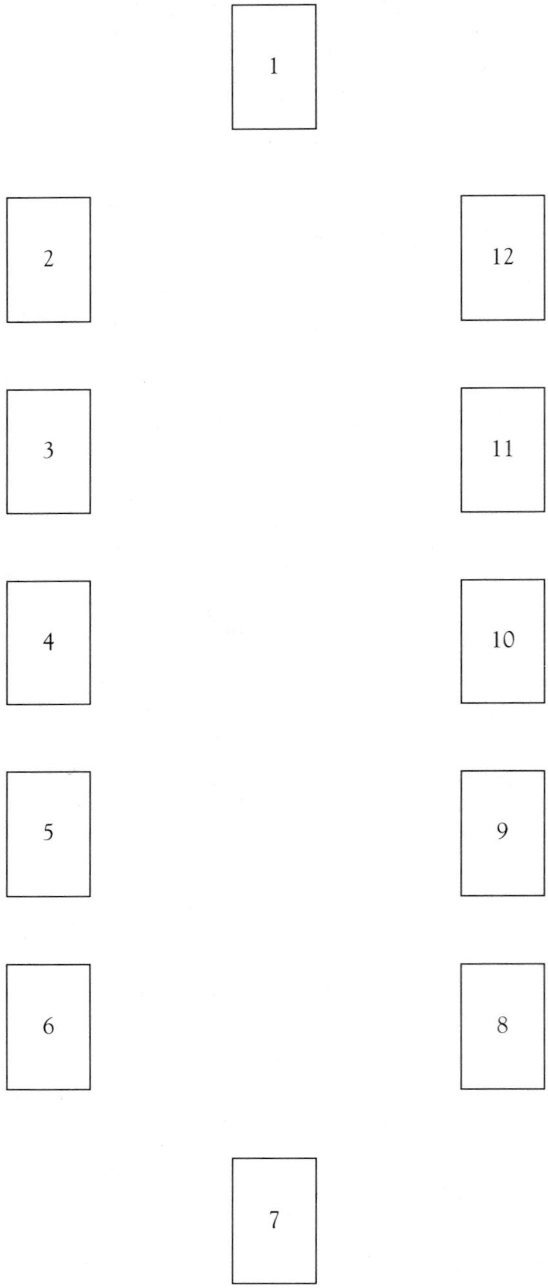

Fig. 15: *Spiral Tower Spread*

revolving. You lay down 12 cards in token of the year you have just lived through. As you do so, the many influences upon your own life become plain to you:

1. Who am I?
2. The way I've handled my resources.
3. The kind of choices I've made.
4. The influence of my home-life/environment.
5. The way I've expressed myself.
6. The way I've worked.
7. The kind of relationships I've had.
8. The legacies I've reaped from actions committed before this year.
9. How I've related to spiritual, legal or philosophical frameworks.
10. How I've responded to society.
11. How my aspirations have been reflected in the world.
12. The part of myself of which I've been unaware.

When you've read and evaluated these cards, the owl-woman mixes all the cards together and dares you to change these patterns for the year to come. It is up to you whether you wish actually to lay down another future spread to do this or not. You may wish her to change one or two specific cards with which you feel dissatisfied. If you choose the latter course, then draw further cards to cover the ones you wish to change and read the pattern again.

The white owl-woman then gives you a gift and you depart.

--------------------------- **LESSON 37** ---------------------------

## *The Grail King, Grail Eight and Nine*

**The Grail King Speaks** *Seeker, pour this cup upon the green stone and let me divine your way for you. I am the keeper of the questing paths, the woodward of the deep forest. Learn to be free of division.*

The Grail King is a strong counsellor and guide to the quest. He is that part of you that patiently listens to the least sign of change in the network of your life, any hint that a new pathway to the Grail may be opening. As the guardian of the Grail, he has been given many mighty resources to draw upon and so is rich in gifts to those who approach him. Some find him and are fearful of his immense power, for he knows by the

shadow of a leaf, by the stir of grass-blade, where you stand in the forest. All that is done in his realm is known to him.

The figure depicted on this card is derived from the Guardian of the Animals who appears in *The Lady of the Fountain*.[8] He is the Way-Shower to adventure for Owain, and directs him to cast water from the hanging bowl on to the green stone. This act provokes a number of changes in weather and season, so that Owain is brought to the goal of his quest much more quickly. The pouring out of water in this story becomes a challenge to 'things as they are', and opens the way for new things to manifest; this is the archetypal action of the Grail.

The Wounded King is one aspect of the Grail King, in his disempowered mode. The Grail King of this card shows him full of power, able to give the Grail's rich gifts to all. His mutable creative character enables him to manifest the Grail in any form - as vessel, cup, cauldron or stone. The shapeshifting elements of the Grail are part of his guardianship, for so he keeps safe the holy vessel from wrongful use.

> **Grail Eight Speaks** *I turn away from whatever is not for me. The holy place I yearned for is not where I should be. I turn away to find a wider path.*

Grail Eight finds the seeker turning away from the obvious pathway to re-evaluate and find a wider way. It is a common experience to work long and hard only to find that our goal and pathway are no longer desired

grail eight

grail nine

or valid for us. Some part of us has developed and we are no longer able to continue doing things in the accustomed way. This can stem from a lingering self-centred stubbornness to do things our way, but more often it involves a deepening maturity of which we have become aware. There may also be elements of unworthiness involved. Retrenchment is the only way forward, in order to evaluate afresh the next approach to the quest. The Grail that spills here may indeed be a false Grail: the wished-for one which does not satisfy.

> **Grail Nine Speaks** *What is your wish? I can grant it. Whatever you need, ask of me. I am the fullness of desire and none goes from me unsatisfied.*

Grail Nine depicts the cauldron that serves the food we most desire and is worth waiting for. The discontinuance of Grail Eight usually modifies itself shortly into a strongly refocused goal which becomes attainable. Grail Nine gives us appetite to continue along our path and feeds our emotional needs in a way which brings greater self-sufficiency and a contentment to trust in our quest. The heart's desire becomes attainable. This experience is often brought about by the simplest everyday things rather than by major spiritual insights.

## Meditation

1. You leave the Spiral Tower and make your way back to the wood where you encounter the Grail King. He is the guardian of the deep Other-world. He questions your progress and tells you to pour water from the bowl on to the green stone. Observe what kind of changes take place around you, for they are indicative of the quest you are upon.
2. The Grail King leads you through the woods to a clearing wherein is the chapel of Grail Eight. He bids you keep watch throughout one night in this place. Upon the altar is an emblem which accords with your own spiritual focus. You remain still and meditate upon this emblem or symbol. How does it equate to the Grail quest upon which you are engaged? After a while, the emblem vanishes and you are left in darkness, with no symbol to sustain your attention. You have no choice but to enter a deeper phase of meditation now. Allow the chapel to reshape and reform itself according to your ideal vision; how would you like it to be? How could this become a holy place for the gathering together of all people/beings? Describe what you experience. At dawn, the Grail King takes you away, saying, 'It is not yet time to drink the cup.'
3. Towards the next evening, the Grail King conducts you to Grail Nine. You may ask to be given your heart's desire from this cauldron. What is it that you truly desire? The Grail King gives you food from the cauldron to eat. Imbibe what is offered to you and experience the fullness of your desire fulfilled.

# ————————— LESSON 38 —————————

# *The Sleeping Lord*

> **The Sleeping Lord Speaks** *I have waited long, turning in my sleep whenever the dangers threatened my land. Yet, though I sleep, my spirit soars above to bring the message to my people: 'I am ever watchful, for I feed on star-fire and wait to the end of the ages. Mine is the voice of the deep earth. I watch with patience and endurance. Speak and act for me, the Once and Future King.'*

The Sleeping Lord is the Arthur who inhabits our imaginations, the awaited 'once and future King' acclaimed by legend and looked for in each generation. Every age and land has its own story of help coming from ancestral levels or of the spirit of the land rising up in heroic form

xx the sleeping lord

to combat enemies or influences which threaten to overwhelm it.

The Sleeping Lord is also our potent selves. We notice that it is Mabon, standing upon the thigh of the land, who wakes the Sleeping Lord with his horn of joy. The voice of youth, of enthusiasm and engaged energies is the one who comes. At the nexus of the ages, the Sleeping Lord turns to listen to that horn and perhaps to manifest again. Here renewal or recapitulation may occur. Lost things may be found again. Great prophetic promises are at last fulfilled.

## Meditation

When you have finished eating from the cauldron, you fall asleep and begin to dream. You see your own land with the Sleeping Lord lying beneath it. A great eagle comes down and lifts you upon its back. You see the history of your own land unfolding from your vantage point: the injustices and the triumphs alike. Describe what you experience. When the unfolding story comes to an end, the eagle flies nearer the earth and you see people of every age and condition assembled, as though awaiting you. One brings you a trumpet with which to awake the Sleeping Lord, so that the people of the earth can be given guidance, prophecy and renewal. Blow and awaken him, and listen for his words. These may come in meditation or at some other unheeded time. The Sleeping Lord also gives you a gift.

## Task

If you want to ask the Sleeping Lord for a specific prophecy or renewal, draw three cards at random to understand his answer.

――――――――――――― **LESSON 39** ―――――――――――――

## *Guinevere*

**Guinevere Speaks** *I weave the soul of the land. The thread that turns under my fingers is blent of many things: peace, contentment, joy and the sweet harmony of creation. I am the mother of all that grows. Wherever I walk, flowers spring up. My mantle of beauty is cast about the shoulders of the land.*

Guinevere is the inner ruler of the court of the Grail. In each of the other inner ruler cards (Merlin, Lady of the Lake and Arthur), the emblems of the stone, sword and spear are clearly visible. There is no Grail depicted on this card because, in the earliest legends, the Grail is not perceived as an object, but as the woman whom the Grail-seeker loves best. (*Peredur* in *The Mabinogion*)

Guinevere is the sovereign lady. As Arthur's Queen and the first lady of the land, she represents all the powers of the Grail in her person. Throughout the many levels of her story, she has a number of appearances and qualities, only one of which is depicted here. She can be a young maiden, as here; a vital and mischievous woman; a powerful queen or a demanding and challenging mistress.

The love that Guinevere represents here is one that accepts the whole of creation for what it is, rather than for any abstract ideas we may have about it. She sits, totally at home in the landscape, allowing it to become one with her. Without love, we none of us can experience compassion. Until we can experience compassion, we will never find the Grail. Guinevere teaches us to be open-handed and loving. She puts into our hands the spindle so that we too can feel the pains and sorrows, as well as the joys, of others. Her secret guardianship of the Grail is well kept.

Many men seek her lineaments in the woman of their heart. Many women seek the confidence that is the pure beauty of Guinevere within themselves. That beauty is easily tarnished by possession, imprisonment and servitude to another's will. For those imprisoned in no-win relationships, Guinevere is a great helper. She supports us also in the search for the roots of our own ungivingness. She is the gift, as well as the giver. This aspect can be over-stressed in our lives. We give so readily and no one seems grateful for our unstinted service. We also need to receive gifts ourselves, but we need to have sufficient self-worth to accept them.

## Meditation

You awaken with the sound of the trumpet still echoing about you. Gawain appears to lead you to Guinevere. She has sat spinning in the field, watching the spiral path of your progress through this realm. As the last piece of wool leaves the distaff and is wound on to the spindle, she looks up and greets you. 'I have ravelled out your thread and see, you are here. Rest now, and be refreshed after your journey.'

She takes up a cup which lies hidden in her skirts and approaches the great white cow which accompanies her. She milks it into the cup and gives you to drink. The milk has the gift of making you aware of your own inner beauty and wealth. Bring to mind all the many gifts that make you the person you are, and make a personal dedication of these gifts to the Queen.

Guinevere blesses your gifts with the ability to expand and grow with greater fulfilment and abundance, and gives you her own gift.

## *The Grail Hallow*

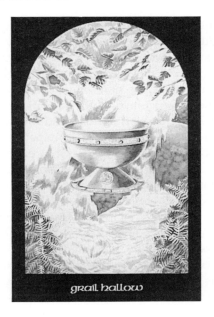

grail hallow

**The Grail Hallow Speaks** *I am the vessel of holy hope and of fair love. I bring the gladness of the new day and the restoration of night's in-gathering. Whoever drinks of me gains healing; whoever wields me brings regeneration to the wastelands. Of my abundance there is no lack. I make the barren fertile, and give nourishment to the starving.*

The Grail is the primal Hallow of the Arthurian legends. It brings regeneration when all seems hopeless, lost or wounded beyond healing. It is the ultimate potential hidden in every action or quality. Its subtle magic cannot be imperiously summoned or commanded, for it will only do the bidding of one who is dedicated to the service of creation. Any attempt to use its gifts unworthily results in the withdrawal of the Grail from ordinary reality. It can be accessed only by those who live to manifest the Grail's influence in the world; only they who are so dedicated can mediate its restorative power.

The realm of the Grail is established in Autumn, wherein our life's gifts are explored in detail. With a good deal of living behind us, we are aware of the need of the gifts of joy and gladness, of the necessity for restoration at all levels of life. The Grail is thus the appropriate symbol of the seeker who has understood the need for compassion in the wasteland of the world.

## Meditation

Filled with confidence from the draught you have drunk, you feel empowered to ask for the Grail. Guinevere asks by what right you make your request, and you respond in your own words. She touches you gently and you become a cow. You follow the other cows in the herd until you come to a sparkling spring. There you see the Grail, which spills out crystal nourishment which the cows imbibe and which is present in their milk. You now bring to mind the places, people and situations that most need healing, in your opinion, and bestow each of them in the Grail. You listen to the voice of the Grail sounding in the swift streaming waters. What does it say to you?

You return to your own shape and bring to mind one whom you have recently encountered, who needs healing. Picking up the Grail, and accompanied by Guinevere's cow, you find the shore where the Wounded King still languishes. The cow bears you on her back. You find him and milk the cow into the Grail, bringing the cup to his lips. As he drinks, you are aware of him also as the Sleeping Lord. Believe that his healing will be accomplished.

The cow bears you and the Grail back across the water to Guinevere. You place the Hallow before her and it fades, leaving only its outline upon the ground. Guinevere gives you the pack of cards and you make the following augury of the Grail.

## Augury of the Grail of Love

For this reading, remove the Grail Hallow, setting it at position 5, and all the Greater Power cards. As you shuffle the remainder of the pack, strongly visualize or gaze at the Grail, putting your trust in its compassion. Ask it, 'How can the Grail of Love be manifest within me?' Then draw four cards from the main pack and lay them on positions 1–4. Shuffle the Greater Powers separately and ask for the augury (prophecy) of the Grail. Draw one card and lay it on position 5, covering the Grail Hallow. Each of the positions in this augury represents some aspect of love, for it is love that the Grail symbolizes. After you've laid and briefly interpreted your reading, ask the central card to act as a guide and travel with it through the other cards, listening to what is said.

1. Represents your imagination. This receiver of inner impressions can be like a mirror of divine things, but only if we reflect it truly back

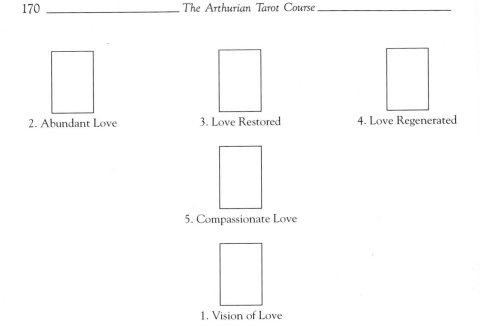

Fig. 16: *The Augury of the Grail of Love*

to our world. Its challenge is 'How do I keep my vision inclusive?'
2. Represents the deep dissatisfactions that create caverns of emptiness in our lives. Without correct nourishment, we grow sick. Its challenge is 'How can I best learn to receive?'
3. Represents the many rejections we have suffered, in relationships and in other ways. This can often make us introspective and unconfident. Its challenge is 'How can the Grail restore me?'
4. Represents your primal joy. Nothing malign can exist when exposed to laughter and the deep confidence of grounded gladness. Its challenge is 'What feeds the springs of spiritual joy within me?'
5. Represents the compassionate heart within you that is always open to love's gift. The Greater Power card represents the initiation of love's action. It challenges you with 'How do I serve the Grail: how does the Grail serve me?'

# LESSON 41

## The Investiture of the Grail

Lay the cards of this Grail Quest about you in the following way:

Fig. 17: *The Inner Court of the Grail*

This is the inner court of the Grail which you have explored on this quest. Guinevere is surrounded by three kingly or warrior figures and by the striking symbol of the lightning-struck tower. Sitting calmly in the middle, Guinevere spins her thread while worlds shatter, kings are wounded and her own husband lies disempowered. Only Gawain defends the realm, alone like Cuchullain at the ford. She is the still centre around which everything revolves. The time has come for the investiture of the Grail.

## Meditation

Visualize the watery western part of your inner landscape that you worked with in Lesson 5. Now superimpose the Grail court upon it. Seeing the Rainbow Path of the Seeker at the centre of your inner landscape, you now enter this Spear quarter, passing through it without fear or difficulty. You may wish to spread the following meditation over several sessions.

Starting with the Grail Maiden, you will meditate on each card in clockwise order until you reach the Sleeping Lord. The Grail Family gives you the following gifts: the Maiden gives a scrying crystal that is tuned to the Grail Hallow; the Knight gives an emblem of twilight; the Queen gives a healing herb; the King gives a golden coin with your own image on one side and the Grail on the obverse. These gifts will prove useful in your future journeys in the Grail realm. Each of the landscape cards gives you a different colour liquid in small vials to place within the Grail. Each of the Greater Powers imparts a special blessing.

Continue meditating on each of the cards until you reach the centre where Guinevere sits, with the Grail Castle behind her and the Grail Hallow before her. You may not enter the Grail Castle until you have shown her the gifts you have collected from the Greater Powers on this quest. The combined energy of these gifts creates a strong path between yourself and the Grail Castle. Kneel before Guinevere and make your personal dedication to the Grail. Then you enshrine the Grail in the Grail Castle, which is the same as the Western Caer of your own inner landscape.

Slowly the images fade and are replaced by that of your own Grail shrine. Open your eyes and formally repeat your inner dedication to the Grail, that its energy may be once more operative in the outer world.

## Assimilation and Examination of Lessons 30-41

You have concluded the Grail Quest, but please turn to p.99 and study the assimilation exercises there. The Grail Court is an inspired family, attuned to the element of water and to the land's autumn face. See how well you have responded to the healing and regeneration of this suit. You can then pass on the next quest, or to Part Three, if you have completed all your quests.

# WINTER:

*And Peredur proceeded towards the castle . . . and he beheld a chess-board in the hall, and the chess-men were playing against each other, by themselves. And the side that he favoured lost the game, and thereupon the others set up a shout, as though they had been living men.*

Peredur ap Efrawc

Our quest begins in the Realm of the Stone, from the Stone Castle and aided by the Stone Family, who act as our guides. Companioned by Taliesin, we gain wisdom from the Grail Hermit, encounter the Washer at the Ford and receive the initiation of the Star. The Stone Hallow itself is guarded by Merlin. You will need the following cards for study:

The entire Stone Suit
Merlin
Taliesin
The Grail Hermit
The Washer at the Ford
The Star of Prophecy

# LESSON 42

## The Stone Realm

stone ten

**Stone Ten Speaks** *The way lies clear across the snow. The fire burns within. Come, learn of the abiding treasury of tradition. Keep Winter Court with us and beat us at our own game.*

The Realm of the Stone is established in Winter. This realm is where our life's commitments are explored. The Stone Castle is clearly indicated from afar, but it lies in the middle of the Winter-gripped land. It welcomes travellers who have a sense of the fitness of things, who understand the formal steps of the game and who are willing to learn of traditional wisdom with humility. The prizes to be won in this game are those to do with rightful inheritance, with gaining establishment, with entering into positive ancestral patterns. Many assume that these prizes entail becoming deadly serious, but, in truth, their accomplishment brings with it the security to exercise our abilities and enjoy working at full stretch, in our assured strength. The magpies remind us that possessions are transitory: there will always be thieves and predators, but the inheritance of wisdom is forever.

The Winter Solstice brings with it the tide of cleansing, when we gradually loose our grasp upon what until then has seemed important to us. We allow ourselves to be stripped of our self-importance and feel open to new influences. The Winter snow and gales help us let go, to be brought nearer to the bone of our essential selves.

But before we submit to the cleansing tide of Winter, we first seek the homecoming of Midwinter in order to be truly enriched. Wisdom, knowledge, wealth and an enduring inheritance are some of the qualities we seek within this castle. As we move through this realm, we will frequently discover these twin themes of riches and dearth. Our best weapon upon this quest is perseverance, without which nothing can be established.

## Questions

1. What wisdom do you seek at this time in your life?
2. Who are the family of your spiritual lineage: from whom have you inherited your current store of wisdom? (These may include characters from books, spiritual teachers, saints, deities etc.)
3. If you were to die tomorrow, what spiritual legacy would you like to leave to the world?

## Meditation

1. Visualize the Seeker's Rainbow Path (see Lesson 2) until you come to a cross-roads. Northern hemisphere students should take the northern road, southern hemisphere students should travel by the southern road. Set out in search of the Stone Castle. Note any animals, people or significant encounters or landmarks on your way.
2. Enter the Stone Castle and explore it. Describe what you find. Who is within it?
3. Within the castle's foundations there is a strong room full of treasure. One piece of this treasure belongs to you and one only; taking a light, you begin your search, yet without knowing what it is that you seek. Suddenly the light blows out and you are plunged into darkness. Calling upon all the people in your spiritual lineage who have helped you in the past and whose support gives you inner strength and comfort to continue your quest, you breathe gently and evenly to stem your panic. Thinking only of the spiritual help you have received, look into the darkness. In the gloom, you can discern a shimmering radiance: you have found your piece of treasure. Look at it carefully, describe it. Ask about its function and qualities. You may not take this treasure away with you on the quest, but you may draw fortitude and encouragement from it. What qualities does your treasure bestow upon you? You may call upon these qualities throughout your quest.

4. To explore the Stone Realm, you can stand upon the battlements and look across the land. If you wish, you can fly over in the shape of a magpie.

# Winter Ceremony of the Stone Hallow

Celebrate this seasonal ritual at the Winter Solstice (21 December in the northern hemisphere, 21 June in the southern). You will need evergreen leaves or Winter crocus to decorate your shrine.

The Winter tide comes in at the Winter Solstice. This is the period of Saturnalia, when everything is reversed and when we stop work and enjoy play and recreation more than at any other time of the year. Most people are more aware of this tide coming in because they have more leisure at Christmas and New Year. The weather is usually cold and calm. The decaying leaves lie on the ground, ready to act as compost for future growth. The Zodiacal earthy sign of Capricorn comes in now. This tide is one of completion and endings. It is the time to finish off projects, to look back on the old year and rest. It is also the clearing out tide, which some people find difficult around February. Think of this period as the 'inner Spring clean'. It is analogous to the time of Lent. The Stone of Wisdom is swept clean of detritus and we see ourselves, as in a mirror.

See the general notes on p.63 for the performance of this ritual.

## 1. The Making Sacred
Standing centrally, facing North,
*In the season of Winter, I dedicate myself to the quest for the Stone of Wisdom.* For the opening ritual see p.64.

## 2. Meditation on the Mystery of the Winter Solstice
*I stand at the gate of the dying year and welcome the inner illumination of darkness and introspection. It penetrates to the heart of doubt and releases the Hallow of the Stone. From this portal stream forth the gifts of wisdom, establishment and attainment. May all that is ignorant, rootless and unaware of its potential find its dwelling place in the soil of new growth, that all creation may benefit from the gifts of this Hallow!*

Sit and enter into silent meditation upon the nature of the season in your land. Contemplate the powers of the Stone as you understand them. Bring to mind the needs of creation: your own circle of family and friends, your land, troubled places in the world, and other global issues. Spend at least ten minutes doing this.

## 3. Invocation and Visualization of the Stone Guardian

Stand facing North:

*I call upon Merlin, guardian of the Stone Hallow, to help and assist me. Mighty Prophet, you are the master who foretells and perceives the destiny of the land. You stand ready to guide the seeker through insight and initiative, into the greater mystery of the Otherworld. I seek the empowerment of the Stone Hallow for the benefit of all beings.* (Visualize Merlin bearing the Stone in his hand. Here you may ask him any question and listen to his words.)

Chant/sing the following (tune on p.254):

> *Ancient guardian of the land,*
> *Take us gently by the hand.*
> *Show us your vision, show us your art,*
> *Show us the wisdom of your heart:*
> *Keep faith with the Seeker.*

See a ray of clear light emanating from his heart to your feet, forming a path between you. Breathe in that light, breathing it up until it reaches your heart. Now call to mind the great need for the Stone of Wisdom in the world, holding that clear light at your heart. When the urgency of the need becomes too difficult to hold in your heart any longer, return a ray of light from your own heart until it touches the Stone. Only need of great magnitude, directed by the earnest seeker, can call forth the Stone.

## 4. The Epiphany of the Stone Hallow

Welcome the Stone in your own words, and see the light from your heart streaming into it. The Stone begins to glow with a great, piercing light that is refracted in every direction. When this happens, be aware of its light streaming impartially through the world to all who need its power. Be aware of the mediation of power. At this point, you may wish to speak aloud the people, issues or needs that are known to you, turning in a circle, so that the light of the Stone is mediated to all.

## 5. Communion

Take the food for your ritual meal and bless it in your own words. Be aware of the land where the ingredients were grown, the elements that went into growing them, and the necessity for spiritual nourishment. As you eat it, make conscious attunement with the Realm of the Stone which you are going to explore in the coming season. A suitable seasonal song can be sung to welcome the Winter.

### 6. Establishing the Stone Hallow Shrine

Bless your empty shrine with the elements and adorn it with Winter crocus, or with bare twigs sprayed gold or silver. Take your chosen symbol of the Stone Hallow: *Let this token represent the power of the Stone Hallow in this place. May it be blessed by the powers of the Great Above and the Great Below, the inhabitants of the ages before the ages. This shrine is established for the restoration of all the worlds.*

Now take your symbol to each of the quarters, starting in the North, finishing West, and say: *Behold the Stone Hallow! May the gifts of wisdom, establishment and attainment be operative in this quarter.* Place it on your shrine with the words: *May the power of the Stone Hallow be the indwelling presence of this shrine.* Make a gesture of homage or service and place your hand on your symbol. *On this day of the Winter Solstice, I dedicate myself to the quest for the Stone Hallow.* Make your own promise or dedication to the principles of the Stone.

### 7. The Return

For the closing ritual see p.67.

---

# LESSON 43

## *The Stone Maiden, Stone Two and Three*

> **The Stone Maiden Speaks** *I bear the head of the chosen sacrifice and speak the words of one who has met the ancestors. Behold, the blood in the snow is the sign for you to act! Do not wander aimlessly upon the earth, but question why and how you walk!*

The Stone Maiden speaks with the voice of experience, surprising in one so young. She is that part of ourselves that is never fooled by confusing messages, but attends to the voice of our mother-wit. As the seer of the Stone she also speaks with the authority of the ancestral earth. Although she is attuned deeply to the mysteries of the Stone, she can awaken our practical ability to act with intention and common sense. She gives the lie to the stereotypical esoteric student who is always dreamy and spaced-out. As a maiden of earth's power, she upholds the virtue of enduring discernment.

This startling image of a maiden bearing a bloody severed head is an ancient one drawn from the story of Peredur.[8] Peredur is the Welsh name

stone maiden

of Perceval. In his wanderings he comes to his uncle's castle where he beholds the procession of the Hallows. The bleeding Spear is brought in, to be followed by two maidens,

> *with a large salver between them, in which was a man's head, surrounded by a profusion of blood. And thereupon the company of the court made so great an outcry, that it was irksome to be in the same hall with them.*

Peredur doesn't ask the meaning of this procession, but he is impelled to continue his quest. In this early story he does not search for the Grail, but rather for self-empowerment through his deeds in the realm of Arthur and in the Otherworld. It is not until the end of the story that he discovers that his deeds have avenged his cousin, whose head was in the dish, slain by the nine witches of Gloucester.

The Stone Maiden alerts us to a primal accountability for our quest: the ancestral loose-ends over which we continually stumble. With the discernment of one totally attuned to the earth, she knows our antecedents and knows what kind of inherited problems we each of us face. Nevertheless, she continues to exhibit endurance and a willingness to overcome all obstacles, however ingrained in our mortal blood, urging us ever onwards to discover her as the Daughter of Wisdom.

**Stone Two Speaks** *Whither shall you wander? Both streams flow to the north: which is best for you? If you wait too long, the ice will freeze them over. Keep your weather-eye on the path and proceed when you've decided.*

Stone Two typifies the over-scrupulous student who has to have all his pencils sharpened before writing up a report, and who cannot settle to meditate before a whole pantheon has been invoked to guard his sacred space, or who keeps finding ever-more exciting groups or books. It can also represent the student who is good at keeping many things in the air at once and who enjoys a good balance of activities. Whichever best describes you, resolve to start your quest today. A tardy beginning often misses many great opportunities.

**Stone Three Speaks** *I am the maker and shaper, I am the crafter of the earth and its ores. If you seek a good master, come to me, for I will impart my craft to all who honour the Great Work.*

Stone Three shows the professional mastery that every seeker on the path wishes to attain. The worker in stone or metal gives us an example of what it is to discover the statue within the marble, how to transmute ores into implements, how to find our true shape in the Mysteries. Here the seeker is inspired by the creative instinct to organize her study in such a way as to reflect the craftsmanship revealed on this part of the path.

stone three

It becomes obvious that only by developing these skills can she succeed to the same degree of excellence.

## Questions

1. What is the best, most practical reason for your quest?
2. Which different spiritual directions or esoteric methods jockey for your attention? Which do you intend to pursue right now?
3. What are the pre-eminent qualities of your spiritual craft? How do you reflect these?

## Task

During this quest you can reconnect with the Stone nightly by making a dedication as you go to bed. This takes only a few minutes before sleep claims you. Visualize the chess-board of the Stone Hallow before you. Each square is a plot of earth into which you can plant the seeds that lie dormant within you. Each night, plant a new seed of intention that can come to fruition in the months ahead.

## Meditation

1. Leave the Stone Castle and journey in search of the Stone Maiden. She is your initiator into the Stone Realm. As a seer, she can tell you

about any part of the quest. She leads you through and within the stone that is beside her, for it is an Otherworldly gateway. Within is a cave containing warm garments and other things that you may need upon your quest. These seem to derive from different eras of history and have been deposited by seekers before you. Take whatever you need for your quest and leave something of your own in exchange, that other seekers may be comforted in this realm.

2. The Stone Maiden leads you back through the stone and brings you to Stone Two. You cannot decide which way to go; suddenly all the manifold indecisions of your life rise up at once. The Stone Maiden instructs you to breathe upon the dark standing stone. Under your breath there appears a short inscription which is for you alone. Read what it says there and act upon it. Continue on your way.

3. You come to less snowy regions and arrive at Stone Three. The great chalk hill figure looms above you in the twilight. He challenges you to state your craft before you pass onwards into the night. Bring to mind the qualities that you bring to your life as a whole, if you have no explicit notion of your craft (spiritual or practical). The smith in the chalk listens to you and then sets to fashion you an emblem which will serve as a symbol of your potential attainment in that craft. Give him thanks and pass onwards.

# ———————— LESSON 44 ————————

## *Taliesin*

> **Taliesin Speaks** *Behold, I change and yet I remain the same, ever true to the tradition. I am the preserver and the inspirer. The song of creation falls from my lips and the very trees listen. I pass the golden links of memory into your hands that you may initiate others into their own story.*

Taliesin is the great poet and preserver of the ancient memories of the roots of time. He can access any point in the creative unfolding and give a relevant story to kindle our imaginations and understanding. He remembers things by formal patterns of verse, music, shape and inter-relation, which is how indigenous peoples have ever remembered their ancient lore. Taliesin's is the voice forever singing, sustaining the connection by a choir of perpetual song, which is the golden chain he gives into our hands. He can become an active teacher of all students

of the tradition: you have only to ask him. [28]

Taliesin acts as the companion and counterpart of Merlin in this court. He is a teller of stories, a fund of tradition. He companions Merlin in Geoffrey of Monmouth's _Vita Merlini_ and explains many profound teachings to him while Merlin is distracted in his madness after the terrible battle he has witnessed. [37]

Taliesin only gained his reputation as a rememberer of tradition through shapeshifting into many forms. This is an important thing to remember when we are inclined to dismiss any kind of tradition or to become petrified within our own: it must change and shift in order to stay healthy and to sustain each new generation. Tradition remains flexible and revelatory only if sustained by inspiration. Our contemporary access to inspiration is circumscribed by those who would codify spiritual traditions into narrow pathways. In these times, we must call upon Taliesin to raise a great wind to blow away such restraints and to reinspire us.

## Meditation

You journey onwards until night falls, when you find a lighted house. Here sits Taliesin who is your guide and companion on this Stone quest. You may call upon him at any point for help or advice. He sits you by the fire and tells you your own story. You see the images form in the smoke of the fire. You see the challenges that helped you grow, though they seemed like predators or dangers at the time. You appreciate the earliest influences that spurred your spiritual growth.

You can meditate separately from the following reading, which may amplify or trigger your realizations.

## Pursuit of the Soul Reading

This reading is based upon the pursuit of Taliesin by Ceridwen. Extract the greater powers from the deck. Shuffle the remaining lesser power cards and lay them upon positions 1-8. Shuffle the greater power cards and

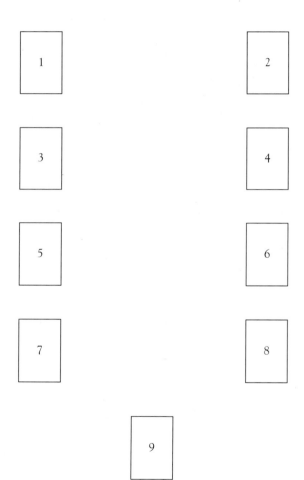

Fig. 18: *Pursuit of the Soul Spread*

lay one on position 9. Read cards 1, 3, 5 and 7 in relation to the emotion generated by the experience you remember; read cards 2, 4, 6 and 8 as broadly as possible in relation to the self-knowledge you were given at those times. Read card 9 as yourself, the sum of these experiences and insights: this transformed self may still be in the process of manifesting.

1. Represents the first betrayal of your childhood imagination, e.g. when adults scorned your play/make-believe/creativity.
2. What lesson this taught you.
3. Represents the first betrayal you suffered in love or friendship.
4. What lesson this taught you.
5. Represents the first time you were inspired to seek a spiritual path.
6. What lesson this taught you.
7. Represents the first time you became aware that you were one of many other seekers who had walked this way before.
8. What lesson this taught you.
9. Represents the transformed self.

Ask Taliesin to make any further comments on your reading. He then gives you a gift.

# LESSON 45

## *The Stone Knight, Stone Four and Five*

**The Stone Knight Speaks** *Through snow and ice the path leads on and I follow it unto the very end. My quest does not stop for day or night. If your heart is determined, take me as guide and I will never fail you.*

The Stone Knight is a trustworthy companion upon the quest. He is that part of you that never gives up, whatever the odds, but is determined to see the end of the matter. As the Way-Shower of the Stone, he passes through much difficult terrain. He continues through the night, and may sometimes act as a guide within the realms of dream. Whatever phantoms of darkness surround us, he is ready to fight them back, using his shield as a defence.

The Stone Knight represents all seekers who have the (often dogged) persistence to keep right on with the quest. In times of difficulty or disruption, he sets a good example of the steady practice of meditation,

stone knight

of methodical reconnoitre, to those who want to give up. He shows a responsibility for his charges which cannot be overset by any circumstances. His stone shield depicts the gaming board, ever reminding him that the quest is a game to be played seriously. He can step upon the black squares of his quest as resolutely as upon the light squares.

His esoteric title is 'Son of the Law', for he defends the law of the land with his life. The law referred to here is not the legal statute but the deep natural law which wells up from the land itself.

> **Stone Four Speaks** *I am the dragon's hoard, the attainment of your dreams. If you would wield the withdrawn Hallows, seek first the treasures that you hoard within. Bring them forth, that others may benefit from them.*

Stone Four typifies the spiritual treasury of the path. The amassing of knowledge can become an end in itself: more books and workshops seem to point to personal fulfilment and the gratification that we are more 'spiritual' than our peers. Spiritual materialism is the chief temptation on this part of the path. The way beyond lies through committing our life and works to the service of creation in a conscious way, by maintaining a strict self-clarification programme to ensure we are not slipping into a form of spiritual materialism.

stone four     stone five

**Stone Five Speaks** *There is no worst! I stand alone in the icy wastes without shelter or means. How can one so rich become so destitute? I seek the bare necessities of life.*

Stone Five comes as a distinct shock after the superabundant plenty of Stone Four. The riches to rags scenario is most often enacted by the seeker who has trusted in her own powers and finds that they are inadequate for real life. This part of the path is also encountered by the student who undergoes a necessary purgation of his life after having dedicated himself to the path. This ritual stripping away of all that makes life worthwhile has been called 'the Dark Night of the Soul' by mystics. But as a bridegroom promises to be faithful in riches or in poverty, so must the student maintain his dedication to the quest.

## Questions

1. What are the best spurs for you to continue a course of action when the way ahead seems impossibly hard?
2. In what ways are you rich and successful?
3. In what ways are you impoverished or insecure?

In questions 2 and 3, concentrate upon your inner qualities as much as your material possessions.

# Task

Spend one morning/afternoon/evening/ this week sorting out one intractable part of your life, for example a messy cupboard, an unruly schedule or plan, or an unresolved inner state of confusion. If you decide upon the latter, make sure you ask yourself many pertinent questions to clarify your condition.

# Meditation

1. You leave the hall of Taliesin and set off, travelling all day until you find the Stone Knight as darkness falls. He is your defender as you enter the Lands Adventurous. He sets you upon his horse and leads you to a quiet lea of the valley where you can both shelter. With a fistful of different coloured pebbles, you play a game upon his shield in the light of the fire. You wager against each other without money, setting the stakes at a form of service you will render the other. What service will you perform for the Stone Knight if you lose? What service will he perform for you? Who wins the game? Whoever loses must render that service within the next month.

2. After you have slept, he leads you to the hill of Stone Four. The Stone Knight invites you to enter the hill. He says you may take one item from the ancient treasury there. What will it be? Take it into your hands and ask the ancestral presences who guard this place to relate the qualities of the item you take. Be aware that if you take this treasure, you become its guardian, responsible for the manifestation of those qualities within your own world.

3. You travel onwards and come to the wilderness of Stone Five. A freezing mist descends, making progress nearly impossible. Isolated in this frozen waste, you are a prey to many doubts. Call upon all the things that make life secure for you and, drawing on the strength which you derive from them, take one step after the other until you approach the solitary stone. It becomes a doorway of help and you step through it into the safety of a wooded glade.

# The Grail Hermit

ıx the grail hermit

**The Grail Hermit Speaks** *I am the voice in the stillness and I am the listening. I welcome all who need counsel, but the idle chatterer can leave my grove. Sit at my fire, be refreshed. Send down your roots and be as my flowering staff: a wonder in the wilderness and a sign of illumination.*

The Grail Hermit is a listener and an interpreter of the experiences that we have along our way. He fulfils an important role in our spiritual quest, which is sometimes inexplicably bewildering. He can be our guide and counsellor, if we let him. In him is the perfect mediation of the inner and outer worlds. He cannot live in the courts of humankind, but chooses the woodland stillness in which to be in communion with both his own and the inner worlds, whose messages he receives and records. His dove sings of the deep peace that can attend the simple daily devotion to the quest.

In our own lives, we encounter many people who act as our guides and counsellors when we are perplexed. We instinctively trust their wisdom because they have experience and maturity. In meditation we also encounter many spiritual helpers and yet, because our society shuns the unseen worlds and distrusts their inhabitants, we often don't accord them the same degree of trust. The Grail Hermit can help us discover the authenticity of our personal experience of the innerworlds and their helpers, and show us how to trust the voice within.

Though the Grail Hermit's task seems peaceful and gentle, it is only taken up after a lifetime spent in quest himself. Whatever inner dangers the seeker encounters, the Grail Hermit also has known them. He guards a mystery which we must all discover.

## Questions

1. Looking over your work so far, what is the clearest theme or message which runs through your diary?
2. Bring to mind the times you trusted or distrusted your inner voice. What led you to trust or distrust yourself at those times? What do you learn from this that you can draw upon in the future?

## Task

Make a list of the many different people in your life who have acted as special counsellors in times of confusion; note what kinds of qualities drew you to consult them, for example, Marion for clarity and kindness, Peter for analysis and dependability.

## Meditation

In the wooded glade sits the Grail Hermit, who welcomes you and shows you his book. It speaks of many dangers and terrors that await the quester, but you are not discouraged. You may ask him to help you trust the process of your quest even when it is hard to understand. He allows you to enter his hut: what lies within? He gives you a gift.

## ──────────── LESSON 47 ────────────

# *The Stone Queen, Stone Six and Seven*

**The Stone Queen Speaks** *Within my mirror I see all guests who come to the Chess-board Castle. Come from the snow-drifted path and play the game of the land with me. Secure the Winter long, you may win a kingdom of your own.*

stone queen

The Stone Queen stimulates a love of the land's own lore. She is that part of us that welcomes new experiences and is interested in their inter-relationship with known experiential resources. As the empowerer of the Stone she spends much time brooding over the 'circuit-board' of the land's memory. She makes provision against times of need, and glories in the abundance of her land. In many ways, she acts as a priestess to the Goddess of Sovereignty, maintaining the guardianship of the land and its laws. She teaches students by way of the gaming or _gwyddbwyll_ board, by which they rehearse the steps of the path and learn the strategy that they will need.

The Stone Queen is based upon the Empress of the Chess-board Castle in _Peredur._[8] Peredur sees a chess-board with pieces that play against each other. The side that he supports loses and, in a fit of temper, he hurls board and pieces into a lake. He has to fight to win it back by overcoming the enemies of the Empress: each of these is an Otherworldly opponent. Peredur is successful in his cause, for he has already served the Empress for fourteen years and she has given him her trust by the token of a ring with a stone of invisibility.

The Stone Queen bestows many gifts upon us, including the sense of comfort and stability in a shifting world. In accordance with her title 'Mother of the Law', she can show us how our every step upon the land carries its own responsibilities.

stone six

**Stone Six Speaks** *I am the circle of sharing, the house beneath the stars. Do not draw away, for all are welcome! Enter here and tell your story. We are the touchstones of good fortune: take what you need and proceed.*

The generosity of Stone Six is not like the sometimes acquisitive superabundance of Stone Four. The circle is truly a place of meeting and equality: a place where the richly experienced seeker shares her insights with students who have just begun to walk the path. In the context of our planetary quest, all seekers need to come together to experience this sharing, that we may all be enriched. This part of the path can often be marked by an encounter such as this, with a fellow-walker of the ways who offers us encouragement and empowerment without patronizing us.

**Stone Seven Speaks** *Which side of the wall should you be on? What does this stone indicate? What does this mean for your life? Do not fear tomorrow's evil, but take the path one day at a time.*

Stone Seven represents the student's dilemma over the path itself. It seems to go on without end and there is always some new problem to face. While it is good to gain the general perspective of Stone Six, it can also lead us into needless anxieties. Spiritual progress is often a case of not being able to see the wood for the trees, but in this card the bare hills on the horizon seem to loom menacingly, to be scrutinized as a

stone seven

possible danger or signifier when, in fact, they're just too far ahead. When this kind of anxiety strikes, it's best to concentrate on the task in hand. It is fruitless to look too far ahead and to try to make arrangements when the spiritual itinerary is not even mapped.

## Questions

1. What is your relationship to the land in which you live?
2. How do you share your gifts and resources with others?
3. What are your personal strategies for keeping things in proportion?

## Meditation

1. Leaving the shelter of the Grail Hermit's glade, you travel onwards until you come to the Stone Queen's castle, which stands at the borders of the Otherworld. The Stone Queen greets you and brings you into the warm. She invites you to play a game with her. On her gaming-board you see the many moves of your life. She will advise you about any problems concerning any specific disempowerment, showing you new strategies to win and retain personal energy. You then look into her mirror and see the image of your potential self. She gives you a magical ring which retains this reflection, to give you inspiration on your quest.
2. She brings you to Stone Six and bids you sit at one of the stones to

await a gathering of other seekers who will come. One by one, they arrive. Together you share your experiences of quest, giving encouragement to each other and sharing the new-found strategies and wisdom you have found. You may visualize these newcomers or you may choose five cards, unseen, from your pack.

3. After a night spent in the company of the other seekers, you pass onwards to Stone Seven. The way seems to drag onwards and you are still no nearer success on your quest. Your resources feel over-stretched and anxiety is strong within you. You find a place in the wall which is broken down. Many dangers might break through at this place. You stop to repair it, finding that the act of concentrated work has relieved your anxiety. It grows darker and you see that the symbol stone is glowing. Upon the stone is written an ancient blessing for the way; you may also hear music. Record what you experience.

# LESSON 48

## *The Washer at the Ford*

xiii the washer at the ford

**The Washer at the Ford Speaks** *You fear me and rightly, for I wait at the crossing places of your life and know everything about you. I*

*wash your seemingly white linen and reveal the map of your life. I can*
*cut you off the loom of life, yet I can also change you. Whoever needs*
*the empowerment of renewal must first kiss me – if they dare!*

The Washer at the Ford is a challenger. All who encounter her receive
the initiation of death, which is renewal. Her appearance in a reading
does not indicate sudden death, rather she represents the katabolic
'breaking-down' action and subsequent release of energy which is at the
heart of all life. Such chaos brings confusion to us, but creation is not
the only side of the picture; destruction or devolution is also necessary.
When we are presented with the possibility of a sudden ending, the doors
to freedom are instantaneously opened to us. Great need is the spur to
discovery. When we want the fullness of spiritual life to the same degree
that we need bread or sex, only then are we able to create something new.

The dynamic struggle between order and chaos is perceived by us in
our daily lives: the breaking down of our ordered existence into muddle
and confusion, the laborious reassembly of a fragmented situation are
both common experiences. To our mortal eyes, death seems to bring
everything to an end. But there is another way of looking at this. Our
birth into our present incarnatory existence is really a death to
Otherworldly reality; our death brings us back into Otherworldly
existence and so is a kind of birth. This is a very difficult concept to
maintain in the face of the death of a loved one. Our lives intermesh with
others so completely that when a partner or child dies, our own lives
are shattered.

Whether we mourn a death or the ending of a situation, the
elimination of the Washer at the Ford brings about new opportunities
and new patterns in our lives. We cannot retain the exact pattern we have
planned so carefully without losing its essential spirit. When the spirit
flies freely, new energies can flow again and revitalize our lives.

## Questions

1. What do you fear most about death?
2. If you had one day of life left to you, what situations, relationships,
   ambitions would be left unresolved?
3. What are you clinging on to that needs to fly free in your life?

## Task

This week, attempt to face up to or bring towards a better resolution,
one factor which your death would leave unresolved.

## Meditation

With the blessing still ringing in your ears, the Stone Queen leads you to a forsaken ford, bidding you to watch alone. As the moon comes out from behind a bloody cloud, the Washer at the Ford appears carrying a bundle of linen. She will not let you pass this ford until you have given up all that impedes your progress. Which of the gifts you have been given on your way do you need least? (Please retain the gifts given you by the Greater Power cards.) You cast it into the waters. The Washer then asks you which aspects of your life are ripe for dismantling. With one harsh word, she transforms you into a raven and sends you to fetch away the carrion from your life. You fly over the inner landscape which represents your life and remove all aspects that have entered the phase of decay. You drop each piece down to the waiting hounds of the Washer, who devour the carrion until there is no more left. You return and are transformed back into your human shape. The Washer gives you a gift and you cross the ford.

---

# LESSON 49

# *The Stone King, Stone Eight and Nine*

stone king

**The Stone King Speaks** *At the centre of the land sit I, the sustainer of the law. By the deep wisdom of the Stone, all things are known to me. Wherever you walk, I know it. Walk wisely upon the earth and uphold its laws.*

The Stone King is the enduring warden of the land's wisdom. He is that part of yourself that patiently abides, husbanding deep reserves of strength in times of adversity. His constancy is maintained because of his deep communion with the Stone, a representation of which hangs about his neck. As the guardian of the Stone, he has a sensitivity to all that passes in the land. By merely touching the Stone he can access both memory and ancient wisdom and act as a voice of the land.

Our society does not have a high regard for traditional values. Popular culture mocks tradition as hidebound. True tradition must speak pertinently to all generations of people and its guardians have a duty to let tradition breathe and evolve; but this must be done with respect and patience. The Stone King is an oracular guardian of tradition transmission, like Bran the Blessed, the many stories, songs and legends which preserve ancestral wisdom.

As the 'Father of the Law', he knows all time's precedents: when a thing was first done or spoken. He acts as a bridge between our generation and the ancestral levels of understanding.

**Stone Eight Speaks** *As the sun sets and your tools are put away, ever heed my precepts: maintain your practice, learn your craft!*

stone eight

Stone Eight depicts the hard work of the apprentice slowly but surely becoming manifest on the physical plane. A little practice each day keeps the student sharp. The incremental learning process brings fresh insights and opens up wiser pathways of opportunity. This process is often arduous and toilsome, but it is a step that cannot be omitted. To gain the thing we most want to achieve, we must be willing to become apprentices: this will mean starting at the bottom, gradually building up our skills until we can attempt our apprentice-piece and earn our freedom as a professional craftsperson.

stone nine

**Stone Nine Speaks** *Behold, all things are easy to the one who is in tune with the many worlds. We are the companions of your solitude, who speak to you in silent fulfilment of your work.*

Stone Eight and Nine show us the culmination of the work of the Winter Stone Court. Stone Nine depicts the supporters of that work, the hidden helpers and totemic beings who accompany our solitary moments. They represent the empowerment of the path which brings the seeker to interior quiet and natural ease – the fulfilment of the long hard struggle. This experience is mundanely seen in the enjoyment that can come from retirement from employment; but for the student of the path, there is no such thing as retirement, only periods of refreshment which deeply nourish and sustain us on our ongoing quest.

# Tasks and Questions

1. What is your definition of 'tradition'? Now, look up the derivation of the word 'tradition' in an etymological dictionary. In what way does its original meaning accord or differ from your current understanding of the word?
2. Looking over your recent life, trace your apprenticeship on the spiritual path. What are its major signposts, achievements and practical applications in your life?
3. In an ideal world, how would you most like to spend your time? What qualities do you derive from practising this/these pursuit/s?

# Meditation

1. You come at dawn to a great circle of trilithons. Seated in front of the Midwinter sunrise sits the Stone King, who is a guardian of the deep Otherworld. He questions you about your journey so far, for he is aware of every step of your quest. He says that you may seek an augury of the stone doorway, for many a true vision is had at this magical hour. Bring to mind an issue or question needing clarification at this time. You must stand, with bare feet, underneath the trilithon which is behind him. Set one hand on either stone of the doorway and close your eyes, saying this invocation:

   > *Sun of the seasons, be a path to my feet.*
   > *Stones of memory, awaken my remembrance.*
   > *Earth of the Winter, give knowledge of my quest.*
   > *Sign and symbol, word and omen,*
   > *Send me a truthful augury.*

   Opening your inner eyes, see what animal, bird or being stands before you. You may ask the Stone King to interpret this augury for you.
2. The Stone King leads you to Stone Eight. In the centre is a stone whereon is roughly traced the emblem made for you by the smith of chalk in Stone Three. Taking up hammer and chisel, complete the emblem until it is perfectly formed.
3. This stone is to be your personal touchstone of accomplishment and is to be set up in the grove of Stone Nine, in place of the stone which is there. As you set it up, many animals (perhaps different ones from those depicted) come to gather in perfect friendship about the stone. They each acknowledge the stone as an emblem of protection for them. In return, they have gifts to give you:

# Gifts of the Totems Reading

For this reading, separate the Greater Power cards from the Lesser Powers. Consciously choose one Lesser Power card to represent a current problem and then shuffle the Greater Powers, laying them on positions 2 - 5 to act as your totemic helpers. You will be reading the cards rather differently here, since you will be directly addressing the totem animal in the Greater Power card, not its main subject.

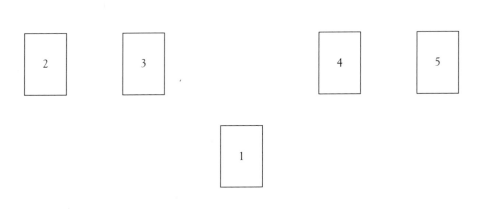

Fig. 19: *Gifts of the Totems Spread*

1. You choose this card, from the Lesser Powers to represent appropriately the problem you are addressing right now.
2. This totem shows you where to look for the gift of joy.
3. This totem shows how to employ the gift of endurance.
4. This totem gives you the gift of faithfulness.
5. This totem helps show you the gift of resourcefulness.

**Diary Example:**      **Reading:**
*5.2.91*                  *Gifts of the Totems*

*I chose Spear Ten to represent the many responsibilities that are weighing on me at present, making it difficult to find time for myself. I feel I've climbed this hill over and over recently. The Owl of the Spiral Tower revealed that I should look for the gift of joy in the present moment and not to keep looking for it in some future time. The Eagle of the Sleeping Lord told me that the gift of endurance was mine if I sought the winds that blow and use their air currents to support me. The Merlin of the Round Table said that the gift of faithfulness was to accept with love the cycles of life and to look for the connections between things with more understanding. The Bee of the*

*Flowering of Logres affirmed that the gift of resourcefulness was already within me and that I could use the knowledge and resources I had already put by from previous work in this field.*

*It's interesting to note that none of the cards I drew are 'people cards' anyway! This was a helpful reading which I can implement when I feel discouraged; I only need call up the animals to remind me of the gifts at my disposal.*

# LESSON 50

## *The Star of Prophecy*

xvii the star

**The Star of Prophecy Speaks** *I offer the gift of deepest insight. I am the heart of the crystal who has seen all. Within you also there is deep knowledge of the oldest kind. Pick up any stone and find within it the history of your earth. You are the stuff of the stars, from deepest space to the intricate spiral of life is but a small step.*

The Star of Prophecy brings fresh hope to us. It promises a new cycle of manifestation wherein the old stagnant patterns will be changed, where new opportunities for restoring things become available. Many see the Aquarian Age in this light and already begin to draw inspiration from its fore-glare. Many others look towards the new millennium with a hopelessness that evokes Armageddon, the end of all things. There are prophets of both camps who seek to elicit our support for their claims. Whether we are pessimists or optimists, the Star of Prophecy reconnects us with the roots of our faith in the universe.

Signs and wonders can be very misleading without skilful interpretation to support them. We are all skilled omen-watchers, whether we are consciously aware of this faculty or not. We are all constantly looking for the miracle that will transform our lives, whether it be a lucky prize in a lottery, or else a vision of a new pathway that will lead to fresh opportunity or spiritual fulfilment. The little signs and wonders of our daily lives form our own private symbolic language of success and failure.

Prophecies have to be attended by constant watchfulness and by faithful service, otherwise they are likely to be fulfilled without our knowledge. The ability to hope and desire is strongly present in this card, but it is not a selfish desire. At critical world-changing moments, we need this inspiration to continue along our chosen path, to create a pathway for manifestation.

## Questions

1. What new cycle do you foresee coming into operation in the next ten years?
2. When all is dark, what are your personal strategies for stimulating hope?

## Meditation

The Stone King leads you to a high rampart of a hill-fort overlooking the Stone Realm, there to keep watch while he rests. Towards deepest midnight, you see the Star of Prophecy. Its meteor-brightness illumines the land beneath and you can see which way you have journeyed. Along one of its pathways comes the vision you saw through the stone trilithon in the last lesson. You may ask this being or animal to give you words of hope on any aspect of your life that seems hopeless. As you listen to the answer, you are bathed in star-dust which gives you inspiration and a refreshment of deep faith within you. Fears and troubles fall from you at the sight of the Star. The cockerel begins to utter its joyous cry of acclaim. The being from the Star lifts you up and you continue through the sky until you are set down on a hillside. The being from the Star gives you a gift.

# Merlin

ꞁ mer̃lꞁꞁ

**Merlin Speaks** *Mine is the mastery of the mystery, and the mystery is my master. At the stone table many worlds have been made, and between the twin towers of my life are many worlds conceived. Only when your knowledge of the worlds within and the worlds without stand in equal measure may you be as I: the initiator who stands in alignment with the creative powers and over whom none has power.*

Merlin is the guardian of our land, wherever we live. He lives on a withdrawn level, observant of the daily changes that occur. Because he has not died, he is in continual communion with the creative powers which shape our world, and can maintain a perceptive over-view of all that passes. He is incorruptible by earthly powers and is opened on a very deep level to the laws of creation. His balanced guardianship is maintained by a free-flow of the dragon-energies, which are traditionally seen as in combat or in sleep. When Merlin awakes the dragons, the land sizzles with the awareness of new life; when they are put to sleep again, so his power ebbs. What Merlin dreams, we think we imagine from our own heads. Imagination is not what we have conceived it to be: not the fantastic speculations of our brain, but a true seeing of the inner reality that can be.

Merlin awakens us to our inner accomplishment as masters and mistresses of skilful wisdom. We do not have to become arcane magicians with miraculous skills to bring about changes in our world. Merlin awakens us to the authority of our own imagination and its power to align and interlink with those things that we want to manifest in the world. He makes sure that we know the difference between manipulation of and co-operation with the powers of the universe. If we are truly aligned with the energies of the earth-dragons, we can find our way to the Otherworldly observatory of Merlin; but if we are committed to imposing our will upon the dragons, we will find ourselves in the collapsing castle of Vortigern.

## Meditation

The Star brings you down to where Merlin is. He has watched your progress upon his map, plotting your journey. He asks if you are willing to fulfil your creative potential by becoming the person who lies potentially within you, waiting to manifest. 'Truth lies at the heart of the stone', he says and moves his hands across the stone table. Upon it appears a crystalline outline of thirteen facets. He invites you look into Merlin's Mirror and describe what you see there.

## Merlin's Mirror Reading

Using the whole pack, lay the following reading, and answer the questions which it poses.

1. What is the face I show to the world?
2. What hidden fears lead me to assume this mask?
3. What do I expect to gain from presenting this mask?
4. What am I doing with my life?
5. Who would I like to be?
6. What is preventing me from becoming like this?
7. What opportunities am I avoiding?
8. How do I envisage my life becoming?
9. Who is the real me?
10. What is my life purpose?
11. What do I still need to assimilate to find the real me?
12. What masks do I need to drop?
13. What is the next step on my life's journey?

After you have read this spread with Merlin's help, he gives you a gift.

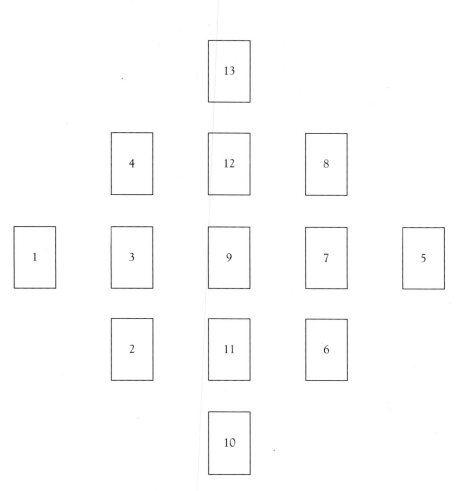

Fig. 20: Merlin's Mirror Spread

# LESSON 52

## The Stone Hallow

**The Stone Hallow Speaks** _I glow in the darkest depths of the earth._
_I am the floor of your dancing step, the ground of your experience. The_
_black squares bring you trials, the white squares bring you realizations:_

*stone hallow*

*step upon both with a light foot. I am the gem of your highest attainment, awaiting discovery.*

The Stone Hallow is the touchstone of wisdom. It is akin to the earth itself as a preserver of knowledge and guardian of tradition. It appears in many guises within legend: as the inauguration stone upon which monarchs were acknowledged, as the perilous seat at the Round Table, as the Stone which fell from heaven, as the gaming board on which kingdoms are won and lost. The gaming board may seem a frivolous emblem for a power that has such important consequences. This fear underpins our insecurity about all issues concerning the wielding of treasures. Prosperity is not an enduring quality to be freely enjoyed at all times by all people. Possessions are lost, destroyed or stolen. There is no abiding security anywhere. Everyday we wager our very lives by our actions. This is where our mother-wit is important, for we do not live our lives by hazarding another's wealth or experience, but by daring our own resources and interacting with the coinage of life itself. We can win all or lose all at any time.

The Stone Hallow abides in darkness in the frozen earth of Winter, keeping its secret treasury safe for all. It is used as a shield for defence, as a receptacle of ancient lore, as an oracle of wisdom. It brings deep wisdom and security to the lost and ignorant. It is the proper symbol of the elder who has a full entitlement of experience to draw upon.

# Meditation on the Stone

With the self-knowledge that arises from Merlin's Mirror, you ask for the Stone Hallow. Merlin asks by what right you make your request, and you answer in your own words. He touches you and you become a young dragon. (If you are a woman, you become a red dragon; if you are a man, you become a white dragon.) You head for the depths of the earth, to your den. Here, in a deep cavern, lies the Stone. You curl yourself around it and listen to its voice which echoes around the vast interior of the cavern. You hear the heartbeat of the earth within the Stone. What does the earth say? What wisdom does it impart to you?

You fold your body about the Stone and bear it back to Merlin. He lays it upon his stone table where it fades, leaving its pattern. Merlin restores you to human shape and you make the following reading.

# The Augury of the Stone of Wisdom

For this reading, remove all the Greater Power cards and put the Stone Hallow at position 5. As you shuffle the remainder of the pack, strongly visualize or gaze upon the Stone, putting your trust in its wisdom. Ask it, 'How can the Stone of Wisdom be manifest within me?' Then draw

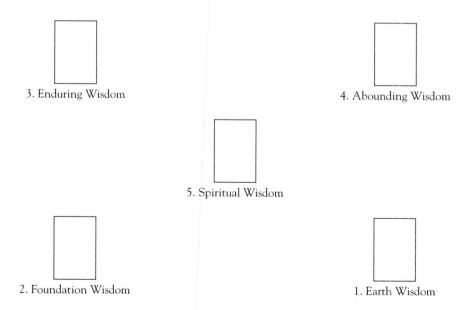

3. Enduring Wisdom

4. Abounding Wisdom

5. Spiritual Wisdom

2. Foundation Wisdom

1. Earth Wisdom

Fig. 21: *The Augury of the Stone Spread*

four cards from the main pack and lay them on positions 1-4. Shuffle the Greater Powers separately and ask for the augury (prophecy) of the Stone. Draw one card and lay it on position 5, covering the Stone Hallow. Each of the positions in this augury represent some aspect of Wisdom. After you've laid and briefly interpreted your reading, ask the central card to act as a guide and travel with it through the other cards, listening to what is said.

1. Represents your instinct, which gives you the first true impressions about anything. Our mother-wit is innate but is often ignored. Its challenge is, 'How do I truly reflect my mother-wit?'
2. Represents the various instabilities and uncertainties that prevent us from building more firmly. As a result our lives often rest on shaky foundations. Its challenge is, 'Where is the ground of my establishment?'
3. Represents the obscurity of ignorance from which we all suffer, often unknowingly. The light often shines briefly in the darkness so that we gain knowledge by touch. Its challenge is, 'What is the touch-stone of knowledge for me?'
4. Represents your ability to attain. With so many factors in life to disempower us, it is important that this primal capacity for abundance be found. Its challenge is, 'What is the gift that lies within me?'
5. Represents the spiritual treasury which is always accessible. The Greater Power card represents the guardianship of the deep wisdom beyond the worlds. It challenges you with, 'What is the wisdom of the Stone and how do I manifest it?'

———————————— **LESSON 53** ————————————

## *The Investiture of the Stone*

Lay the cards of the Stone Quest about you as shown opposite.

This is the inner court of the Stone, where Merlin is surrounded by the guardians of Arthurian realm and its destiny. The Star of Prophecy foretold the coming of the Pendragons, Taliesin preserved the lore of the Arthurian realm, Blaise as the Grail Hermit was Merlin's own teacher, while the Washer at the Ford is one who brings us Merlin's prophetic insight, acting as the initiator of every person's life. In this gathering of wise ones during the dark time of Winter, we are enabled to ask counsel of the assembled company and stand ourselves in the place of Midwinter's illumination.

Fig. 22: *The Inner Court of the Stone*

# Meditation

Visualize the northern part of your inner landscape that you worked with in Lesson 5. (Readers in the southern hemisphere visualize the southern part of their landscape.) Now superimpose the Stone court upon it. Seeing the Rainbow Path of the Seeker at the centre of your inner landscape, you now enter this Stone quarter, passing through it without fear or difficulty. You may wish to spread this meditation over several sessions.

Starting with the Stone Maiden, you will meditate on each card in clockwise order until you reach the Star of Prophecy. The Stone Family gives you the following gifts: the Maiden gives you a scrying crystal that is tuned to the Stone Hallow; the Knight gives an emblem of midnight; the Queen gives you a healing herb; the King gives you a golden coin with your own image on one side and the Stone on the obverse. These gifts will prove useful in your future journeys in the Stone Realm. Each of the landscape cards gives you a differently coloured gem-stone. Each of the Greater Powers imparts a special blessing.

Continue meditating on each of the cards until you reach the centre where Merlin sits, with the Stone Castle behind him and the Stone Hallow before him. You may not enter the Stone Castle until you have shown him the gifts you have collected from the Greater Powers on this quest. The combined energies of these gifts creates a strong path between yourself and the Stone Castle. Kneel before Merlin and make your personal dedication to the Stone Hallow. Then you enshrine the Stone in the Stone Castle, which is the same as the Northern Caer of your own inner landscape.

Slowly the images fade and are replaced by that of your own Stone shrine which is before you. Open your eyes and formally repeat your dedication to the Stone, that its energy may be once more operative in the outer worlds.

# Assimilation and Examination of Lessons 42~53

You have concluded the Stone Quest, but please turn now to p.99 and study the assimilation exercises there. The Stone Court is a serious family, attuned to the earth and to its Winter face. See how well you have responded to and understood the introspection and wisdom of this suit. You can then pass on the next quest, or to Part Three, if you have completed all your quests.

## PART THREE

# The Way of the Hallows

*Now we can see the real use of the Tarot pack.
It is for living in and arranging our lives with.
The cards are the exchange-symbols between
Inner and Outer life. The way we arrange
and link them Inwardly will reflect into our
Outer living.*

William Gray *Magical Ritual Methods*

You have concluded all four quests. Now it is time to make sense of what you have experienced and to implement your findings in your own world. This section concludes the book, integrating the findings and realizations of the course and giving suggestions for further work. The purpose of this part is to bring together the fourfold landscape into a holistic inner cosmology.

You have probably found that one or more of your seasonal quests was easier than the others. This is important to your self-assessment for it shows the areas and principles to which you are naturally attuned, and which ones need more attention. Below are outlines of the four natural kinds of seekers. If one of these accurately pin-points yourself, it shows that you need to amplify your potential. Follow the instructions below to help broaden out your experience. If you feel that you are better described by a combination of these outlines, then rejoice, for you may have achieved a broader integration. However, no one can afford to rest on their laurels. It is very easy to lose focus and to slip into cosy habits which shore up the ego and never stretch it. Note that the astrological associations in the definitions of seeker given below *do not imply* that all those born under Pisces, for example, are *ipso facto* natural Grail seekers. Few of us are archetypally definable in the purest astrological sense.

Study the Bach Flower Remedies listed on pp.255-258. These are assigned to each card of the tarot and offer suggested avenues of changing stale personality patterns from which seekers may suffer.

## The Sword Seeker

The Sword Seeker retains her simplicity and directness throughout her life. She usually chooses what she is going to do at an early age and rarely deviates far from this choice. There is a measure of integrity within her that is pure gold. The Sword Seeker must beware of becoming fanatical or obsessive in her quest, and learn to balance serious intent with childlike playfulness. She often finds that a tendency to brood in silence can lead her into subtle retaliations and self-deceits, especially when she perceives the easy conquests of more confident peers. These niggling jealousies and unfair comparisons require a great deal of personal responsibility to balance them. The Sword Seeker equates to the Air signs of the Zodiac: Gemini, Libra and Aquarius.

The Sword Seeker should practise a form of meditation that stresses her connection to the rest of creation; this will counteract the tendency to see the world as an enemy or herself as a solitary individual. Meditate upon the Grail to encourage a more compassionate outlook, on the Spear to bring a little more warmth into your life, and on the Stone to give you a firmer basis for living.

## The Spear Seeker

The Spear Seeker is easy to distinguish. His early career is prodigious and assured, things come easily. However, this seeming ease is often a recapitulation and reassimilation of knowledge learned in past incarnations. The latter half of his career may be less assured and can be problematic, as bad habits and over-confidence begin to mar the way. The Spear Seeker's progress is often erratic: things move on very speedily, but this is immediately followed by long periods of assimilation. He usually spends a lot of time taking issue with methodology or ideology. The Spear Seeker equates to the Fire signs of the Zodiac: Aries, Leo and Sagittarius.

The Spear Seeker should practise patience and analyse the situation in a slow and considered light, rather than resorting to instant decision. He can learn from the Spear by facing up to innate weaknesses earlier on, exercising the habit of self-clarification; this will build character and stamina. Meditate upon the Stone to bring calmness and stability, on the Sword to pin-point things more accurately, and on the Grail to learn how healing and gentleness can soften blows.

## The Grail Seeker

The Grail Seeker is often idealistic and dreamy. Major issues will be about how reality is perceived and how he should react to this. The Grail Seeker's progress is often marked by extraordinary vision and is sustained by deep creative springs: this is fine while these springs keep flowing, but, in the course of life, these often dry up and the seeker is left bereft of inspiration. The dark times that follow can be most severe: the Grail Seeker is prey to self-pity, doubts, disillusion and lethargy. In such times, it is important that he remembers his connections with all life, and continues to perform the routine meditations and practices which align him: this may often feel like marking time or treading water, but the Grail Seeker has a strong tendency to give up. The Grail Seeker equates to the Water signs of the Zodiac: Cancer, Scorpio and Pisces.

The Grail Seeker should cultivate friends who will give encouragement and companionship, and learn to share the inner vision which will give great gladness and inspiration to others. Meditate upon the Sword to sharpen up the focus, upon the Spear to bring dynamism, and on the Stone to discover sources of strength and nurture.

## The Stone Seeker

The Stone Seeker is one of the great givers. Careful and sometimes plodding, she will find a good thing and really research it before committing herself to its service. Stone Seekers are rarely discouraged by most obstacles, although it may seem to them that their work is neither fully appreciated nor gives its fullest reward. This can be a source of great trouble to the Stone Seeker, who can sometimes turn in on herself and begin to hoard her discoveries. It is the little daily worries and details that are the last straw, and a tendency to become over-scrupulous should be kept under control. The Stone Seeker often finds the rewards of walking the path faithfully after a lifetime of methodical practice: an unshakeable technique and a professional mastery gives her the confident ability to guide others and share their wisdom. The Stone Seeker equates to the Earth signs of the Zodiac: Taurus, Virgo and Capricorn.

The Stone Seeker should practise non-attachment to the material things in life, which can sometimes exercise a great attraction. She should seek out people who are unconventional, perhaps a little crazy, as well as those who know how to have fun in order to counteract a tendency to over-seriousness. Meditate upon the Spear to encourage speedier intuition and verve, upon the Grail for imaginative nourishment, and upon the Sword to be reminded of first principles and humility.

——————— LESSON 54 ———————

## _The Protection of the Powers_

In the succeeding chapters, you will be using the cards in more creative ways, calling upon the energies which they represent in ritual and ceremony.

We all need to perform rituals at certain points in our life: to celebrate a festival, to mark a coming of age or a new aspect of our life such as retirement, illness, leaving school, or divorce. Ritual reconnects us with the source of our spiritual impulse and helps us over difficult periods of transition.

Remember, *ritual should not attempt to manipulate the universe in any way.* Rather, it accesses and co-operates with the universal divine power and creates a burning glass for change. Ritual is a statement of need, celebration or remembrance that aligns us with sacred time and space.

Creative use of ritual is something open to us all: it doesn't need a special priest, minister or expert to perform it, nor does it need lots of equipment and costumes. Determine your need, work out what sort of ritual is required and perform it with that object in mind. Keep it simple. Ritual is always performed with intention, and a sacred space is created by formal demarcation to enclose it.

When you need to create sacred space for a ritual or for deep meditation, you can use the Greater Powers only as a ritual opening and closing, arranged in the following order: III, V, VIII, XIII, IV, XI, II, I, XIX, XVIII, XVII, X, XX, XIV, O, XXI, VII, VI, XVI, IX, XII, XV.

Set the cards down in order, as you invoke them. You can use your own words rather than those below. Clearly visualize the powers you are invoking, acknowledging their presence, feeling their help and guidance. When you withdraw the powers, visualize them departing.

## Invoking the Powers

*This day I intend to do the following* (the ritual/meditation/work) *for* (the spiritual intention of the ritual). For example, a ritual of self-clarification after an outburst of temper, in order to gain better self-control; or a ceremony of new beginnings after a divorce, to close old doors and open new ones.

*I invoke the Protection of the Powers!*

(Turn to each direction as you speak.)

*In the East: I invoke Gwenhwyfar and Taliesin ~ may the loving power of the Flower Bride and the inspirational presence of the Sweet Singer be present.*

. *In the South: I invoke Gawain and the Washer at the Ford ~ may the transformative power of the Raven Queen and the guarding presence of the Strong Protector be present.*

*In the West: I invoke Arthur and Sovereignty ~ may the power of the Goddess of the Land and the presence of the Pendragon be present.*

*In the North: I invoke the Lady of the Lake and Merlin ~ may the power of the Foster Mother and the presence of the Guiding Father be present.*

*Above me are the great luminaries of the Sun, the Moon and the Star of Prophecy: may enthusiasm, vision and hope light my way.*

*Around me is the Round Table: may all that I do and intend be in accordance with the universal law.*

*Beneath me are the Sleeping Lord and the Maidens of the Cauldron: may I be ever true to the powers of renewal and regeneration.*

*I am the Seeker in the Wasteland who shall help it Flower again.*

*Three guardian animals unlock for me the power of the three worlds: the Boar of the Underworld gives me the key to ancestral knowledge;*

*the White Hart of the Plain gives me the key to knowledge of Middle Earth;*

*the Owl of the Spiral Tower gives me the key to Otherworldly knowledge.*

*Three strong protectors are my guides in Middle Earth:*

*the Grail Hermit who is the voice of the earth;*

*the Wounded King who guards the blood of the earth;*

*the Green Knight who is the keeper of the earth.*

*May the Protection of the Powers be about me on every side!*

*The Withdrawal of the Powers*

(You perform this after the ritual: it is discourteous and ritually messy to invoke powers and then forget to thank them and ask for their withdrawal!)

*I give thanks for the Protection of the Powers!*

*Thanks to the three strong protectors: to the Grail Hermit, the Wounded King and the Green Knight.*

*Thanks to the three guardian animals: the Boar of the Underworld, the White Hart of the Wide Earth and the Owl of the Spiral Tower.*

*I give thanks for the illumination of the Sun, the Moon and the Star of prophecy; for the stability of the Round Table and for the enduring strength of the Sleeping Lord and the Cauldron.*

*In the North I give thanks to the Lady of the Lake and to Merlin.*

*In the West I give thanks to Arthur and to Sovereignty.*

*In the South I give thanks to Gawain and to the Washer at the Ford.*

*In the East I give thanks to Gwenhwyfar and to Taliesin.*

*For I am the Seeker in the Wasteland who shall help it Flower again.*

*In conclusion, I offer this (ritual/meditation/work) as part of my service to the Hallows. May its healing go forth to all in need. May I receive the inspiring grace of the Hallows and go forth as a Grail-bearer into the wastelands of the world!*

## Self-Protection

This opening and closing ritual can itself also be used for personal protection when you feel low in self-esteem or power, for example before a challenging interview, or before appearing in court as a defendant or witness. Don't forget also to thank and ask the powers to withdraw after you have drawn on their protection. As a self-protective measure, this ritual should be used only in the short term and not as a daily event. If you need that much protection, then you need to address the problem in a much more preventative and radical way.

## Meditation

1. Choose one of the combinations of cards from this ritual protection, e.g. Grail Hermit, Wounded King and Green Knight, and meditate on them. As in Part Two, you can enter each card or else ask the protagonists of each card to dialogue with you.
2. Spend at least one day each meditating upon the Underworld, Middle Earth and the Upperworld. The Underworld is the realm of the ancestors and the place of our power. It is *not* analogous to the Christian Hell. Ask the Boar of Prydwen to help you understand its purpose and to find your personal power. Middle Earth is the realm where our lives are lived out, the here and now. Ask the White Hart to help you understand how you can best relate to it. The Otherworld or Upperworld is the source of inspiration and knowledge. Ask the Owl to show you how to access this realm.

## Task

Create your own simple ritual and use the Protection of the Powers to begin and end it. Use any current situation that needs attention. Write up your ritual and your experience of it.

———————————— LESSON 55 ————————————

## *The Sanctuary of the Hallows*

In this lesson, we are going to create an inner sanctuary using the Four Hallows. Look back over your notes from Lessons 17, 29, 41 and 53. You will see that you have keyed each of the Hallow castles - Sword, Spear,

Grail and Stone Ten cards – into the fourfold inner landscape you meditated upon in Lesson 5. The time has now come to connect these.

Up until now, we have considered each of the seasonal landscapes as a separate realm, but of course they do join together to make a composite year and an integrated landscape. Now we take this experience deeper and relate to further dimensions of the Hallows which are forever guarded in the realms within.

In the following meditation we recombine the cards in different ways to create four inner companies. Each Hallow suit, with its accompanying Greater Powers, is invited to the central Caer of your inner landscape. Each company is dedicated to and illuminated by one of the celestial Greater Powers:

Grail Company of the Terrestrial World illuminated by the Sleeping Lord.
Sword Company of the Lunar World illuminated by the Moon.
Spear Company of the Solar World illuminated by the Sun.
Stone Company of the Stellar World illuminated by the Star.

We have so far only meditated upon the four Hallows as they relate to our own realm; but here we discover their deeper correlative upon other levels. This is a long meditation which should be performed at your own speed in as many sessions as necessary.

## Meditation

1. Taking the Rainbow Bridge of the Seeker, enter the inner landscape of Lesson 5 once more and stand at the centre. You see the four Caers or towers at the four directions wherein you enshrined the Hallows that you achieved on your seasonal quests. You now turn your attention to the central Caer, which you have still not fully explored. You ascend the straight central stairway and come to a narrow, winding stair which leads to a trap-door above. Go through it and you find yourself at the heart of the Caer in a central room of great honour, currently unfurnished. The trap-door opens in the centre of the floor. The central area of the room is lower than its four sides, which are raised by four steps on each side. There is no way into this room, save through the trap-door. Stretched across each of its four walls there is a semi-transparent veil. As you come out you see that at its entrance hangs a horn. Towards it run four pathways, from each of the directional Caers. Keep meditating upon this unit of the meditation until it is very clear to you, and begin each of the following sessions with this preliminary composition of place.

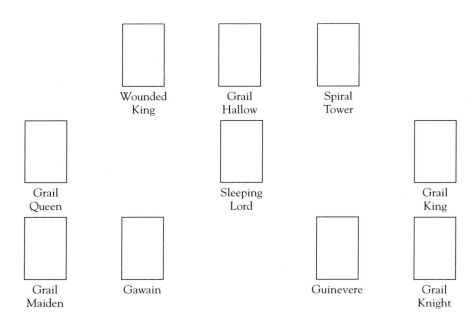

Fig. 23: *Grail Company of the Terrestrial World*

2. The time has come to establish the Sanctuary of the Hallows. You blow the horn towards the West to invite the power of the Grail into the Sanctuary. From the Western Caer comes the Grail family, with the Knight riding before and the Maiden following with the Grail in her hands. Behind her walk the Queen and King. You stand aside as they enter the Caer and ascend to the central room. After a short time, the trap-door is lowered and you also enter.

Hanging across the western wall is a semi-transparent veil from floor to ceiling. Upon it is depicted the Sleeping Lord. In front of the veil stand Gawain and Guinevere, attended by the Grail Maiden and Grail Knight respectively (see Fig. 23). The Grail Queen and King stand either side of the veil.

The Grail Maiden and Knight come forward in invitation and bring you to stand between Gawain and Guinevere who are the guardians of the Mystery of the Terrestrial World. The Terrestrial World is the realm of forms which you inhabit, the planet earth itself. Gawain and Guinevere tell you to look upon the Sleeping Lord upon the veil. It seems that you see the whole history of the earth, being enacted and replayed over and over. You are aware of the many protectors of the earth in every era. Spend some time in contemplation of the Sleeping

Lord and what he signifies for you. As you look upon him, the image fades and you see the globe of the earth, spinning in space. Contemplate your planet and what it means to you. You become aware that a hawk and a cow are at your side. When you hear the cry of an eagle overhead, the veil is raised by the Grail Queen and King and you pass beyond the veil.

Before you is the glory of the Grail Hallow itself. To one side of it is the Wounded King, on the other is the Spiral Tower. You look upon these three images in combination and ask, 'What is the Mystery of the Terrestrial World?' (Do not look up the meanings of the cards themselves, but let a story or impression come to you, without forcing anything.) You may ask clarifying questions of the hawk and the cow. Accept the realizations that you have and record them.

As you look upon the Wounded King, you sense the presence of Gawain. What is the significance of the King's wound to the earth? How does Gawain guard the earth? As you look upon the Spiral Tower, you become aware of the presence of Guinevere. What is the message of the Spiral Tower for the earth? What is the significance of Guinevere's spindle in relation to the Tower? Finally, you contemplate the Grail. What is the action of the Grail in the Terrestrial World? Be aware of it as a sacred gift of wholeness that remains always for the healing of the earth. The hawk and the cow lead you back through the veil, which closes behind you. Give thanks to the Company of the Terrestrial World and leave the Caer. Make sure that you are well earthed (see p.23).

3. You blow the horn towards the East to invite the power of the Sword into the Sanctuary. From the eastern Caer comes the Sword family, with the Knight riding before and the Maiden following with the Sword in her hands. Behind her walk the Queen and King.

You stand aside as they enter the Caer and ascend to the central room. After a short time, the trap-door is lowered and you also enter.

Hanging across the eastern wall is a semi-transparent veil from floor to ceiling. Upon it is depicted the Moon. In front of the veil are the Round Table and the Lady of the Lake, attended by the Sword Maiden and Sword Knight respectively (see Fig. 24). The Sword Queen and King stand either side of the veil.

The Sword Maiden and Knight come forward in invitation and bring you to stand between the Round Table and the Lady of the Lake who are the guardians of the Mystery of the Lunar World. The Lunar World is the realm of vision, imagination and fertile growth which influences our dreams and our fertility cycle. The subtle influences of the Moon touch the parts of us that are hidden or lie *in potentia*, waiting to germinate. The Round Table and the Lady of the Lake tell

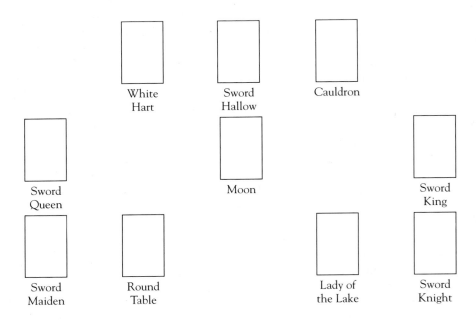

Fig. 24: *Sword Company of the Lunar World*

you to look upon the Moon that appears on the veil. It seems that you see patterns of influence which the Moon sets in motion. You are aware of the cycles of fluctuation, growth, increase and fallowness in all life forms. You are also aware of the many gifted ones who have given inspiration in every era. Spend some time in contemplation of the Moon and what it signifies for you. As you look upon it, the image grows even stronger, becoming a silver globe of light spinning in space. You become aware that a merlin falcon and a crane are at your side. When you hear the rippling waters of a flowing stream before you, the veil is raised by the Sword Queen and King and you pass beyond the veil.

Before you is the vibrant Sword Hallow itself. To one side of it is the White Hart, on the other is the Cauldron. You regard these three images in combination and ask, 'What is the Mystery of the Lunar World?' (Do not look up the meanings of the cards themselves, but let a story or impression come to you, without forcing anything.) You may ask clarifying questions of the merlin and the crane. Accept the realizations that you have and record them.

As you look upon the White Hart, you sense the presence of the Round Table. What is the role of the White Hart in stimulating vision of the Lunar realm? What is the significance of the Round Table in the cycles of growth? As you look upon the Cauldron, you become aware of the presence of the Lady of the Lake. What part of yourself is brewing in the Cauldron? What is the relationship between the Cauldron maidens and the Lady of the Lake? Finally, you contemplate the Sword. What is the action of the Sword in the Lunar World? Be aware of it as a sacred gift of guardianship that sheds the clarifying light of the moon upon all who quest for vision. The merlin falcon and the crane lead you back through the veil, which closes behind you. Give thanks to the Company of the Lunar World and leave the Caer. Make sure that you are well earthed.

4. You blow the horn towards the South to invite the power of the Spear into the Sanctuary. From the southern Caer comes the Spear family, with the Knight riding before and the Maiden following with the Spear in her hands. Behind her walk the Queen and King. You stand aside as they enter the Caer and ascend to the central room. After a short time, the trap-door is lowered and you also enter.

Hanging across the southern wall is a semi-transparent veil from floor to ceiling. Upon it is depicted the Sun. In front of the veil are Arthur and Sovereignty, attended by the Spear Maiden and Knight, respectively (see Fig. 25). The Spear Queen and King stand either side of the veil.

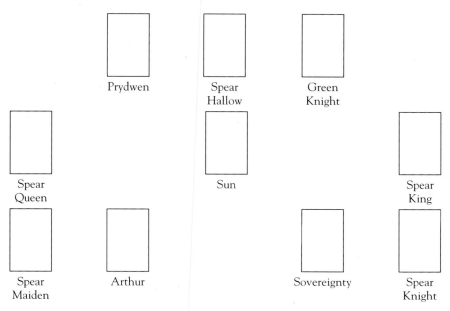

Fig. 25: *Spear Company of the Solar World*

The Spear Maiden and Knight come forward in invitation and bring you to stand between Arthur and Sovereignty who are the guardians of the Mystery of the Solar World. The Solar World is the realm of creativity, enlightenment and wholeness, wherein we receive the radiation of life-energy. The bright influence of the Sun brings us the height of our powers, kindling enthusiasm for life and showing us the way to illuminate the darkness. Arthur and Sovereignty tell you to look upon the Sun that appears on the veil. You see the radial influence of the Sun which warms all things. You are aware of the many illuminated ones whose charismatic quality has brightened the spiritual path. Spend some time in contemplation of the Sun and what it signifies for you. As you look upon it, the image grows even stronger, becoming a golden globe of light spinning in space. You become aware that a chough and an ermine are at your side. When you hear the thunder of hooves before you, the veil is raised by the Spear Queen and King and you pass beyond the veil.

Before you is the vibrant Spear Hallow itself. To one side of it is Prydwen, on the other is the Green Knight. You regard these three images in combination and ask, 'What is the Mystery of the Solar World?' (Do not look up the meanings of the cards themselves, but let a story or impression come to you, without forcing anything.) You may ask clarifying questions of the chough and the ermine. Accept the realizations that you have and record them.

As you look upon Prydwen, you sense the presence of Arthur. What is the role of Prydwen in stimulating energy in the Solar realm? What is the significance of Arthur's descent to the darkness of the Underworld? As you look upon the Green Knight, you become aware of the presence of Sovereignty. What is the role of the Green Knight in the cycle of the solar year? What is the relationship between Sovereignty and the Green Knight? Finally, you contemplate the Spear. What is the action of the Spear in the Solar World? Be aware of it as a sacred gift of creativity that directs a beam of solar light upon all who quest for wholeness.

The chough and the ermine lead you back through the veil, which closes behind you. Give thanks to the Company of the Solar World and leave the Caer. Make sure that you are well earthed.

5. You blow the horn towards the North to invite the power of the Stone into the Sanctuary. From the northern Caer comes the Stone family, with the Knight riding before and the Maiden following with the Stone in her hands. Behind her walk the Queen and King. You stand aside as they enter the Caer and ascend to the central room. After a short time, the trap-door is lowered and you also enter.

Hanging across the northern wall is a semi-transparent veil from floor to ceiling. Upon it is depicted the Star of Prophecy. In front of

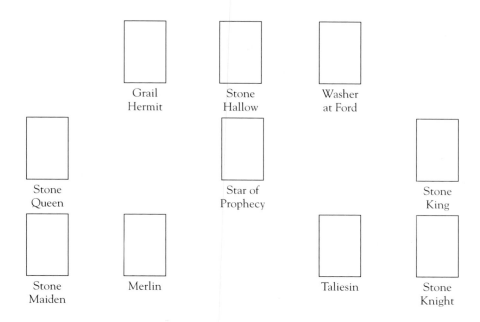

Fig. 26: *Stone Company of the Stellar World*

the veil are Merlin and Taliesin, attended by the Stone Maiden and Knight respectively (see Fig. 26). The Stone Queen and King stand either side of the veil.

The Stone Maiden and Knight come forward in invitation and bring you to stand between Merlin and Taliesin, who are the guardians of the Mystery of the Stellar World. The Stellar World is the realm of origination, wherein primary principles are stored. We are all made of the dust of the stars and this wisdom lies awaiting within us. These star-seeds are triggered by faith and hope, they are conceived in the womb of the universe and called forth by watchful trust and patient duty. The stellar influences upon our lives herald great change and bring crystalline awareness into the night of doubt. Merlin and Taliesin tell you to look upon the Star that appears on the veil. You see the crystalline influence of the Star, which illuminates all things and shows the primal pattern underlying them. You are aware of the many deep beings whose mystic awareness connects us with the originative source. Spend some time in contemplation of the Star and what it signifies for you. As you look upon it, the image grows even stronger, becoming a crystal shaft of light transecting space. You become aware that a pair of dragons and a lark are at your side. When you hear the crowing of a cockerel before you, the veil is raised by the Stone Queen and King and you pass beyond the veil.

Before you is the vibrant Stone Hallow itself. To one side of it is the Grail Hermit, on the other is the Washer at the Ford. You regard these three images in combination and ask, 'What is the Mystery of the Stellar World?' (Do not look up the meanings of the cards themselves, but let a story or impression come to you, without forcing anything.) You may ask clarifying questions of the dragons and the lark. Accept the realizations that you have and record them.

As you look upon the Grail Hermit, you sense the presence of Merlin. What is the role of the Grail Hermit in connecting us with the influences of the Stellar World? What is the relationship between the Grail Hermit and Merlin? As you look upon the Washer at the Ford, you become aware of the presence of Taliesin. What is the role of the Washer in the originative patternings of the Stellar World? What is the relationship between Taliesin and the Washer? Finally, you contemplate the Stone. What is the action of the Stone in the Stellar World? Be aware of it as a sacred gift bestowing knowledge of the stars upon those who go on quest for wisdom. The dragons and the lark lead you back through the veil, which closes behind you. Give thanks to the Company of the Stellar World and leave the Caer. Make sure that you are well earthed.

There is considerably more meditation work to be done within your Sanctuary of the Hallows, of course. Use it as a place of communion with the qualities of the Hallows, where you go to regenerate your energies, and where you meet problems or issues that go beyond your human ingenuity to solve. The celestial veils hide great sources of help and power, which may be brought to bear upon situations in the external world.

## Task

Consider the cycles of the Hallows in your life and make a series of blessings that will commemorate them throughout each day and keep you in contact with the Sanctuary you have helped create: e.g.,

> As I begin my day, I take up the Sword of Light: may it illuminate me.
> As I rest from my work at midday, I take up the Spear of Life: may it guide me along the pathway of the day.
> As I return to my home, I take up the Grail of Love: may its nurture bless all whom I meet.
> As I lie down to sleep, I take up the Stone of Wisdom: may my dreams be enriched by its lore.

# LESSON 56

## Earth Guardianship

Throughout this course, you have walked through the Lesser Power landscape cards and have incorporated them into your meditations. Now we will relate them directly to earth guardianship. We are becoming aware of a greater need for personal responsibility in our life on earth: ecological awareness, curbing our consumer greed, sharing and conserving resources with other countries and honouring non-human forms of life are all important issues. In a traditional society we would have grown up knowing these things naturally and living in better harmony with creation; in an urban society, we are less aware and more careless.

Using the Lesser Powers, we can become more aware of our responsibility towards our environment and simultaneously activate positive messages to our own land, its peoples and species. For each of these meditations, you will need to separate the Lesser Powers numbered 2-10 from the pack and arrange them in nine sets with all the same numbered cards together, so that, for example, all the threes will be laid together. You then place each set down in the following way; the numbers below relate to the questions on pp.228-231.

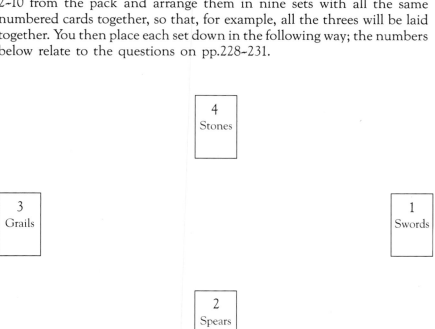

Fig. 27: *Plan for the Circuits of the Land Meditations*

Below are listed the uses of each numbered landscape card for creative magical synthesis of the land's energies. Meditate upon at least one combination in this lesson. Each set is suitable for addressing specific issues which threaten the earth in some way. This is a very useful way of working, since each set combines each of the Hallow energies and weaves together the landscapes within which you have already travelled.

# The Circuits of the Land Meditation

Stand at the centre of these sets, entering each card in meditation, considering them in relationship to your own land and its current situation or a particular issue facing it. Each set represents a level of the land's life, while each card is a seasonal counsellor, able to give answers. When you have asked the first four questions given, turn to the space within the four cards and see the Seeker and the Flowering of Logres cards, back to back: these depict the Seeker at the beginning and end of his quest and can reveal different aspects of the issue at hand. Read the five cards in combination, first with the Seeker then with the Flowering of Logres at the centre.

Lastly, you may also visualize a tree, plant or flower which is indigenous to your own land to be the energy-container for each set. You have been used to speaking with the totem animals of the Greater Power cards; now, you designate your chosen representative of the green realm, rooted in the soil and culture or your country, to speak for your land. Ask it the fifth question and receive an oracle of the land. You can also choose to work with personal issues using this method, in which case you should rephrase the fifth question as 'What does my soul say?' or 'How does my soul speak?'

## Sword, Spear, Grail and Stone Twos
Twos concern pledges, promises, commitments, resources, and directions. Work with this set when peace is threatened, when ethical concepts are being forgotten, when leaders neglect their promises etc.

1. What is preventing implementation?
2. What is the dynamic drive underlying the issue?
3. What factors/personalities need to reciprocate?
4. Which aspects need to be borne in mind?
5. How can the pledge be redeemed, how can the promise be kept to the land?

## Sword, Spear, Grail and Stone Threes
Threes concern formalization, concepts, planning and clarifying. Work

with this set when creative solutions are needed, when education fails to educate, when practical skills are required.

1. How receptive is the time for this issue?
2. How can the issue's appeal be broadened?
3. Where is the joy and fulfilment here?
4. How can creative skill be best used?
5. What is the appropriate shape/container/home for this in the land?

## Sword, Spear, Grail and Stone Fours
Fours concern manifestation and trying out ideas. Work with these when doorways to opportunity need to open, when life-changing directions beckon, when adventurous roads must be trodden.

1. What are the potentials and limitations behind this issue?
2. Which strengths are likely to lead to a harmonious completion?
3. Which areas have become stagnant and unmoving?
4. What material security underlies this issue?
5. How will the land accept the reality of this?

## Sword, Spear, Grail and Stone Fives
Fives concern modification, adjustment, problems, set-backs, and challenges. Work with these when open hostility prevents progress, when energy is blocked, when things are not working smoothly.

1. What divisive tactics threaten the issue?
2. How is jealousy and competitiveness causing obstruction?
3. How can we learn from failure and limitation here?
4. What insecurity underlies the issue?
5. How does the land judge this issue?

## Sword, Spear, Grail and Stone Sixes
Sixes concern harmony, satisfaction, natural rhythm and attunement. Work with these to pin-point how resources can be shared, how combining forces creates strength, where the natural patterns fall.

1. Which intuitive perceptions cleared the way here?
2. What has been achieved?
3. How does this issue link to traditional values?
4. How can good fortune be shared?
5. How does the heart of the land accept this?

## Sword, Spear, Grail and Stone Sevens

Sevens concern specialization, extension and variety. Work with these when the issue is beleaguered by a host of distractions, when experts can't agree, when strength is scattered by disunity.

1. What causes effort to be unstable here?
2. What strongly held beliefs are keeping the gates of possibility open?
3. What kinds of unrealistic fantasies are getting in the way?
4. What immediate action will keep attention on the task in hand?
5. How can the land perfect and harmonize this?

## Sword, Spear, Grail and Stone Eights

Eights concern organization, reorientation and re-evaluation. Work with these to hasten completion of a project, when radical retrenchment is needed, when a new burst of energy is needed to refuel.

1. What out-worn patterns need to be discarded here?
2. What is the vision underlying the need for haste?
3. How can this issue be re-evaluated in a more universal way?
4. What kinds of methodical craft can bring completion?
5. How can the network of the land communicate this?

## Sword, Spear, Grail and Stone Nines

Nines concern integration, flexibility and self-worth. Work with these when you want to discover true strength, when disparate energies need weaving into the plan, when full integration of an issue is incomplete.

1. What doubts or depressions are still shadowing this issue?
2. What is the true purpose and strength of this?
3. What is most satisfying about this?
4. What kind of freedom and accomplishment does this bring?
5. How does the land treasure this?

## Sword, Spear, Grail and Stone Tens

Tens concern culmination and conclusion of a pattern. Work with these when conditions are prime for containing energy, when issues of conservation and sharing are under discussion, when experts gather to decide the fate of the earth, of the family, of the nation.

1. Where is the life or death edge of this issue?
2. How can the responsibilities be best shared?
3. How can the issue bring a single vision of universal/family/national unity?

4. What legacy will this leave for our descendants?
5. How will the land benefit?

**Diary Example:**     **Reading:**
*22.9.92*            *The Circuits of the Land*

*I choose to meditate upon the morale of the country following the recent economic upheavals using the Nine set.*

1. *A complete inability to take responsibility seemed to dog this issue, said the young Seeker. But the mature Seeker reminded me that this card is about great daring in dark times.*
2. *The strength and purpose of the land is obstinately enduring and will use this as wisdom to fight another day.*
3. *There seems little satisfaction here, only an empty pot and little or no security. But the mature Seeker said that we needed to go after our heart's desire with more energy. Hunger is a good sauce, they say!*
4. *This does give us a strange kind of freedom, to discover simple pleasures that don't cost a fortune, to turn to our deep creative needs. This period of 'short commons' might indeed bring a more concerted vision of accomplishment.*
5. *The Seeker faded away and was replaced by a White Chestnut tree. I asked: 'How does the land treasure this?' It spoke on behalf of the land, saying: 'I stand tall and am a wide treasury of wisdom. I feel the vibrations of this and am not concerned, because there are deep wells which my roots draw upon for nourishment. Now you will begin to pay attention to me again and learn the old ways.' I found myself calmer than I'd been for days after this, as though some mysterious message of help had reached me in a remote and embattled region.*

# LESSON 57

# *Building the Tarot Tree*

Many spiritual systems use a method of alignment with the innerworlds. This is most often expressed by the central Tree which interconnects all the worlds, sometimes called the axile tree or Cosmic Axis. In Eastern esoteric tradition, this axis of alignment is understood to be present within the body itself within the chakras. The chakras, or wheels, are vortexes of energy within the subtle body: they both receive and dispense energy. We cannot discuss the complex teachings that surround the chakras here, but these subtle energies which intermesh the body with the universe are also commonly expressed in many other modes of esoteric understanding. [31] The sevenfold nature of creation is clear to us in the seven colours of the rainbow, the seven major notes of music, the seven alchemical metals, the seven planets of classical astrology, the seven sacraments of the church, the seven vices and virtues etc. This archetypal pattern is found worldwide, and is also present within Western Qabalistic tradition as the seven levels of the Tree of Life. In this lesson, you will be exploring yourself as a whole person and realigning yourself with the universal axile tree.

On p.159 of *Hallowquest*, we read about the seven Arthurian Mysteries, wherein the Greater Powers are combined in triads as containers of deep teachings. These combinations can also be related to the chakras and to any other sevenfold system of esoteric understanding. In this lesson we examine our potentialities in relationship to the sevenfold triads of the Greater Powers. Here they are assigned to each of the chakras:

| | | |
|------|-------------------------------------------------|--------------|
| I | Merlin, Gawain, Green Knight | Base |
| II | Lady of Lake, Grail Hermit, Spiral Tower | Sacral |
| III | Guinevere, Round Table, Star | Solar Plexus |
| IV | Arthur, Sovereignty, Moon | Heart |
| V | Taliesin, Wounded King, Sun | Throat |
| VI | White Hart, Washer at the Ford, Sleeping Lord | Brow |
| VII | Prydwen, Cauldron, Flowering of Logres | Crown |

*Note:* The Seeker is excluded from this patterning because s/he is the loom around which these energies are woven. Readers who prefer to work from the Western Qabalistic tradition can alternatively equate these seven levels with the Tree of Life. [5] Again, there is no space to discuss Qabala, which is a discipline all by itself. The sephiroth (lights or vessels of the Tree) are given here with their Hebrew and English titles:

| | | |
|------|--------------------------|-------------------------------|
| I | Malkuth | (Kingdom) |
| II | Yesod | (Foundation) |
| III | Hod and Netzach | (Reverberation and Eternity) |
| IV | Tiphareth | (Beauty) |
| V | Geburah and Chesed | (Judgement and Mercy) |
| VI | Binah and Chokmah | (Understanding and Wisdom) |
| VII | Kether and the Supernals | (Crown) |

Each tarot triad can be considered as a distinct council or tribunal for that chakra or level of the Tree. If you are experiencing problems relating to any particular level, you can meditate within your chosen triad and confer with the appropriate tribunal. The short outlines of the chakra and Qabalistic levels given below are not definitive, but are merely intended to help the reader focus on the issue in hand. The numbering of the cards below and the accompanying questions refer to the reading in Fig. 28.

## Level I

The Base Chakra, located at the perineum, is about survival, to do with stability and grounding. Malkuth equates to effective manifestation, to matters concerning the body and to physical action.

1. Merlin prepares the ground on which we live. What is the stability or basis for your existence?
2. Gawain defends the ground of our existence. How do you best defend your existence?
3. The Green Knight challenges that ground. What threatens your existence?

## Level II

The Sacral Chakra, located in the sacrum, denotes inner creativity and generative power as well as desire and pleasure. Yesod equates to the generation of images and inner vision, it is the power house of our energies. It governs psychological matters and triggers deeper connection.

4. The Lady of Lake fosters the inner vision. What quality of creative enchantment is reflected by your deepest desires?
5. The Grail Hermit nourishes the vision with wise counsel. Which prime circumstances best nourish your desires?
6. The Spiral Tower liberates and transfigures the vision. How do your desires transcend your limitations?

## Level III

The Solar Plexus Chakra is about will-power, the persona, self-confidence and the emotions. Hod and Netzach equate to skill and craft, to sequential and cyclic movements, to the perceptions attendant on memory and attraction.

7. Guinevere maintains the concord of self-esteem. Who are you?
8. The Round Table regulates the fulfilment of vocation. How do you use your personal power?
9. The Star of Prophecy synthesizes and refreshes innate skills. How can your skills be better employed?

## Level IV

The Heart Chakra is expressive of the true self and of compassion. Tiphareth equates to harmony and service, to the equipoise of the essential self.

10. Arthur reveals the self as true sovereign. How do you manifest compassion?
11. Sovereignty maintains the integrity of self-government. How do you maintain your integrity?
12. The Moon reflects the changing patterns of the self's expression. What is the pattern of your service to creation?

## Level V

The Throat Chakra is concerned with creativity and communication, with synthesizing ideas into a symbolic expression. Geburah and Chesed equate to justice tempered by mercy, of critical perception balanced by magnanimity, of stripping away inessentials and building up essentials.

13. Taliesin guards the deep traditions. What is your inner voice telling you?
14. The Wounded King offers himself as a sacrifice to better communication. What are you failing to express?
15. The Sun defends harmony of expression. What is the watchword of your life?

## Level VI

The Brow Chakra, located between the eyes, is about vision, insight, prophecy and intuition. Binah and Chokmah denote receptive understanding and dynamic wisdom, inner maternal and paternal energies in generative embrace, containing and envisioning ideas and inventions.

16. The White Hart shows the vision that guides you. What is your quest?
17. The Washer at the Ford reveals wisdom in the darkest night. What must you let go of to achieve your quest?
18. The Sleeping Lord announces the prophecy of your potential. How will the world be renewed by the fulfilment of your quest?

## Level VII

The Crown Chakra, located at the top of the head, governs mastery, fulfilment and completion; it expresses transcendence and full enlightenment. Kether and the Supernals equate to full alignment with the divine will, with creation and knowledge, with primal origination.

19. Prydwen exemplifies the ability to live with discipline and courage. What is your spiritual focus?
20. The Cauldron exemplifies the ability to transmute our lives. What aspects of yourself need regeneration?
21. The Flowering of Logres exemplifies the ability to achieve and restore. How can your spiritual focus bring healing to the world?

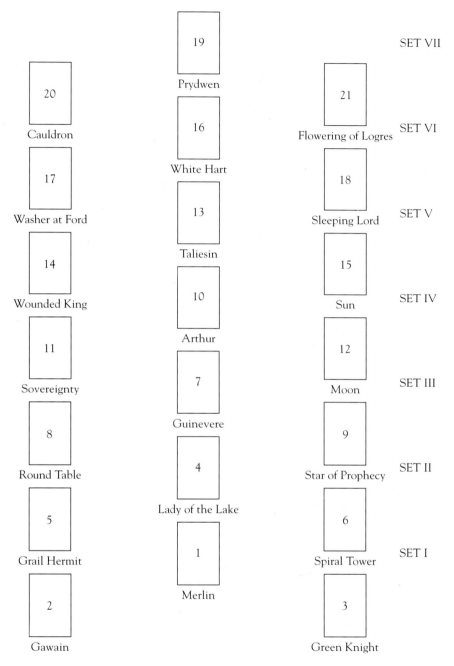

Fig. 28: *Tarot Tree Spread*

*Note:* The numbers on this diagram refer to the order of layout, not to card-numeration; position names are shown for clarity.

# Tasks

1. Lay out the Greater Powers as in Fig. 28. Firstly look at the three lines formed by the layout. How does the centre feel to you? How do the left-hand and right-hand lines feel? Do each have a specific character? Now look at the inter-relations of the triads and make your own assessments of each, without referring to the book. What power does each hold, what gifts are available, what challenges do they set?
2. Using the full tarot, either do a complete Tarot-Tree reading using all 21 positions, OR address a specific issue, using one of the seven sets above, laying one card on each position of the triad chosen. Draw an extra card, sight unseen from the pack, to indicate the key that releases the energy. In both instances, shuffle the full pack and lay one or more cards on each position, asking the questions above.

# Meditation

Meditate on each of the levels in turn, visualizing Merlin, the Lady of the Lake, Guinevere, Arthur, Taliesin, the White Hart and Prydwen over each of the chakra points on your own body. Do not focus upon your chakras themselves, but rather relate each of these Greater Powers to the energy levels associated with each level.

**Diary Example:**          **Meditation**
*14.11.91*                  *Guinevere*

*Problems with self-esteem led me to meditate upon my Guinevere level. With impatience and some frustration, I watched her calmly spinning. She told me to breathe through the angry knot in my stomach and let her untangle it, spooling it off with great equanimity on to her distaff ~ she says she can use well-directed energy in a creative way. She advised me to think of her when I'm being attacked or criticized, to hold my sovereign centre of deep concord and selfhood. During this my 'Arthur level' was encouraging and supportive of her words ~ I could see Arthur nodding furiously in affirmation!*

## *The Council of the Clans*

In this lesson, we will examine the nature of the 16 court cards and take council with the Hallow families in a new combination. As you've worked with the cards, you may have found that you particularly resonate to one or more of these which reflects your own personality very closely. This lesson seeks to shake you out of accepted archetypal patterns into finding new dynamics within your life.

Below are four councils, drawn from the Hallow clans. They can be used both for meditation and for meditative spreads. The magical titles of the Hallow clans are given here, drawing upon the fourfold primal energies of the Hallows themselves, which reflect the creative powers of the universe. Swords denote Life, which is exemplified by air or the breath of life. Spears denote the Light, exemplified by the brightness and light of fire. Grails denote Love, exemplified by the unceasing flow of water. Stones denote the Law, exemplified by the stability of earth. Here we must understand Law in its archetypal sense as the primal defender and guardian of the triple principles of Life, Light and Love, rather than as an oppressive legalistic principle.

To be fully developed individuals, we must integrate the powers of childhood, youth and adulthood, as depicted in the Maidens and Knights, Queens and Kings, for they are all present within us. Women have the dynamism of the Knight within them, just as men can have the feminine insights of the Queen within them. Apply these principles without getting caught up on gender, for these aspectual colorations apply to *all* people.

The elemental combinations of the Hallow clans are given below.

## The Council of Maidens

This council comprises the four seers of the Hallow families. Maidens represent the clarity and integrity of childhood. Their primal ability to risk, to clarify cluttered 'grown-up' patterns, is very useful when we are confused. They are our inner voices upon quest. This is a council that addresses the elemental level of earth within us; it helps us find our true foundation and inner security. Before meditating upon this council, access your inner child. Enter a circular earth-bank wherein the Maidens meet, then dialogue with each one, using the questions below to get you started. These questions are addressed to you personally.

The Sword Maiden is Earth of Air, the Discerning Daughter of Life. *Child of the Sword, what perceptions do you bring to our council?*

The Spear Maiden is Earth of Fire, the Enthusiastic Daughter of the Light. *Child of the Spear, what energy do you bring?*

The Grail Maiden is Earth of Water, the Imaginative Daughter of Love. *Child of the Grail, what dreams do you bring?*

The Stone Maiden is Earth of Earth, the Pragmatic Daughter of the Law. *Child of the Stone, what skills do you bring?*

Try to answer each question from the basis of your inner child. What is the combined insight of this council, including yourself? Record your impressions.

## The Council of Knights

This council comprises the four way-showers of the Hallow families. Knights represent the verve and dynamism of youth. They help us to get moving and be adventurous, to focus our commitment upon the task in hand. They are our companions upon quest. This is a council that addresses the elemental level of fire within us. Before you meditate upon this council, first access your inner youth, then enter a ring of fires where the Knights meet, and dialogue with each one, using the questions below to get you started. These questions are addressed to you personally.

The Sword Knight is Fire of Air, the Incisive Son of Life. *Young One of the Sword, what rights do you defend in this council?*

The Spear Knight is Fire of Fire, the Energetic Son of the Light. *Young One of the Spear, what adventures do you seek?*

The Grail Knight is Fire of Water, the Meditative Son of Love. *Young One of the Grail, what realizations do you bring?*

The Stone Knight is Fire of Earth, the Patient Son of the Law. *Young One of the Stone, what trust is your banner?*

Try to answer each question from the basis of your inner youth. What is the combined insight of this council, including yourself? Record your impressions.

## The Council of Queens

This council comprises the four empowerers of the Hallow families. Queens represent the inner, feminine maturity of adulthood which nurtures our visions and helps us integrate them into our lives. They show us how to recognize and claim our power upon quest. This is a council that addresses the elemental level of water within us. Before you meditate upon this council, first access your inner feminine, then enter an island, moated by water where the Queens meet. Dialogue with each, using the questions below to get you started.

The Sword Queen is Water of Air, the Intelligent Mother of Life. *Lady of the Sword, what understandings do you bring to this council?*
The Spear Queen is Water of Fire, the Committed Mother of the Light. *Lady of the Spear, what service do you uphold?*
The Grail Queen is Water of Water, the Intuitive Mother of Love. *Lady of the Grail, what sympathies do you bring?*
The Stone Queen is Water of Earth, the Nurturing Mother of the Law. *Lady of the Stone, what nourishment do you offer?*

Try to answer each question from the basis of your inner feminine. What is the combined insight of this council, including yourself? Record your impressions.

## The Council of Kings

This council comprises the four guardians of the Hallow families. Kings represent the outer, masculine maturity of adulthood which gives us authority and encourages our true ability. They show us how to manifest and wield the power we have found upon quest. This is a council that addresses the elemental level of air within us. Before you meditate upon this council, access your inner masculine, then enter a circle where the Kings meet, which is surrounded by censers or by fissures from which steam arises. Dialogue with each King, using the questions below to get you started.

The Sword King is Air of Air, the Just Father of Life. *Lord of the Sword, what truth do you uphold in this council?*
The Spear King is Air of Fire, the Passionate Father of the Light. *Lord of the Spear, what healing do you bring?*
The Grail King is Air of Water, the Generous Father of Love. *Lord of the Grail, what gift do you bring?*
The Stone King is Air of Earth, the Enduring Father of the Law. *Lord of the Stone, what wisdom do you bring?*

Try to answer each question from the basis of your inner masculine. What is the combined insight of this council, including yourself? Record your impressions.

# Healing the Land

One of the reasons we have been meditating upon the Hallows is to mediate their qualities to our own land. In this lesson, you are offered the opportunity of reconsecrating and healing the land. Each land over the whole earth is suffering major pollution and abuse. When the earth suffers, so does everything living upon it. The following healing of the land ritual accesses the healing energies of each of the four Hallows.

## Task

Obtain a square or rectangle of plain white cotton or linen about 2 feet (60 cm) square or 2 feet by 3 feet (60 cm by 1m), and a packet of fabric crayons or fabric paints. These will allow you to draw freely upon the material. Draw the outline of your own country with fabric crayons, making a large map of it which covers your fabric. Mark the most sacred site (in your opinion) with a star or other symbol. Draw four rectangles in the four corners ~ these points will represent the four caers of the elemental powers and Hallows, where you will be laying your cards. You may also make an attractive border to the cloth, or decorate it in some other way which reflects your cultural heritage.

Dedicate your cloth to the spirits of your land in your own way. You can call into the cloth the archetypes or deities closely associated with your land and seal the cloth with oil to dedicate it. This should be done simply and with intention. When you have done this you can proceed to your augury of the land reading.

Lay the cards in five packs, with the four Hallow suits at each of the four quarters of your cloth, placing the central pack of Greater Powers on your chosen sacred place. Meditate upon the nature of the healing needed by your land at this time, then shuffle each pack, holding the healing-needs of the land in your heart, drawing one card from each pack and laying it face upwards. Read the cards in relation to the questions below.

Sword Pack: What healing gift does the Sword Hallow give?
Spear Pack: What healing gift does the Spear Hallow give?
Grail Pack: What healing gift does the Grail Hallow give?
Stone Pack: What healing gift does the Stone Hallow give?
Greater Power Pack: Which Power will implement this healing?

Read the cards as best you can, making a complete story or scenario in which the cards drawn from the Hallow packs can be combined by the Greater Power you have drawn. You may sometimes find that before healing can be effected, a good deal of clarification and clearing away is needed, so don't be surprised if your reading seems to offer destructive solutions. The cycles of life must be allowed to operate: the cleansing and preparation of Winter must always precede Spring. If you are unhappy or uncertain about the cards drawn, ask the Greater Power to clarify or explain.

The reading can be repeated when you feel your land needs special healing. But, remember, the cloth is now a sacred talisman of power, so treat it with respect. It cannot be used for any mundane purpose now. Many spiritual traditions 'keep such items guarded, others immediately return ritual objects to the elements by burying, by giving them to water, fire or air. You must decide what is best for you. You may wish to dedicate it for use as your own spread cloth, to use in future readings, to remind you of your own sacred duty to your land. This is a valid use of your cloth, since, in the words of the Russian proverb, 'The earth remembers and witnesses all.' If you feel that it is not for the gaze of other eyes, you can reserve it for private work only.

*Note:* To retain the designs on your piece of material you will need to follow the instructions on the fabric crayons or paints – the cloth may need special treatment before washing, such as to be ironed, in order for the colours to become permanent.

# LESSON 60

## *The Path Ahead*

Congratulations on reaching the end of this course! It may have taken you considerably more than a year to journey to this point and you may well be wondering what you might do next or how you are going to utilize this work.

Firstly, your dedicated commitment to daily meditation and personal study will always sustain you and can be invoked to assist you during periods when concentrated work is essential. Secondly, you now have unlimited access to an inner landscape which you have personally explored and made your own. Extend your researches into whatever area of your life seems most appropriate. Thirdly, you have a degree of self-knowledge that will give you confidence and self-esteem in a world that is always trying to disempower you. Remember, you have the experience of the quest and are able to mediate the quality of the Hallows to all situations.

Practically, although there is much more work you can do with the cards, you need to focus on your life's path. You can use the tarot as a daily focus of your activities and keep a diary of inner influences. You can use the tarot to help others by giving readings. You can create new rituals for yourself and friends, based on the insights you have gained.

The guardianship of the Hallows remains in the inner world, but the guardians cannot mediate their powers unless we keep open the channels by which the Hallows are manifested to the outer world. The path of personal responsibility for our thoughts, actions and visions must still be trodden by us all. Don't forget to live with intention; learn to co-operate with the universe and not manipulate it. Those who manipulate do not serve the Hallows but themselves.

Many possibilities lie before you. You may choose to establish your own group, or join with another, to work through this material in another way. You may want to go on and receive a formal esoteric training with a mystery school or individual teacher, or you could remain as you are and learn of life itself. In whatever land you live, relate closely to its tutelary inner guardians and learn to work with their co-operation. If the Arthurian legends are not the native stories of your land or culture, then turn your attentions to the myths and legends that inform your land and people. If you live in a land where your people are in-comers, then approach the land's inner guardians and stories with respect, always asking permission to work with those energies; ask the land's guardians to show you how to work seriously with them. All who ask in service, ask the Grail question that heals the Wasteland; all who ask that question become members of the Hallows Family and inherit a deeper trust of the earth's tradition.

## The Games of Sovereignty Reading

I would like to share with you a special spread which was specifically written for the *Hallowquest* course, which I led with John at Hawkwood College, Gloucestershire, in December 1990. The spread was the central core of the ritual masquing in which all the Greater Powers were represented by the participants. The Seeker encountered the first six Greater Powers who interpreted the reading in turn. This spread can be used as a life-purpose reading, to be done at least once a year or once a quarter. Each set of cards is under the aegis of an Arthurian power and can be read in relation to it. Shuffle the full pack by laying it on the floor and moving the cards round in a large circle. Gather them together and

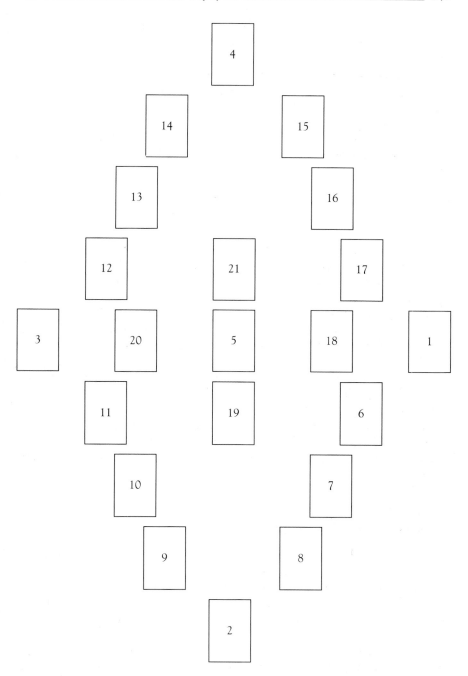

Fig. 29: The Games of Sovereignty Spread

lay them in order, face down, turning over each set and interpreting them as you go. Card 21 is drawn, sight unseen and at random from the pack, laid under card 5 and read last of all. I have not given appropriate questions for this reading - you are now quite experienced enough to create your own. The outlines given below should give you clues.

## Meanings of Positions

### Exploring the Lands Within
Merlin governs cards 1-5. He scans the four directions and the place within.

1. Air, East - powers of thought. Mind.
2. Fire, South - powers of intuition. Psyche.
3. Water, West - powers of emotion. Heart.
4. Earth, North - powers of instinct. Soul.
5. Centre - spirit of the land. Spirit.

### Shapers of Destiny
The Lady of the Lake governs cards 6-8. She perceives the nature of our life energy.

6. The intrinsic nature of our destiny, its source or hidden nurture.
7. Obstacles, problems.
8. What factors need to change.

### Weavers of the Web of Life
Guinevere governs cards 9-11. She sees the patterns that lie in our make-up.

9. One's purpose, life-potential.
10. Recurrent patterns in alignment with cosmic purpose.
11. Future life pattern.

### Service to the Land
Arthur governs cards 12-14. He perceives the nature of our service in the physical world.

12. One's daily actions and interactions.
13. One's service to the earth.
14. One's future service.

## Knowledge of Inner Worlds

Taliesin governs cards 15-17. He perceives the nature of our dedication to the Otherworld.

15. Tradition, inspiration, the ancestors.
16. Healing the worlds.
17. The true self. Vocation.

## Challenges on the Quest

The White Hart governs cards 18-20. It sees the kinds of interaction we have upon our quest.

18. Love and friendship.
19. Enemies and opponents.
20. Rebirth of self.

## The Avalonian Barge

Morgen as the Washer at the Ford governs the last card which will carry us over to the next initiation of our life.

21. The key or bridge to the possession of true sovereignty.

# Meditation

This course ends with a final meditation: the Vigil of Dedication in the Sanctuary of the Hallows. Look back on your diary for Lessons 16, 28, 40 and 52 and see which Greater Power guardians you drew in the four Hallow auguries. Now you may have drawn the same Greater Powers more than once, but you will need *four separate helpers* for this vigil, so decide the most appropriate assignment of that duplicated card, separate the Greater Power cards and draw another one for the Hallow with no current helper. For example, if you drew Gawain for the Auguries of both Sword and Stone, Guinevere for Spear and the Star for Grail, you might decide that Gawain was better suited to represent the Sword, and might draw Taliesin sight unseen from the pack to represent the Stone.

**Diary Example:**　　**Reading:**
*3-6 July 1992*　　*Greater Power Guardians*

　*The augury helpers I drew in Part Two were:*

　*Sword Hallow*　　*The Green Knight*

| Spear Hallow | The Washer at the Ford |
| Grail Hallow | The White Hart |
| Stone Hallow | Merlin |

1. I was aware of a great cold wind blowing the Lunar veil aside and through it came the Green Knight. He showed me that the Sword cuts both ways and that my wit and intellect must be sharp enough to be a good guardian. He challenges my integrity.
2. The Solar veil before the Spear became the bloody linen of the Washer. She showed me that there is much corruption in the world of creativity which needs to be purged from the mirror of imagination. An impression like a solar eclipse came to me. I had the feeling that this was a worthy task indeed which I would enjoy fulfilling.
3. The coming of the White Hart brought tears to my eyes, it was so beautiful. The Terrestrial veil became the forest of the earth. It bounded out with great joy and its liquid eyes filled me with an ecstasy of understanding for which there are no words. It was like the glance of a unicorn to my inmost heart. Only poetry could express this experience.
4. The Stellar veil was parted by the two dragons who stood over and around Merlin. He gave into my hands a great tablet of stone and bade me carve upon it. A symbol like a snake with its tail in its mouth appeared on the stone, denoting the eternal circle of wisdom from age to age. He pointed to a path and gave me a little push, as if to say: 'Well, get on with it!'

*Although I feel alone sometimes, I know that these teachers are at my side to help me. I hope they have patience with my efforts!*

Perform each of the sections below in order on separate sessions.

1. Enter the Sanctuary of the Hallows with a candle. It is night and you light the central lamp of crystal which hangs from the ceiling. The room is unfurnished save for the four veils, which sway gently in the dim light, and a low stool. You have come to keep vigil and ask for a teacher to help illuminate the path of the Sword. Be seated, facing the East, and ask your teacher to appear. Whichever Greater Power card you drew in the Sword Augury of Lesson 16 comes to you. Ask your Sword teacher to reveal to you your destiny as a guardian of truth, innocence and justice. Listen well, record your conversation and any impressions. When you have finished, extinguish the lamp.
2. Illuminate the central lamp of the Sanctuary of the Hallows. You have come to keep vigil and ask for a teacher to help illuminate the path

of the Spear. Be seated, facing the South, and ask your teacher to appear. Whichever Greater Power card you drew in the Spear Augury of Lesson 28 comes to you. Ask your Spear teacher to reveal your destiny as a guardian of creativity, energy and healing. Listen well, record your conversation and any impressions. When you have finished, extinguish the lamp.

3. Illuminate the central lamp of the Sanctuary of the Hallows. You have come to keep vigil and ask for a teacher to help illuminate the path of the Grail. Be seated, facing the West, and ask your teacher to appear. Whichever Greater Power card you drew in the Grail Augury of Lesson 40 comes to you. Ask your Grail teacher to reveal to you your destiny as a guardian of grace, abundance and spiritual joy. Listen well, record your conversation and any impressions. When you have finished, extinguish the lamp.

4. Illuminate the central lamp of the Sanctuary of the Hallows. You have come to keep vigil and ask for a teacher to help illuminate the path of the Stone. Be seated, facing the North, and ask your teacher to appear. Whichever Greater Power card you drew in the Stone Augury of Lesson 52 comes to you. Ask your Stone teacher to reveal your destiny as a guardian of craft, spiritual treasure and wisdom. Listen well, record your conversation and any impressions. When you have finished, extinguish the lamp.

You can call upon each of these Hallow teachers at any time. You have chosen each other and they will continue to be your helpers and guides as you proceed upon the spiritual path you are walking.

Thank you for walking this far with me. I hope that you've enjoyed yourself and have found many new and interesting ways of using _The Arthurian Tarot_. May the blessings of the Hallows keep you ever true to the path!

# Appendices

# Appendix 1

# Study Programme

The following study programme is given as a suggested outline. Each lesson takes about a week. The dates given below are intended to show how a course of study would work.

## *Part One: Preparing for the Quest*

Everyone starts with this part, since it gives guidelines for meditation, study and practical work. Regard these lessons as the run-in to the main course. They do not have to be studied at any special time of the year.

| | | |
|---|---|---|
| Week 1 | Lesson 1 | Meditation and Diary-Keeping |
| Week 2 | Lesson 2 | The Seeker in the Wasteland |
| Week 3 | Lesson 3 | The Goddess of the Land |
| Week 4 | Lesson 4 | The Flowering of Logres |
| Week 5 | Lesson 5 | The Four Realms |

When you have finished these lessons go on to Part Two.

## *Part Two: The Quest for the Hallows*

The four seasonal sections can be worked in order from Lesson 6~57 or the student can choose to work through each section at the appropriate season. If you choose to do the latter, you need to start each season on the appropriate quarter day. There are a few days at the end of each section for rest and assimilation.

# Spring: The Quest for the Sword

| 21 March | Lesson 6 | The Sword Castle. Spring Equinox Ceremony |
| 28 March | Lesson 7 | The Sword Maiden, Sword Two and Three |
| 4 April | Lesson 8 | The White Hart |
| 11 April | Lesson 9 | The Sword Knight, Sword Four and Five |
| 18 April | Lesson 10 | The Round Table |
| 25 April | Lesson 11 | The Sword Queen, Sword Six and Seven |
| 2 May | Lesson 12 | The Cauldron |
| 9 May | Lesson 13 | The Sword King, Sword Eight and Nine |
| 16 May | Lesson 14 | The Moon |
| 23 May | Lesson 15 | The Lady of the Lake |
| 30 May | Lesson 16 | The Augury of the Sword Hallow |
| 6 June | Lesson 17 | The Investiture of the Sword |
| 7–20 June | | Assimilation and examination of Lessons 6–17 |

# Summer: The Quest for the Spear

| 21 June | Lesson 18 | The Spear Castle. Summer Solstice Ceremony |
| 28 June | Lesson 19 | The Spear Maiden, Spear Two and Three |
| 5 July | Lesson 20 | Prydwen |
| 12 July | Lesson 21 | The Spear Knight, Spear Four and Five |
| 19 July | Lesson 22 | Sovereignty |
| 26 July | Lesson 23 | The Spear Queen, Spear Six and Seven |
| 2 August | Lesson 24 | The Green Knight |
| 9 August | Lesson 25 | The Spear King, Spear Eight and Nine |
| 16 August | Lesson 26 | The Sun |
| 23 August | Lesson 27 | Arthur |
| 30 August | Lesson 28 | The Augury of the Spear Hallow |
| 6 September | Lesson 29 | The Investiture of the Spear |
| 13–20 September | | Assimilation and examination of Lessons 18–29 |

# Autumn: The Quest for the Grail

| | | |
|---|---|---|
| 21 September | Lesson 30 | The Grail Castle. Autumn Equinox Ceremony |
| 28 September | Lesson 31 | The Grail Maiden, Grail Two and Three |
| 5 October | Lesson 32 | Gawain |
| 12 October | Lesson 33 | The Grail Knight, Grail Four and Five |
| 19 October | Lesson 34 | The Wounded King |
| 26 October | Lesson 35 | The Grail Queen, Grail Six and Seven |
| 2 November | Lesson 36 | The Spiral Tower |
| 9 November | Lesson 37 | The Grail King, Grail Eight and Nine |
| 16 November | Lesson 38 | The Sleeping Lord |
| 23 November | Lesson 39 | Guinevere |
| 30 November | Lesson 40 | The Augury of the Grail Hallow |
| 7 December | Lesson 41 | The Investiture of the Grail |
| 14–20 December | | Assimilation and examination of Lessons 30–41 |

# Winter: The Quest for the Stone

| | | |
|---|---|---|
| 21 December | Lesson 42 | The Stone Castle. Winter Solstice Ceremony |
| 28 December | Lesson 43 | Stone Maiden, Stone Two and Three |
| 5 January | Lesson 44 | Taliesin |
| 12 January | Lesson 45 | The Stone Knight, Stone Four and Five |
| 19 January | Lesson 46 | The Grail Hermit |
| 26 January | Lesson 47 | The Stone Queen, Stone Six and Seven |
| 2 February | Lesson 48 | The Washer at the Ford |
| 9 February | Lesson 49 | The Stone King, Stone Eight and Nine |
| 16 February | Lesson 50 | The Star |
| 23 February | Lesson 51 | Merlin |
| 2 March | Lesson 52 | The Augury of the Stone Hallow |
| 9 March | Lesson 53 | The Investiture of the Stone |
| 16–20 March | | Assimilation and examination of Lessons 42–53 |

The whole of Part 2 takes at least one year and is completed in full before moving on to Part Three.

## Part Three: The Way of the Hallows

This section concludes the book, bringing together the fourfold landscape into a wholistic inner cosmology. These lessons should be worked in numerical order to the end; they may be worked through at any time after the completion of Part Two.

© Caitlín Matthews

*Tune for the Four Seasonal Hallow Rituals*

# Bach Flower Remedies in Combination with the Arthurian Tarot

The following Bach Flower Remedies are given as suggested correlations which resonate with features of each tarot card. Please do not assume that the remedies given here are fixed or immovable; if you are prescribing these for yourself or another, determine the appropriate remedy by carrying out a full diagnosis first. Possible uses of these remedies are for students who find certain features of this course difficult or challenging, or who discover inadequacies or emotional turmoils within themselves as a result of insights gained through meditation.

The process of self-discovery does indeed raise many problems: these are neither rare nor insuperable. Every student will occasionally find her work barren, his life disrupted, their relationships stormy. The Bach Flower Remedies act as catalysts of change and transformation at such times, working on the subtle body where they are supremely influential. Something so simple is often despised but, as in the alchemical Mysteries, it is the stone that has been rejected that proves to be true gold.

To learn the use of the remedies, it is helpful to analyse any reading you have done for yourself and read each of the remedy outlines, seeking for correlations between your reading and the emotional undercurrents that underlie it by referring to the remedy types.

Although more than one remedy is given for each card, you may not necessarily need all of those mentioned. There are doubtless other correlations which I have not seen. These remedies are harmless in effect if wrongly prescribed; they are also non-addictive.

### Greater Powers

**Seeker** Clematis for dreaminess, Aspen for fear of the unknown, Wild Oat for finding vocation

**Merlin** Cerato for intuitional distrust, Elm for being overwhelmed by one's task, Walnut for oversensitivity to influences

**Lady of Lake** Cerato for ability to listen to our inner voice, Water Violet to correct proud self-sufficiency, Wild Rose for reawakening our purpose

**Guinevere** Elm for the over-altruistic, Chicory for the over-possessive

**Arthur** Red Chestnut for over-concern for others, Vine to counteract dominating personality

**Taliesin** Honeysuckle for those stuck in the past, Chestnut Bud for stimulating openness to change and learning old lessons

**White Hart** Holly for envy and jealousy, Wild Rose for lovelessness

**Prydwen** Larch for those who find the way difficult, Oak for the grimly determined

**Gawain** Impatiens for impatience and tension, Oak for endurance

**Grail Hermit** White Chestnut for an over-active brain, Heather for the poor listener

**Round Table** White Chestnut for breaking persistent patterns, Chestnut Bud for accepting incarnational lessons

**Sovereignty** Willow for bitterness and resentment, Scleranthus for poise, Centuary for those who need to maintain clear boundaries

**Wounded King** Pine to purge guilt, Gorse for acceptance, Crab Apple for self-disgust

**Washer at Ford** Crab Apple to cleanse old life patterns, Olive for renewal of energies, Gorse for when all seems dead

**Cauldron** Olive for regeneration, Hornbeam for recombining one's resources

**Green Knight** Vine for inflexibility, Hornbeam for stagnation, Larch for fear of failure

**Spiral Tower** Star of Bethlehem for shock, Oak for those who need to face their limitations, Rock Water for those unable to adapt

**Star of Prophecy** Gorse for those needing renewed hope, Gentian for those with doubts

**Moon** Scleranthus for indecision, Holly for suspicion and negativity

**Sun** Wild Oat for those who scatter their energies, Vervain for the over-enthusiastic

**Sleeping Lord** Chestnut Bud for stimulating change, Oak for those who have endured too long

**Flowering of Logres** Star of Bethlehem for healing trauma, Clematis for creative fulfilment

### Lesser Powers

**Sword Hallow** Aspen for those fearful of unknown evils, Gentian for perseverance

**Sword Two** Scleranthus for indecision

**Sword Three** Holly for those who brood on slights, Star of Bethlehem for consolation after grief or disappointment

**Sword Four** Olive for restful recuperation, Impatiens for those who need time for self-assessment

**Sword Five** Holly for jealousy, Vine for misuse of power

**Sword Six** Walnut for clearing blockages and for protection

**Sword Seven** Scleranthus for clarifying motives

**Sword Eight** Walnut for those who are easily influenced and breaking up stagnant patterns

**Sword Nine** Rock Rose for nightmares, Aspen for premonitions, Mustard for depression

**Sword Ten** Red Chestnut for the over-protective, Chestnut Bud for acknowledgement of karmic debts

**Sword Maiden** Centuary for the self-sacrificing

**Sword Knight** Red Chestnut for calm in emergencies

**Sword Queen** Holly when suffering from malicious thoughts, Beech for the intolerant

**Sword King** Rock Water for the over-idealistic

**Spear Hallow** Crab Apple for cleansing pollution of mind, body or spirit, Wild Rose for lack of purpose

**Spear Two** Larch for lack of confidence, Scleranthus for lack of organization

**Spear Three** Rock Water for wider outlook, Wild Rose for fresh zest

**Spear Four** Wild Rose for the joyless, Willow for those who don't mix well

**Spear Five** Vine for the unyielding, Rock Water for the dogmatic

**Spear Six** Gorse for those who give up, Larch for the impotent

**Spear Seven** Oak for those who have battled long, Walnut for protection

**Spear Eight** Impatiens for those who react hastily, Chestnut Bud for assimilating information more deeply

**Spear Nine** Olive when energy reserves are depleted, Oak for perseverance

**Spear Ten** Elm for those overwhelmed by responsibilities, Vine for those who need to delegate

**Spear Maiden** Impatiens for impatience, Vervain for over-enthusiasm, Beech for the hypercritical

**Spear Knight** Cherry Plum for rage, Impatiens for the over-hasty

**Spear Queen** Willow for bitterness, Water Violet for the emotionally withdrawn, Sweet Chestnut for despair

**Spear King** Pine for the self-sacrificing, Red Chestnut for over-solicitude

**Grail Hallow** Gorse for creative stagnation, Water Violet for getting in touch with emotions

**Grail Two** Heather for the determinedly solitary, Vine to encourage team work

**Grail Three** Star of Bethlehem for comfort, Chicory for unselfish support

**Grail Four** Wild Rose for apathy, Hornbeam for finding fresh hope in the daily round

**Grail Five** Chestnut Bud to help learn from mistakes, Pine for regret

**Grail Six** Honeysuckle for nostalgia or atavism and for developing a balanced appreciation of things past

**Grail Seven** Crab Apple for disproportionate fantasies, Clematis for focusing scattered energies

**Grail Eight** Rock Water for mental flexibility, Chicory for self-pity

**Grail Nine** Willow for dissatisfaction, Wild Rose for discovering new springs of life

**Grail Ten** Walnut for family transitions, Chicory for generous sharing with others

**Grail Maiden** Wild Rose for renewed interest in life, Cerato for renewed trust in one's intuitions

**Grail Knight** Clematis for the dreamy, Walnut for trust in the quest

**Grail Queen** Red Chestnut for over-concern for others, Chicory for giving love in service

**Grail King** Walnut for overcoming illusions, Aspen for fear of the unknown on quest

**Stone Hallow** Honeysuckle for realization of past wisdom, Wild Oat for realizing inner treasures and skills

**Stone Two** Scleranthus for indecision, Crab Apple for over-scrupulosity

**Stone Three** Clematis for focusing creativity, Hornbeam for revitalization of one's craft/work

**Stone Four** Chicory for a miserly spirit, Larch for under-achievers

**Stone Five** Mimulus for fear of destitution or disempowerment, Star of Bethlehem for comfort

**Stone Six** Water Violet for ability to share good fortune, Walnut for transformation of matter into spirit

**Stone Seven** Larch for fear of failure, Impatiens for taking one day at a time

**Stone Eight** Vervain for patience in learning/teaching, Chestnut Bud for re-evaluating past mistakes as teachers

**Stone Nine** Centuary for giving space to fulfill oneself, Water Violet for those who are too withdrawn from life

**Stone Ten** Honeysuckle for valuing ancestral qualities, Wild Oat for those who have no permanence

**Stone Maiden** Cerato for those who need to listen to their inner voice

**Stone Knight** Oak for those who plod, Hornbeam for fresh spontaneity

**Stone Queen** Water Violet for greater emotional involvement, Chicory for the dominating manipulator

**Stone King** Chestnut Bud for learning new lessons from life, Oak for revitalizing one's duty

# Resources

For details of tapes which accompany this course, and other tapes by Caitlín and John Matthews, send an SAE or two IRCS to BCM HALLOWQUEST, London WC1N 3XX, U.K.

## Quarterly Newsletter

We produce a quarterly newsletter detailing forthcoming books, courses, events, and workshops. Current yearly subscription: 8 first class stamps (within U.K.) or 8 international reply paid coupons (outside UK) available from post-offices; send to address above.

## Bach Flower Remedies

Remedies and relevant information can be obtained from:

### In U.K.

The Bach Flower Remedies Ltd, The Bach Centre, Mount Vernon, Sotwell, Wallingford, Oxon OX10 0PZ, U.K. (tel: 0491 39489)

### In USA/Canada

Ellon (Bach USA) Inc., PO Box 320, Woodmere, NY 11598, USA (tel: 516 825 2229)

### In Australia

Martin & Pleasance Wholesale Pty Ltd, PO Box 4, Collingwood, Victoria 3066, Australia (tel: 419 9733)

## In Europe

Mechthild Scheffer HP, Bach Centre ~ German Office, Eppendorfer Landstrasse 32, 2000 Hamburg 20, Germany (tel: 040/46 10 41)

# Bibliography

All titles were published in London unless stated otherwise.

1. Byrne, Francis J., *Irish Kings and High Kings*, Batsford, 1973
2. Chrétien de Troyes, *Arthurian Romances*, trans. D.D.R. Owen, Dent, 1987
3. Fortune, Dion, *Aspects of Occultism*, Aquarian Press, Wellingborough, 1962
4. Gray, William, *Magical Ritual Methods*, Helios Books, Toddington, 1971
5. Halevi, Z'ev Ben Shimon, *Tree of Life*, Rider, 1972.
6. Lewis, C.S., *That Hideous Strength*, Bodley Head, 1945.
7. Lonegren, Sig, *Labyrinths: Ancient Myths & Modern Uses*, Gothic Image Press, Glastonbury, 1991
8. *Mabinogion*, ed. Lady Charlotte Guest, Ballantyne Press, 1910
9. Malory, Sir Thomas, *The Morte d'Arthur*, University Books, New York, 1961
10. Matarasso, P.M., *The Quest of the Holy Grail*, Penguin, Harmondsworth, 1969
11. Matthews, Caitlín, *Arthur and the Sovereignty of Britain: King & Goddess in the Mabinogion*, Arkana, 1989
12. Matthews, Caitlín, *The Celtic Book of the Dead*, Aquarian Press, 1992
13. Matthews, Caitlín, *The Elements of Celtic Tradition*, Element Books, Shaftesbury, 1989
14. Matthews, Caitlín, *The Elements of the Goddess*, Element Books, Shaftesbury, 1989
15. Matthews, Caitlín, *Mabon and the Mysteries of Britain: An exploration of the Mabinogion*, Arkana, 1987
16. Matthews, Caitlín, *Sophia: Goddess of Wisdom*, Mandala, 1991
17. Matthews, Caitlín and John, *The Arthurian Book of Days*, Sidgwick & Jackson
18. Matthews, Caitlín and John, *The Arthurian Tarot*, illus. Miranda Gray, Aquarian Press, Wellingborough, 1990

19. Matthews, Caitlín and John, *Hallowquest: Tarot Magic and the Arthurian Mysteries*, Aquarian Press, Wellingborough, 1990

20. Matthews, Caitlín and John, *Ladies of the Lake*, Aquarian Press, 1992

21. Matthews, John (ed.), *The Arthurian Reader*, Aquarian Press, Wellingborough, 1988

22. Matthews, John (ed.), *At the Table of the Grail*, Arkana, 1987

23. Matthews, John, *The Celtic Shaman*, Element Books, Shaftesbury, 1991

24. Matthews, John, *The Elements of the Arthurian Tradition*, Element Books, Shaftesbury, 1989

25. Matthews, John, *The Elements of the Grail Tradition*, Element Books, Shaftesbury, 1990

26. Matthews, John, *Gawain, Knight of the Goddess*, Aquarian Press, 1990

27. Matthews, John, *The Grail: Quest for the Eternal*, Thames and Hudson, 1981

28. Matthews, John, *Taliesin: the Shamanic and Bardic Mysteries in Britain and Ireland* (with additional material by Caitlín Matthews), Mandala, 1991

29. Matthews, John (ed.), *World Atlas of Divination*, Headline, 1992

30. Matthews, John and Green, Marian, *The Grail Seeker's Companion*, Aquarian Press, Wellingborough, 1986

31. Ozaniec, Naomi, *The Chakras*, Element Books, Shaftesbury, 1990

32. Photius, *Life of Pythagorus*, n.d.

33. Stewart, R.J., *Advanced Magical Arts*, Element Books, Shaftesbury, 1988

34. Stewart, R.J., *Earth-Light*, Element Books, Shaftesbury, 1992

35. Stewart, R.J., *Living Magical Arts*, Blandford Press, Poole, 1987

36. Stewart, R.J., *The Merlin Tarot* (illustrated by Miranda Gray), Aquarian Press, Wellingborough, 1988

37. Stewart, R.J., *The Mystic Life of Merlin*, Arkana, 1986

38. Stewart, R.J., *The UnderWorld Initiation*, Aquarian Press, Wellingborough, 1985

39. *Trioedd Ynys Prydein*, trans. Rachel Bromwich, University of Wales Press, Cardiff, 1961

# Index

(Major entries for individual cards, meditations etc. are in **bold**.)

*Of further interest . . .*

# THE ARTHURIAN TAROT

## A Complete Package of Book and Cards

## Caitlín and John Matthews
### Illustrated by Miranda Gray

*The Arthurian Tarot* represents the ultimate in Tarot design. Steeped in the sheer unequalled magic of the legends, history and traditions of Arthurian Britain, these exceptional cards capture in 78 frames all the wonder and beauty of King Arthur's realm. Conceived and designed by Caitlín and John Matthews and beautifully executed by Miranda Gray, this original pack reveals the ancient traditions of the Arthurian Mysteries as a living mythos for creative visualization and personal transformation.

This exclusive pack comes complete with *The Arthurian Tarot: A Hallowquest Handbook,* a fully illustrated guide to the divinatory and archetypal meanings of the cards – the 22 Greater Powers and the 56 Lesser Powers. The suits of Sword, Spear, Grail and Stone, corresponding to the four elements of Western esoteric tradition as well as to the four seasons, empower the reader through the sacred quest for the Hallows. The book also gives original methods for reading and using the Tarot, including the Merlin's Mirror and Excalibur spreads, with sample readings to show their practical significance.

# HALLOWQUEST

## Tarot Magic and the Arthurian Mysteries

# Caitlín and John Matthews

*Hallowquest* takes you deeply into the realm of King Arthur. Drawing on the rich mythology of the Celtic-Arthurian legends, Caitlín and John Matthews unlock the subtle levels of the Arthurian Mysteries by means of Tarot magic.

This complete companion volume to the exceptional *Arthurian Tarot* describes the Celtic derivation of the Arthurian legends and their correspondences with early medieval stories, giving the reader a firm traditional foundation to work from. The four empowering Hallows of the Sword, Spear, Grail and Stone appear in the four Tarot suits and form the basis of a modern Grail Quest.

You will meet the gods and symbolic forms which underlie King Arthur's magical realm, as well as encouraging the kings, queens, knights and maidens of each of the four castles which stand as elemental guardians of the Arthurian realms. In the course of the many practical rituals, meditations and shamanic journeys included within this book, you will become acquainted with your own inner landscape.

*Hallowquest* presents a complete initiatory system into the Arthurian Mysteries as well as providing new ways of using the Tarot, including story-telling, ritual and shamanic exploration.

# THE DREAMPOWER TAROT

## A Complete Package of Book and Cards

## R. J. Stewart

### Illustrated by Stuart Littlejohn

Tarot cards often have secret paths within them, leading to the Underworld of our deepest spiritual and magical transformations and traditions. *The Dreampower Tarot* takes us down into these realms on a voyage of exploration of the hidden depths within us. Drawing on profound ancient traditions, its powerful and unique images depict the powers and people we may meet on our way.

This brand new pack of beautifully illustrated cards comes together with an explanatory book and may be used for meditation, vision and reading. Conceived and designed by R. J. Stewart, originator of the best-selling *Merlin Tarot*, the exciting images have been skilfully realized by Stuart Littlejohn and will provide Tarot enthusiasts with a rich source of inspiration.

| | | | |
|---|---|---|---|
| HALLOWQUEST | 0 85030 963 8 | £8.99 | ☐ |
| THE ARTHURIAN TAROT PACK | 0 85030 843 7 | £20.00* | ☐ |
| THE DREAMPOWER TAROT PACK | 1 85538 300 4 | £20.00* | ☐ |
| THE CELTIC TAROT PACK | 0 85030 920 4 | £20.00* | ☐ |
| THE NORSE TAROT PACK | 0 85030 792 9 | £17.99* | ☐ |
| THE MERLIN TAROT PACK | 1 85538 092 7 | £20.00* | ☐ |
| THE MAGICKAL TAROT PACK | 1 85538 093 5 | £20.00* | ☐ |
| THE SHAKESPEAREAN TAROT PACK | 1 85538 054 4 | £20.00* | ☐ |
| THE SERVANTS OF THE LIGHT TAROT PACK | 1 85538 001 3 | £20.00* | ☐ |
| THE SHINING WOMAN TAROT PACK | 1 85538 098 6 | £20.00* | ☐ |
| THE PREDICTION TAROT PACK | 0 85030 476 8 | £20.00* | ☐ |

* including VAT @ 17.5%

All these books are available from your local bookseller or can be ordered direct from the publishers.

To order direct just tick the titles you want and fill in the form below:

Name: _____

Address: _____

_____

_____ Postcode:_____

Send to: Thorsons Mail Order, Dept 3, HarperCollins*Publishers*, Westerhill Road, Bishopbriggs, Glasgow G64 2QT.

Please enclose a cheque or postal order or your authority to debit your Visa/Access account —

Credit card no: _____

Expiry date: _____

Signature: _____

— up to the value of the cover price plus:

**UK & BFPO:** Add £1.00 for the first book and 25p for each additional book ordered.
**Overseas orders including Eire:** Please add £2.95 service charge. Books will be sent by surface mail but quotes for airmail despatches will be given on request.

**24 HOUR TELEPHONE ORDERING SERVICE** FOR ACCESS/VISA CARDHOLDERS — TEL: **041 772 2281.**